Emotions
and Social
Relations

SAGE has been part of the global academic community since 1965, supporting high quality research and learning that transforms society and our understanding of individuals, groups and cultures. SAGE is the independent, innovative, natural home for authors, editors and societies who share our commitment and passion for the social sciences.

Find out more at: **www.sagepublications.com**

Emotions and Social Relations

Ian Burkitt

Los Angeles | London | New Delhi
Singapore | Washington DC

Los Angeles | London | New Delhi
Singapore | Washington DC

SAGE Publications Ltd
1 Oliver's Yard
55 City Road
London EC1Y 1SP

SAGE Publications Inc.
2455 Teller Road
Thousand Oaks, California 91320

SAGE Publications India Pvt Ltd
B 1/I 1 Mohan Cooperative Industrial Area
Mathura Road
New Delhi 110 044

SAGE Publications Asia-Pacific Pte Ltd
3 Church Street
#10-04 Samsung Hub
Singapore 049483

Editor: Chris Rojek
Editorial assistant: Gemma Shields
Production editor: Katherine Haw
Copyeditor: Jane Fricker
Proofreader: Dick Davis
Indexer: Anne Fencott
Marketing manager: Michael Ainsley
Cover design: Shaun Mercier
Typeset by: C&M Digitals (P) Ltd, Chennai, India
Printed by: Replika Press Pvt Ltd

Library of Congress Control Number: 2013947746

British Library Cataloguing in Publication data

A catalogue record for this book is available from
the British Library

ISBN 978-1-4462-0929-5
ISBN 978-1-4462-0930-1 (pbk)

Loan Receipt
Liverpool John Moores University
Library Services

Borrower Name: Millward,Peter
Borrower ID: ********

Emotions and social relations /
31111014635807
Due Date: 30/09/2016 23:59

Total Items: 1
13/07/2016 14:33

Please keep your receipt in case of
dispute.

Contents

About the Author

Ian Burkitt is Professor of Social Identity at the University of Bradford where he teaches sociology and social psychology. His research interests are in the areas of social theory, theories of identity and embodiment, and the social and psychological understanding of feelings and emotions. In his work he has pioneered a relational understanding of the self and of emotions, and future projects include the application of this approach to the understanding of agency. He is the author of *Social Selves: Theories of Self and Society* (2nd Edition, Sage 2008) and *Bodies of Thought: Embodiment, Identity and Modernity* (Sage, 1999).

Acknowledgements

I would like to thank all the people who have supported me in the writing of this book. Mary Holmes was instrumental in suggesting that I begin to write it in the first place and not just muse about it. My friends and colleagues at the University of Bradford were also tremendously helpful, particularly Paul Sullivan and Nathan Manning who took the time and trouble to read and comment on the second major draft of the book. Jason Hughes also gave incredibly helpful macro and micro comments on the full draft. Friends outside of academic life provided the distractions and emotional support necessary for sustaining a project like this, especially Alan Scott, Charles Stones, John Smith and Yasar Amin.

The publishers and the author wish to express their thanks to SAGE Publications for kind permission to reproduce extracts from 'Powerful Emotions: Power, Government and Opposition to the War on Terror', *Sociology*, 39: 4, 2005.

1

Introduction: Feeling and Emotion as Patterns of Relationship

> ... the relationship between the self and others, and the relationship between self and environment, are, in fact, the subject matter of what are called 'feelings' – love, hate, fear, confidence, anxiety, hostility, etc. It is unfortunate that these abstractions referring to *patterns* of relationship have received names, which are usually handled in ways that assume that the 'feelings' are mainly characterised by quantity rather than by precise pattern. This is one of the nonsensical contributions of psychology to a distorted epistemology. (Bateson, 1973: 113)

What Bateson says above is something we still need to ponder 40 years after his words were first published, because the nonsensical contribution not only of psychology but also of our commonsense language to the misapprehension of what feelings and emotions are really about still persists to this day. Because feelings and emotions have received names like love, hate, fear and anxiety, we tend to think about them as though they are 'things' in themselves, entities that exist and can be known if only we can accurately trace their roots back to a causal origin. In commonsense terms, because feelings and emotions are registered first of all by our bodies, we think and speak as if the source of emotion was our own individual bodies and minds. As Bateson says above, it is as if feelings were quantities that existed inside us, ones that we struggle to express and quantify in words. A mother may say to her child, 'I love you more than I can say', telling the child both what her feelings about it are and also measuring that love as a quantity, in this case one that is off the scale of verbal measure. Or we may say to a loved one, 'I love you more than anyone else in the whole world', showing that our love for that particular person is greater than for anyone else.

Where our commonsense language misleads us by naming specific feelings and emotions is by encouraging us to feel and think about them as if they were private entities that originate in our bodies or minds. But if we think more about the brief examples given above in Bateson's terms, we can see that what we refer to when we express feelings and emotions is our *relationship* to other people. When we say to a child or a lover that we love them more than words can say or more than anyone else, we are saying something about not only the bodily feelings they evoke in us but also the special nature of our relationship to them and how this is different from our relations to others. What our feelings and emotions are the subject matter of, then, are *patterns of relationship* between self and others, and between self and world. It is not only other people we can fall in love with; we can love a landscape, our homes, a treasured personal possession, a piece of music – the list could go on. Our love expresses our relationship to our world and specific people or things within it. It is not wrong, then, to identify feelings and emotions as occurring in the body, because in part they do so: we could not feel without a body and mind which register our feelings and are conscious of having them. The problem comes when the explanation of emotion stops there, with the feeling itself as a thing that is not connected to the wider world of relations and the pattern of relationships.

This problem also exists in psychology, as Bateson said above, for the discipline has tended to fall into commonsensical assumptions about emotions, contributing to our distorted understanding of them. In general terms, most psychologists assume that the words we have for emotions refer to entities that can be described in neuropsychological terms, as to do with underlying neuro-circuitry or cognitive predispositions to certain emotional responses. It is these underlying body–brain systems and networks that produce the emotion, or more to the point, they *are* the emotion. This explanation misses the patterns of relationships in which those emotions emerge in the first place and in which they make sense. Because psychology is a subject that focuses on the individual, the emotion is seen as something to do with what is happening in the individual's body-brain, rather than understanding the embodied person – and their emotional experiences – within patterns of relationship.

Let me give an example to illustrate this. In the 1990s a BBC television science programme called *Wot You Looking At* focused on aggression and violent acts committed by young men. Like in so many similar programmes concerning human behaviour, the central issue was framed as whether aggression is something learned or innate. The programme quickly dismissed the idea that aggression in men has genetic causes, an explanation that would attempt to show how, for example, some men are more aggressive than others because of genes inherited from their parents that influence the level of chemical neurotransmitters in the brain like dopamine or serotonin, leading to aggressive responses to situations. This was dismissed because twin studies do not provide the evidence to show that twin brothers are both equally or similarly predisposed to aggressive or violent behaviour. Instead of this the programme alighted on the explanation that aggressive responses to situations had to do with learning from 'the environment', in particular the learning of a cognitive style of thinking we call 'paranoia'. That is to say, aggression was seen as the result of a style of thinking in which other people's behaviour is seen as having a negative intent towards the person concerned, and to that person only. In a revealing interview, one young man, in prison for a series of violent offences, was questioned about his behaviour and recounted an incident on a train with a stranger. The man had got on a train with his pregnant wife to find a woman sitting in one of the seats they thought they had booked. An argument developed with the woman, who was said to have got really upset, and although there were other empty seats in the carriage, the man dragged the woman out of the seat and onto the floor and spat on her. The interviewer asked why he'd acted in this way and the man replied it was because of, 'The way she was talking to me, the way she looked down on me'. When asked how he knew the woman looked down on him, he replied, 'The way she was talking to me like a stuck-up snob. She might come from a posh house and a posh area but she got up my nose and I let her fucking know about it 'n' all. ... I thought I'm not having you telling me where my wife's sitting. My wife'll sit there if she fucking wants.'

Psychologists involved in the programme explained this in terms of paranoia because, without any objective justification, this man had interpreted the woman's actions as specifically directed against him, as belittling him. Someone else could have shrugged this off as a simple misunderstanding or confusion and found another empty seat. But this man saw himself as being belittled and had to take a stand, one that restored his status through an aggressive act. Indeed, talking about his string of violent offences and his childhood, the man recalled a formative incident when he was 11 years old. At primary school another child had punched him on the nose and he went home crying to his father, who told him, 'Don't you come crying to my door'. Instead the father – who was described as a 'very violent man' – instructed his son to pick up a milk bottle from the doorstep, go back to the school and smash the bottle over the head of the child who had punched him. If he didn't do this his father told him, 'Don't come back to my door again'. Although as a child he felt frightened doing this, he did as his father told him and 'it solved the problem'. This then set up a pattern that lasted throughout his life to that point, which he summarised as, 'you've got a problem, you get into a fight, you go out of your way to hurt 'em'. The psychological explanation here is that a paranoid cognitive style of thinking was developed in this man's life which regularly resulted in aggression in order to right the wrongs he felt that others, and the world, were doing to him.

Although I will argue here that such explanations are not entirely wrong, I do believe they are limited, for a number of reasons. First, this is because to look for the cause of aggression will be always a futile search because we are assuming aggression is a thing which has a cause. Many years ago the social psychologists Sabini and Silver (1982) argued there is no such thing as aggression that can be isolated and studied, because aggression is not a thing but a moral evaluation we make of people's actions. Aggression is the name we give to a certain act where, for a variety of reasons, someone or something is attacked, physically or verbally, in a way that a moral community finds unjustifiable. If you are walking home at night and you are attacked and robbed in a subway, this would be seen as an act of aggression. However, if you fight back, provided that the force you use is seen as proportionate, you will not be labelled as aggressive: like the old lady fighting off her attackers with a walking stick or shopping bag, you might even be seen as a hero. So it is not an act of violence or even the feeling or motive behind it that constitutes 'aggression': rather, it is the context in which the act occurs and how this is evaluated in moral terms. A headline in a newspaper which read 'Aggressive victim fights off attacker' would not make sense, not because it is ungrammatical in linguistic terms, but because it is ungrammatical in moral terms. This also means, though, that not everyone will agree on what is an act of aggression. Was the invasion of Iraq in 2003 an attack and occupation, or the liberation of the country from dictatorship? What your answer to this question is will depend on your own moral and political views. If, though, there is no objective standpoint on what constitutes an act of aggression, how can it be studied objectively by a science like psychology and a cause for it found which then might be treated?

The second problem I have with psychological explanations of feelings and emotions is that they ignore patterns of relationship. To consider this let's go back to the example above of the young man on the train and the reaction to the woman sitting in his seat. His explanation of his behaviour, that it was provoked by the fact she was looking down on him and being snobbish, reflects a wider pattern of social class relations in society in which this young man was brought up. In fact, the TV programme in which he featured noted that aggressive acts like his are often committed by men from a lower socioeconomic background. He perceived the woman he attacked as being of a higher social class, as being snobbish and looking down on him, meaning that he felt she considered him of lesser worth. Moreover, she was telling him what to do, or at least that's what he thought, maybe like so many middle-class people he'd encountered in the past, and now he was having none of it. His act of retaliation was certainly aggressive, in that it was morally unjustifiable, and other things he said in the interview showed he realised that himself after the fact. But to say that the act resulted from a cognitive style that can be classified as paranoid is limited, as it looks only at the *psychological* context of the act. After all, everyone checks the looks, gestures and words of those around them and interprets what they might possibly mean, what those people might be thinking or feeling about us. And our interpretations of those looks and gestures can be wrong. What made this particular young man feel he was being looked down on was his perception of his own social class and that of the woman in his seat. Indeed, what is often thought of as paranoid forms of thinking can make more sense when they are put back into the wider context of class relations in society and the social background and relationships of those labelled as paranoid (Cromby and Harper, 2009). In the situation above, patterns of class relations formed a backdrop against which this particular drama played itself out in the immediate relations between three people in a particular situation on a train. Overlapping this was also the biography of each person concerned and the way that orientated them in this situation, in terms of how they related to each other; the patterns of relationships from their past, embodied in their habits of orientation to others, particularly situations of conflict and how they dealt with them, and their bodily dispositions and forms of perception of others and the world, fed into the creation of the drama.

In the case of the young man on the train, his biography is partly composed of the pattern of relationships in which he had lived, in particular his relationship to a violent father. The lesson his father taught him, that a man can restore his pride and dignity through an act of violence, was just one small recounted incident from an entire childhood. To see the learning of such lessons in terms of a cognitive-behavioural style of conditioning ignores the wider social context and the patterns of relationship in which they are set. Given that these kinds of 'random' acts of aggression and violence are mainly committed by *some* men – but still only a minority – from the lower socioeconomic orders, could it be that violence is an easily accessible way of restoring pride and controlling your world – especially the people around you – in a society that denies this group other resources for power and advancement, such as economic, educational, or other cultural resources? Furthermore, the perpetrators of such acts are mainly men, and thus they cannot be divorced from the more hegemonic forms of masculinity (Connell and Messerschmidt, 2005) – portrayed in innumerable cowboy and war movies – in which it is seen as part of the nature of masculinity to be able to protect one-self (including one's honour as a man), one's home and family, and the nation-state, by the use of violence. In certain localities and subcultures, a man's use of violence may not only restore his status but win a higher status within that community, although it may get him into trouble with mainstream morality and the law (Marsh et al., 1978).

Overall, though, the argument I am running here is one that I will build throughout this book. That feelings and emotions cannot be under-stood as things in themselves which, as such, can be isolated and stud-ied. Feelings and emotions only arise in patterns of relationship, which include the way we look at and perceive the world, and these also result in patterns of activity that can become dispositions – ways of acting in particular situations that are not wholly within our conscious control and are, thus, partly involuntary. I say here they are not 'wholly' within our conscious control and are 'partly' involuntary because I think that the study of feelings and emotions calls into question any rigid distinction between consciousness and unconsciousness, and between voluntary and involuntary control. In that sense the idea I will develop here of emotional dispositions is set within this framework, in that by dispositions I do not mean a determination to act in certain ways, or of acts oriented to a given outcome, but a *tendency* to act in particular ways that is highly sensitive and oriented to certain situations as they develop. In this I will follow the pragmatist philosopher John Dewey (1922/1983), who thought that habits of action were flexible responses adaptable to unique situations, rather than mechanical responses with a given outcome. Thus as Dewey said, a person disposed to anger may commit murder only once. That is to say, someone disposed to anger *may* commit an act of violence, but they are not *bound* to: indeed, they may never do so. Yet dispositions such as this are part of what characterise us as individuals, in that our emotional dispositions form part of what others recognise as our personality: Paul is a laid-back kind of guy, while Joe is uptight and anxious.

But in my desire to give you a flavour of the book and the line of thinking I will build, I am getting ahead of myself. In talking about feel-ings and emotions I need to say something about what they mean and how I will use these terms throughout the book, along with other terms that will be important.

Feeling, Emotion and Affect

In ordinary, everyday language we regularly run the words 'feeling' and 'emotion' together, as in statements such as 'I feel love' or 'I feel angry'. Indeed, emotion is defined by the *Oxford English Dictionary* (2nd ed.) (or OED) as a 'strong feeling deriving from one's circumstances, mood, or relationships with others' and I want to stick to something like this definition in this book, as it emphasises my view of emotions as relational, although I do not think that emotions necessarily have to be strong feelings. It is not the strength of a feeling that makes it into an emotion. All emotions, though, seem to be certain types of feeling, but not all feelings are emotions. Someone may feel caution about a business deal or nervous before a job interview, but we do not usually class caution or nerves as emotions: more often than not we would just refer to them as feelings. And there are other feelings that are not thought of as emotions at all, such as feeling hungry or feeling pain. In this vein, Cromby (2007) has claimed that there are three categories of feeling: first, feelings experientially constitute the somatic, embodied aspect of emotion, such as the lightheaded sensation in the first flush of love: second , there are extra-emotional feelings like hunger, thirst, or pain, and some feelings like being tickled that have an emotional dimension but are not themselves emotions: third, there are more subtle, fleeting feelings like William James described as the feeling of hesitancy when we say words like 'if' or 'but'. In this latter sense, feelings give us a 'sense of our embodied relation to the world, and their influence is continuous' (Cromby, 2007: 102). Because of this we cannot separate out feelings, or emotions for that matter, from our bodily ways of perceiving the world, as perception is the ability to see, hear, or become aware of something through senses such as vision, hearing and touch. But sense is more than the organs of sense perception, as the term 'sense' also means a feeling that something is the case. Thus, sense in all its meanings, including sense perception, is to do with the bodily relation we have to the world and to other people within it, and feeling and emotion is part of this too.

In fact, what distinguishes feeling and emotion is not just that feeling is the bodily sensation which is central to all experiences of emotion. It is also to do with the social meanings we give to perceptual experiences and the context in which they arise. This is why certain bodily feelings are felt as emotions while others are experienced as feelings. The queasy feeling we get before a job interview – the butterflies in the stomach – we experience as 'nerves', whereas the lightheaded feeling and sense of restlessness we get after meeting someone special we experience as an emotion called falling in love. What distinguishes feeling and emotion, then, is not the strength of feeling, because before a big occasion 'nerves' can become overwhelming, even though we wouldn't normally class them as an emotion; nor is feeling a bodily sensation while emotion is not, for as Cromby showed feelings are central to emotions. Rather, it is social meaning and context that distinguish what we feel as an emotion or some other type of experience. If I'm walking down the street and feeling lightheaded and disoriented yet I haven't just met that special someone, I may start to think I'm coming down with the flu rather than falling in love. As John Dewey said, emotions do not get experienced initially as emotions, intrinsically defined as such; rather, 'some cases of awareness or perception are designated "emotions" in retrospect or from without' (Dewey, 1929/1958: 304). When Dewey says here that bodily awareness or perception is designated as emotion, or feeling, in retrospect or from without, what he means is that it is designated in terms of its contextual reference and its social meaning. I would also underline the *relational* quality of what we define as emotion or feeling. It is in relation to others or to certain situations that feelings are identified as specific emotions: that is the reference point by which we can say that I'm in love, am angry or nervous. What is interesting, then, about feeling and emotion is that they are prime examples of how the body and bodily sensations are always fused with social meanings in the patterned relational weavings of our immediate social encounters. Given this, what I will develop throughout this book is an *aesthetic understanding of emotion*, in the sense of aesthetics not as art theory but as the study of how humans make and experience meaning, and how the body is a fundamental element in this (Johnson, 2007).

Indeed, our feelings and emotions, along with other bodily perceptions, are the means by which we meaningfully orientate ourselves within a particular situation, as well as in relation to others who are part of that situation. Throughout our lives we may develop habitual ways of acting and responding emotionally in given situations, but these habits are themselves the sedimentation of past patterns of relationships and actions, and they must be open to change and adaptation to the situations we encounter. None of us are blank slates emotionally, for even in early infancy we have ways of responding to the world that characterise us as emotional beings. Yet as we enter new situations our emotional habits have to be fluid and open enough for us to be able to interpret our circumstances and to reorientate and adjust ourselves according to our changing feelings and thoughts about such circumstances. If we can't do this, we run into trouble. This is something that I hope to develop throughout this book.

There was, though, another term in the OED's definition of emotion above, which was that emotion is a feeling deriving not only from circumstance and relationships, but also from *mood*. Here, I will follow Denzin's (1984) definition of mood, in that it refers to an emotion that lingers in our dispositions to action and habit, and in our outlook on the world, long after the situation that created it is over. Thus mood is an emotional disposition, both bodily and psychological, that people bring with them from past situations into new ones that may not have relevance to that emotion. We have all experienced this on occasions where a group of people is cheerful and happy and someone comes into the group bad tempered or grumpy. Normally we would say this person was in a bad mood and, not knowing what the reason for this is, we say things like 'what's got into them?' or 'what's eating them today?' A mood, then, is an emotional hangover from other situations that can be long lasting.

Another term that has become increasingly popular in social and psychological research on emotions in recent years is that of 'affect'. However, I do not want to substitute the term affect for emotion, as I have my own definition of emotion as discussed above. Instead, I will use the term affect with reference to the word's subtle shading of three meanings. First, according to the OED, 'affect' means 'to have an effect on' (and note the difference between the terms 'affect' and 'effect', the former meaning something that makes a difference to something else, while the latter means the result of an influence) or 'make a difference to'; this includes the meaning of to 'touch the feelings of' or 'move emotionally'. Here, affect means being changed by a feeling or emotion in relation to someone or something else, so that one is *moved*, quite literally as well as metaphorically, from one state to another. This accentuates the relational aspect of feeling and emotion because it underlines that it is other people and things that we are related to (other bodies and bodily selves) which can affect us, just as we can affect them. Indeed, the word 'emotion' derives from the French *émouviour* (excite), which in turn is derived from the Latin *emovere*; *movere* meaning 'move'. Emotion, then, is a word derived from the sense of e-motion. My view of emotion is not of a static state or a thing in itself – such as a psychological phenomenon – which then moves us to act, but as movement itself within relations and interaction. In these interactions we are constantly being affected by others, being moved by them to other actions, in the process constantly feeling and thinking – being moved from one feeling or emotion to another.

The second meaning of 'affect' is that we can pretend or enact a particular emotion to have an effect on others, in the sense of *affectation*. The latter term is defined by the OED as 'behaviour, speech, or writing that is pretentious and designed to impress' and as 'a studied display of real or pretended feeling'. In this sense, we can put on a show of how we feel or perform an emotion for particular effect, especially to draw the required emotion from others or to impress them in some way. When going to shake hands with the bereaved family on the way out of a funeral, one would hardly console them with a big beaming smile and a slap on the back. It would be unacceptable under the circumstances. If one smiled, it would be in a consolatory fashion and usually accompanied with such required words as 'I'm sorry'. In this ritual there is a knowing sense in the use of emotion, especially if one was not close to the deceased and is not feeling any deep sense of grief. This has led some to argue that the production of all emotion is scripted in this way and produced by the 'actor' as required for the situation they find themselves in. Emotion, it is argued, is affected according to the 'feeling rules' for each familiar scenario, which is why emotion has to be regarded as a social construction.

I dispute this account of the production of emotion, although I do not dispute that emotion can be affection in certain circumstance. My argument will be that the first meaning of affect is primary in our experience: a feeling or emotion that *takes us* or *moves us* in ways that we cannot help or prevent. From the experience of the infant wailing and crying for food or for consolation, for satisfaction or protection, to *falling* in love (and such metaphors are significant as I will explain in Chapter 3), the primary experience of feeling and emotion is one of helpless absorption in the experience. Affect in the second sense, meaning affectation, is a secondary phenomenon that occurs only after we have learned to feel. Then, and only then, can we produce emotions to order, ones that are expected of us under certain conditions. In this case it could be said that we produce or perform emotion according to the required feeling rules, but this does not mean that feeling rules produce or construct all social emotional experience. This is just wrong thinking, as I will argue in Chapter 6.

The third meaning of 'affect' in the OED is one related to psychology, that of 'emotion or desire as influencing behaviour'. In psychology this often means emotion as a cognitive or physiological state motivating or driving a particular behaviour. For example, in a recent article, Duncan and Barrett have argued that affect is not the opposite of cognitive styles of thinking or of processing information mentally, but affect actually plays a role in cognition. Thus affective reactions are the means by which 'information about the external world is translated into an internal code or representation', and the term 'affect' itself, rather than 'emotion', is used to denote 'any state that *represents* how an object or situation impacts a person' (Duncan and Barrett, 2007: 1185, my emphasis).

However, as in the case of paranoia that we have just discussed, affect is defined *only* as a *mental representation* that is either the affect itself or the affective response it provokes, as paranoia provoked aggression. But this explanation is framed only in terms of how mental states *represent* the impact of an object or person upon us; it takes no account at all of the bodily relations we have to other people and things, which is to say the way we are *actually* related to them in a shared social world. I do not dispute that the way we relate to people and things leads to mental imagery and the whole realm of the human imagination, as I show in Chapter 3, but I do dispute that the latter is all there is to affect and emotion. In this book I argue against the cognitive way of seeing and understanding emotion as a mental representation, instead putting forward the case for understanding emotion as arising from a context, a set of circumstances and relationships with others and things.

However, it is important to clarify this use of terminology right at the beginning because the term 'affect' has so many different uses in social, psychological and cultural studies. In this last discipline the 'turn to affect' has been highly influential in the last 10 years, and once again the term 'affect' takes on a characteristic meaning within cultural studies (Blackman and Venn, 2010). Just as the 1980s was characterised by the 'turn to language' or to 'discourse' in many of the social sciences, now many in cultural studies are turning away from language as a key to the meaning of human cultural interchange and focusing on affect instead. Following Massumi (2002), in cultural studies the term 'affect' is defined as being about the *intensity* of experience rather than its quality or its discursive meaning. Thus, the quality of an experience is to do with the emotion associated with it, something which can be expressed in language or discourse, while affective intensity is non-representational and non-conscious, therefore escaping all attempts to articulate it. Unlike in the psychological sciences, affect is seen as relating to the body rather than the conscious mind, and is concerned with the flow of intensities that pass and circulate between bodies, almost like a contagion. Because of this, affect is also characterised as non-rational and accounts for the irrational forces that can grip whole communities, such as outbreaks of mass hysteria or panic which affect a collective body as well as an individual one. As Seigworth and Gregg state,

> ... affect is found in those intensities that pass body to body (human, nonhuman, part-body, and otherwise), in those resonances that circulate about, between, and sometimes stick to bodies and worlds. ... Affect, at its most anthropomorphic, is the name we give to those forces – visceral forces beneath, alongside, or generally *other*

than conscious knowing, vital forces insisting beyond emotion. (Seigworth and Gregg, 2010: 1, emphasis in original).

The danger in this view is that affect, seen as a force, intensity or valence, comes to be understood as being like electricity as it passes through a circuit; a current with its own charge that comes to 'stick' to bodies and worlds. But if affect is generated by bodies affecting other bodies in a relational patterning, affect is not something separate from bodies that can stick to them. Affect is not a mystical force or a charge akin to an electrical current, but is a material process of its own kind created by body-selves acting in relational concert. This idea can be accommodated in some studies of affect, such as Henriques' (2010) account of the affect of music – its vibrations, frequencies and rhythms – on the bodies of dancers in a dancehall in Kingston, Jamaica, allowing them to feel their body movements in a syncopated pattern. This is a material process that emerges from the patterned figuration of dancing bodies responding to the music, especially the low-pitched bass-line of reggae, and to other bodies in the room. The material frequencies and vibrations of the amplitudes and timbres of sound resonate with the corporeal rhythms of the crowd pulsating with kinetic dance rhythms. These are felt in the body as frequencies that translate into the collective movements of dance.

But this also raises questions about affect as being something other than conscious knowing; indeed something which is inassimilable and always in excess of consciousness. This is because those people moving their bodies in the dancehall 'know' full well what they are doing: it is just that this is not an intellectual form of knowing, like knowing about the gravitational forces by which the earth revolves around the sun (gravitational forces themselves being generated by moving bodies in space and time that do not stick to them), nor is it a practical kind of knowing, like knowing how to make a meal from a learned recipe. It is more a knowing on the level of a feeling for the rhythm and how to move your body in sync with it and with other bodies – although some have a better feel for this than others. This calls into question the rigid distinction between the conscious and unconscious, as feelings are a primary element of consciousness itself (Peirce, 1902/1966). Moreover, the joy that people can feel in situations where they are dancing with others is not simply a named conscious emotion, because central to the experience is the feeling of life and freedom of movement that *is* joy. Furthermore, I do not think we can separate out the intensity of such experiences from the quality of them, for the greater the quality of the experience of a night out dancing, the more intense the experience will be. How we are affected by this quality of the experience as a whole will also influence what emotions we feel, whether that is joy, or feelings such as euphoria or transcendence. It therefore seems to me impossible to separate out terms such as affect, emotion and feeling as standing for different experiences that exist in different realms, i.e. the unconscious as opposed to the conscious, the bodily as opposed to the discursive.

Although it is true that we cannot always name what we feel, either as distinct feelings or as emotions, it is a wrong move to then say that feeling or affect is something other than the discursive and the conscious, belonging in the realm of the body. This is because, if we adopt Merleau-Ponty's view, language itself is not a disembodied phenomenon, belonging in the realm of abstract linguistic or grammatical rules. Language is not learned by children as an intellectual exercise, although that may be true of learning grammar in school; primarily, though, language is learned habitually *as a practice* before it can be contemplated intellectually. This is how we know what we are going to say before we have actually said it, without articulating the words first of all for ourselves or for others: it is because speech is 'a certain use of my phonatory apparatus and a certain modulation of my body as being in the world' (Merleau-Ponty, 1945/2012: 425). Speech and thought does not *represent*, it is an expression of my bodily belonging to the world and the situations within it. Thus in circumstances where I feel surprise, reactions like 'Oh no!' or 'Look out!' are not verbal or mental representations that then need to be expressed; rather, they are bodily expressions of my being in that particular situation at that time and how I am affected by it. It is the way I feel that speaks in such circumstances, meaning that feelings and emotions can speak – they have a voice and a specific intonation. As in reactions of surprise, utterances like 'Oh no!' or 'Look out!' will have a sense of bodily urgency to them, illustrated here on the page by my use of exclamation marks. Likewise, if I'm deeply in love with someone I may end up blurting out the words 'I love you' despite my best efforts to suppress it. These spontaneous uses of language are learned, just as the words they utilise are learned, but they become as 'second nature' to us because they are as natural as many other uses of our bodies (like dancing in the dancehall).

As William James noted, more subtle feelings are also involved in the bodily use of language, written or spoken, especially where we *feel* the hesitancy in words like 'if' or 'but'. So while Massumi (2002) defines affect as to do with the body's capacity for movement and change, in contradistinction to the idea of the body in theories of discourse which freeze it in a static discursive position, this is a critique of just one *particular* post-structural informed view of discourse and language. Another view, such as Merleau-Ponty's phenomenological understanding of language, fuses the body and the many ways it can be affected with bodily movement and the bodily use of language.

What this means is that throughout this book I will not take a position where the term 'affect' means something radically different from emotion. This does not mean I have no affinity with some elements of the theories of affect in cultural studies, as I am also attempting to view emotion in terms of relationality and embodied movement. However, I do not take the view that the embodied capacity to be affected by other bodies, human or non-human, takes us beyond emotion, language and consciousness in its various forms. I side more with the view of Wetherell (2012), who has developed the concept of 'affective practice' to argue that affect is to do with embodied meaning-making that has both pattern and order, while also being capable of creating conditions which open us up to fluid, indeterminate and radically shifting possibilities. The idea of affective practice also constantly orients us to the view that affect and emotion, as embodied meaning-making, is something that we *do* within social life, instead of being subject to unconscious forces and intensities that flow through relational figurations. Wetherell also wants us to look at the cycles and rhythms of affective practices, although these are never clearly explained; thus, 'affect does display strong pushes for pattern as well as signalling trouble and disturbance in existing patterns' (Wetherell, 2012: 13). However, I want to think of pattern as patterns of relationships and that affect does not push for this or disturb it (how could 'it' if affect is not a thing in itself and is about practice) but is part of relational configurations and, as such, is a complex phenomenon.

Complex Emotions

I have no doubt that affect is an aspect of human practice, but looking at emotional or affective practices in isolation is not so telling. Indeed, one of the problems in studying emotion is there seem to be so many aspects to experiencing emotion that focusing on one in isolation gives only a partial picture. But then how do we account for them all, especially when many aspects of emotional experience, such as cognition or embodied emotion, are often taken as in opposition to each other? My solution is to view emotions as complexes, where the many different components of emotions are configured to form the whole emotional experience. Here, when I say emotions are complex phenomena I mean 'complex' in both senses of the term. First, that emotions are complex in that they consist of many different aspects of experience which are connected together, albeit temporarily, to create an emotional experience. And, second, emotions are complex in that they are not easy to understand because they are complex and intricate phenomena.

In the first sense of the term 'complex', I mean that emotions are complex in that they are composed of different but interrelated aspects of experience, and some of these I have already touched on, such as the bodily, the psychological, the discursive or linguistic, and the biographical. However, simply lumping these together and saying that they somehow overlap to create emotions would be highly unsatisfactory. *My argument here is that we are always in patterns of relationship to other people and to the world, and feelings and emotions form our embodied, mindful sense of different aspects of those relationships.* Without that relational sense there would be no feeling or emotion. I cannot love or hate someone or something without reference to the way I am related to them and they are related to me in given, specific situations and contexts. It is this that gives my feelings meaning and sense, in that when we love or hate someone it is usually for a reason to do with the way they have affected us or the way they have behaved in a certain situation. At the same time, though, we would not *feel* these things were it not for our body-minds which register these feelings at some level, in the case of love not only as an interpersonal attraction but often as a physical attraction as well. That does not mean that these feelings, some of which are emotions, are 'natural' in the sense that they are biologically given and then simply expressed or understood through social meanings and language. Rather, because we grow up as social language users, speech, like feeling, is one of the uses and modulations of our body, so that what we feel and think is never something different from the sense of speech and, more generally, of language and social meaning. Like the man on the train who behaved aggressively to the woman sitting in his wife's seat, his emotional response cannot be understood separately from the social meaning the situation had for him, of social status positions and his fear of being belittled. These situations are complex because they involve human bodies and minds in socially meaningful situations; without the body-mind we could not *feel* our situations and patterns of relationship with others, yet without the social meaning of these relations and situations our feelings and emotions would be random and meaningless. Attempts to reduce the understanding of emotion to psychological, physiological, neurological, or even to social situations in themselves, will only ever be partial and unsatisfactory. *A complex understanding of emotion allows us to understand how socially meaningful relationships register in our body-minds and, at some level of awareness, are felt.* Emotions always have elements of the socially meaningful and discursive as they are embodied in specific situations.

Emotions, then, are also complex in that they are complicated and intricate phenomena. However, there is also a third meaning to the word 'complex', which is its reference to someone overly preoccupied or fixated with an idea, usually about themselves, as in, 'He's got a complex about his weight' or 'She's got a complex about her lack of education'. In psychoanalysis the term has been used to denote a psychic condition in which repressed or partly repressed mental contents cause internal conflict which is manifest as unusual or abnormal ideas or behaviour. In this way, neurotic or hysteric behaviour is understood as the result of complexes. This is an explanation that I reject, largely because, once again, it rests on certain emotional or behavioural states as being the result of mental processes only. Yet in my understanding of feeling and emotion complexes can have a meaning if we do not define these only as mental processes. So, for example, a complex could involve a certain pattern of relations in a given situation – like someone sitting in my seat on a train – which creates a configuration of feelings and emotions drawn from past relational patterns that dispose me to act in certain ways, such as – 'they're always getting at me', 'why does this always happen to me', 'they're looking down on me', 'I'll show them'. Alternatively, the complex could go like this – 'someone's in my seat, what do I do?', 'shall I ask them to move?', 'nah, there's lots of free seats in the carriage'. Although this is expressed in verbal terms, when in the immediate situation these responses may just be feelings, it does illustrate how a complex may play out in specific situations; a complex formed from a social situation and my relationship to it in terms of my own bodily disposition to feelings and thoughts stemming from past patterns of relationships in my biography.

Our control over a complex will depend on the unity and strength of a situation and also of our dispositions – the unity and strength of our feelings – within it. As Buytendijk (1965/1974) pointed out, in emotion we often feel as if we are at the mercy of an alien power, something we cannot control, and at times this is felt to be our body. So in instances of blushing or of panic in an examination, we are *overcome* by emotion as we lose poise, memory and control of our bodies and thoughts. This is a compulsion that is brought on by a particular situation – social clumsiness in front of others or an examination – that is not experienced as a physical disease, but is dis-ease in another sense: it is the *sign* of personal confusion and loss of poise. As Buytendijk says, 'what evokes the shyness or fear is a *sign*, emerging from the periphery in the field of encounter, from the *possibility* of bodily disorder and personal impotence', so that the bodily reaction confirms that 'the personal *e-motio* was already indicated situationally' (Buytendijk, 1965/1974: 177, emphasis in original). Here, a complex emerges from the situation which is read as containing the possibility of the loss of poise, and the bodily disposition – 'a tentative sketch of our existence' (Buytendik, 1965/1974: 179) towards that loss of control in such circumstances. The different reaction of individuals to the same situation is based on the different meanings it will have for them, depending on past biographical experiences. As Buytendijk points out, the physiological responses themselves have no purpose, such as the reddening face when we are blushing, yet they represent for the person the bodily, lived sense of the emotion-making situation.

For Buytendijk, though, 'being emotional' or becoming emotional always exists in the experience of being out of control, of being taken over by the situation in ways similar to the ones above. The fact that a feeling or emotion can completely overwhelm us and take us over, as in a panic attack or *falling* in love, challenges the idea that our consciousness of what happens to us is unified and continuous, along with the illusion that we are always in control and that our willpower is supreme. However, this is not the only way in which we experience feelings and emotions. There are situations in which we are conscious of what we are feeling in the moment and have the power to control it to some degree. As I said above, this may depend on the unity and strength of a situation and also the unity and strength of our dispositions in that situation, or it may depend on the nature of our relationship to the people and things in it and how they affect us. For example, if a boss at work is scathing about my capabilities and I'm about to give the job up anyway, I'm more likely to feel sanguine about this than if I desperately need or want the job – in which case I'm more likely to feel angry or upset. In some cases affect may become affectation, as when we show concern for the misfortune of someone we really do not know well. What I want to develop here, then, is the idea that there is a range of experiencing feeling and emotion, and that our control of these experiences will vary across a range, from being helplessly affected at one end to being very much in control and affecting the required responses at the other end.

Emotions and Relationships

Having defined many of the key terms I will be using throughout this book I now need to say something about what I mean when I refer to the term 'relationships', and thus to emotions as patterns of relationships. Kenneth Gergen has pioneered research in the relational context of emotion, suggesting in a similar fashion to Bateson that 'communities generate conventional modes of relating; patterns of action within these relationships are often given labels. Some forms of action – by current Western standards – are said to indicate emotions' (Gergen, 1994: 222). Like me, Gergen claims that emotion is not a thing or a substance that exists separately from relationships; rather, he suggests that we perform emotion within relationships, a bit like actors perform emotions on stage. In particular cases, patterns of relationship can be viewed as *emotional scenarios*, which are informally scripted patterns of interchange. It is within such scenarios that individuals perform emotions, which are not under the control of the individual but are called for by the particular relationships in that scenario. To explain this, Gergen draws on research by Pearce and Cronen (1980), as well as on a study he completed with Linda Harris and Jack Lannamann, to show how domestic violence between couples is an unwanted repetitive pattern of hostility that escalates within relationships, ending in physical violence that was not the original intention of either of the parties. The view also emerged that under certain conditions, such as one party being excessively critical of the other, violence was more likely to occur even if it is not acceptable. What Gergen is pointing out, though, through these small examples, is that in certain scenarios a violent act is not the result of an emotional state contained within an individual, such as anger or rage, but that these emotions emerge as part of the relational scenario itself; in this case, mounting hostility and decreasing opportunities for conciliation. While options for transforming or altering the course of the emotional scenario are always possible once it is in play, these options are limited by cultural traditions which prescribe the possibilities for intelligible action.

However, there are limitations to the view of emotions as scripted performance, as I will show in Chapter 6. Although it is true that people do informally script their emotional scenarios in the context of current relationships, they also bring their own biographies and dispositions into the scenario or situation, as did the man and woman on the train in my earlier example. Perhaps these scenarios are best understood as the acting out of dispositions from the past as much as 'performances' created according to an unfolding script. So while I have great sympathy with the intent behind Gergen's relational view of emotions, I have disagreements about the concepts he deploys to understand emotions in a relational context. Moreover, he does not define what he means by 'relationships', taking it for granted that we know what is meant by that term. There are personal relationships, like those Gergen refers to above, and wider social relations. I will come to this in a moment.

Briefly, I want to mention one other point on which I differ from Gergen, which is his rejection of 'experience' as being important in emotional life. Gergen rejects this term because he feels it is individualistic and detracts from the focus on relationships. However, if we follow John Dewey's ideas about situations and the experiences within them, there is no need for this to be so, because the term 'experience' does not denote something purely subjective and private, but instead is taken to mean the interaction between a person and their environment, involving other people and objects. For Dewey, experience is therefore about activity and interaction in the world which is not primarily subjective, but is relational in that it is constituted in relations to others as well as to the whole context of one's immediate situation. Thus, experience is a continually evolving process in which interactions are nested in dynamic relationships identifiable within particular situations (Dewey, 1934/1980). This is the definition of experience I will follow in this book and is the reason why the term figures so largely in what follows.

To return to the issue of relationships, what do I mean here when I talk about relationships and about emotions only appearing in particular relational contexts? I agree with Crossley (2011), that an understanding of relations has to be centred on *interaction*, which is to say primarily the interaction between people, or perhaps that between people and things, such as inanimate objects, or the interaction between people and other living creatures. In this sense, 'a social relation is not an object, akin to a bridge, but rather a shifting state of play within a process of social interaction' (Crossley, 2011: 28). This means that social relations are never static, remaining in the same state, but unfold over time in a process of continual change. They are dynamic, unpredictable and co-created, so that no one person is ever in complete control over the way the relation will evolve.

The relational approach I will develop here follows that of Emirbayer (1997) who argues that relational sociology *does not* see the social world as consisting primarily in substances or 'things' (the substantialist perspective) that constitute the fundamental units of enquiry; rather, the relational perspective understands the terms or units of enquiry (such as emotions) to derive their meaning, significance and identity from their location in social relations, the latter being conceived as dynamic, unfolding processes that are never completely finalised. It is these relations that are the primary unit of analysis rather than the constituent elements in themselves. Although Emirbayer calls this approach transactional, following Dewey and Bentley (1949), as opposed to interactional – the latter term being conceived in the substantialist terms of the interaction of static entities, similar to the Newtonian understanding of the causal interaction between fixed entities in the universe – like Crossley I shall continue to use the term interaction here. This is partly because this is the familiar term in the social sciences, but also because by it I do not mean interaction in the Newtonian sense, rather in the relational sense used by the pragmatists (including Dewey in his early work). That is, interaction is a relational process that goes on between elements that are not understood to be independent at any point in the process, because each takes on their meaning and identity in relations: furthermore, their meaning and identity changes in relational processes. This is true of emotions, which, in the approach I am advocating here, are not substances but only come into existence and take on a meaning in relational processes between people. Likewise with human identities, that (as I will argue in Chapter 5) are not to be understood as fixed entities, but as polyphonic selves that take their form within and act upon complex, fluid, dialogical social relations.

In this sense relations can be understood as patterned figurations, just as Norbert Elias (1939/2000) conceives of figurations as being like a dance in which the patterned activity is created by the dancers acting in concert. While the dance cannot be independent of the dancers, it can be independent *of any particular dancer*, in that different styles of dancing are communicated and learned in a social process in which the dance style came to be a relatively enduring and recognisable pattern of movement through which individual dancers learned to dance. This is the way that dances spread, endure, multiply and are transformed, through myriad individual and collective variations of the practice. But the dance is also material because it is a practice that is dependent on embodied social learning; on the repositories of movement lodged in muscle memory that enable, with intense practice, the effortless flow from one body position to the next.[1] In a similar way, affective practices can spread through myriad social relations, conceived not as absolutely bounded entities, such as sealed off 'societies', but as relations between classes, groups and factions which are themselves not bounded entities; rather, they are multiple and intersecting networks of interactions and practices. These, too, rest on material and economic factors, as I will show in Chapter 2, that support different types of relationships and thus enable different types of affective practice. But this means that the emotional scenarios in which dramatic encounters occur are the relational settings in which wider cultural styles come into play, just as the setting on the train was infused by social class and gender relations – the different styles of masculinity and femininity, and the different bodily displays of status and social distinction that helped script the drama. Because networks of relations intersect and overlap, there is no way of separating the macro – the relations between classes, groups and factions – from the micro – the face-to-face interactions of particular situations – that take place in the broader framework of social relations.

Perhaps social relations and the scenes of interaction can really only be understood as 'a temporally embedded process of social engagement', that is 'informed by the past (in its habitual aspect), but also oriented towards the future (as a capacity to imagine alternative possibilities) and towards the present (as a capacity to contextualise past habits and future projects within the contingencies of the moment)' (Emirbayer and Mische, 1998: 963). As Raymond Williams (1977) commented in his essay on 'structures of feeling', culture and society seen as monolithic blocks are an expression of an habitual past tense, as fixed objective and explicit forms, whereas the present moment is more active, subjective and flexible as it moves towards a future which is not defined in absolute terms. The fixed forms of the past – society, culture, a dance – become active and part of practical consciousness 'only when they are lived, actively, in real relationships, and moreover in relationships that are more than systematic exchanges between fixed units' (Williams, 1977: 130). In the moment of active relations 'we are concerned with meanings and values as they are actively lived and felt', a process in which there is no distinction between thought and feeling in practical consciousness. Instead, in the moment of interaction there are 'characteristic elements of impulse, restraint, and tone; specifically affective elements of consciousness and relationship: not feeling against thought, but thought as felt and feeling as thought: practical consciousness of a present kind, in a living and interrelating continuity' (Williams, 1977: 132). Williams talks about these as *structures* of feeling because they are not mere flux; they are sensed as a pre-formation of new meanings, open to articulation when new semantic figures are created that can give them full expression. However, the important thing for us here is that in the present moment of interaction, feeling and thought are one and the same; they are part of practical consciousness which brings into play and experiences socially given meanings from the past, but is capable of creating new meanings in the present moment and as it imagines the future. I will explore these ideas in Chapter 3 as I further develop the aesthetic understanding of feeling and emotion.

As I said above, though, within these relations there are varying degrees of power, so that some may have more influence than others, meaning relationships are never completely harmonious. There are conflicts, tensions and rivalries in all relations to some degree or another, or at the very least there is the possibility for these to emerge. Once again, the example of the young man on the train serves to illustrate this, as the interaction between people from different social backgrounds and with very different perceptions of the situation can lead to miscommunication and lack of attunement in emotional situations. What we also saw in this example is that particular situations in which people relate to each other and interact are intersected by wider social relations that stretch across societies, such as relations and conflicts between social classes and genders. This list could also include different ethnicities or religious groups that might affect the relationships between individuals in local contexts, depending on the perceptions, attitudes or prejudices of the particular people involved. Local contexts are influenced by the wider networks of social relations, but not in any over-determined way; in fact, as we will see in the next chapter, local contexts might provide a haven from wider relations of conflict. I will call these local contexts 'emotional situations' and locate them within the broader social relations within societies as a whole. I hope to illustrate this in the next chapter, which looks at the historical and cultural relations in which emotions develop and evolve. Before that I want to give a brief summary of what is to follow in each chapter of the book.

Chapter Summaries

The idea of emotions as patterns of relationship and of emotion as complex is threaded throughout what follows. In the next Chapter (2) I look at historical and anthropological evidence which suggests that emotion has changed as social relationships have changed, a view that goes against the idea that there are a number of 'basic emotions' which are universally found in all human societies and cultures. There is a vast amount of historical and anthropological work, some of it supporting the idea of universal emotion while other work emphasises its variability, to the extent that it is impossible to review all of this in one chapter. Instead, I focus on the history of romantic love as it emerged in western societies in the 12th century, suggesting that what we understand today as a natural, timeless emotion has a history stemming from a certain time and place when significant changes in social relations occurred which, in turn, supported new social practices that allowed the feelings to emerge that we associate with being in love. Similarly, I look at changes in the emotion we call aggressiveness throughout the Middle Ages in the west, and finish by looking at anthropological work done on the emotion of grief in a Brazilian shantytown. My purpose in this is to show how emotions are embedded in social relations and how emotion is a complex phenomenon that also involves the body and various feelings, not just the discursive understanding of emotion as it changes between historical periods and across different cultures.

This theme is then taken up in Chapter 3, which develops the aesthetic theory of feeling and emotion, in that they are seen to be at the centre of the bodily process of making and experiencing meaning. Here, I argue for the complex understanding of emotion, in which for emotional experience to occur there has to be both a bodily response to a particular situation fused with a mindful realisation of that experience as expressed in language, word meanings and metaphors. My argument is that we need to account for the whole of this complex phenomenon to understand how emotions are composed of different feelings, and, in turn, how these feelings occur. This leads me into a consideration of work in contemporary neuroscience in Chapter 4, in particular that of Antonio Damasio, who has attempted a neuroscientific understanding of emotion which also unites the mind and the body, something that is ignored by most other works in neuroscience. However, in my critique of Damasio, I find his work falls short of the complex view of the emotions I am aiming for, as it fails to understand the way emotions are created in social relations. Instead, a cognitive-behavioural model of emotions is adopted by this form of neuroscience which I find to be inadequate. I do, though, at the end of the chapter, look at work currently emerging in neuroscience which might be more adaptable to the kind of explanation of emotion I am developing here.

Some of these themes are continued in Chapter 5, as Damasio has attempted not only to challenge the dualism between body and mind in the study of emotion, but also the dualism between reason and emotion. I take this forward throughout this chapter, but in a very different way, drawing on the work of pragmatist thinkers like Dewey, Mead and Cooley, alongside the Russian theorist Mikhail Bakhtin. My argument here is that emotion is not something separate from what we call 'rational' thought but is integral to it, along with other factors like the imagination which we often hold in opposition to 'reason'. Furthermore the self, which is so central to emotional experience and is founded on feeling, is not understood in this approach as a cognitive phenomenon – a form of representation – but as a polyphonic and dialogic individual that takes shape in and acts upon complex, unfinished social relations and bodily interactions in particular situations. This works against current cognitive theories of affect that are being developed in psychology, which understand emotion and the self to be factors in the cognitive processing of information.

Chapter 6 changes gear again slightly to look at sociological work on the emotions, in particular studies of the 'emotional labour' of service workers, stemming from Arlie Russell Hochschild's seminal work which began the study of emotional labour and emotion work. While this has been hugely influential in the social sciences and beyond, there has been little attention paid to the actual theory of emotion developed in the concept of emotional labour. In this chapter I take a critical view of Hochschild's concepts, such as emotional labour, emotion work and the feeling rules that govern emotional situations, going on to develop a different view of the way emotion and emotional life occurs, not just in work but in the whole of our lives, based on the relational and complex understanding of emotion I am advancing here. I then apply this to the way emotion is central to our working lives using a study of nursing practice in the NHS in Britain.

Finally, in Chapter 7 I study the role of emotion in power relations and in politics. I look at the way emotion has figured in theories of power and technologies of government, focusing on a case study of the popular protests against the impending Iraq war in 2003. My thesis here is that despite the attempts of those in power to govern emotions through instilling fear during the 'war on terror', this was not entirely possible as emotions among large populations of people are unpredictable in advance. I also conclude by drawing together the themes of the book, which are that emotion is a response to the way in which people are embedded in patterns of relationship, both to others and to significant social and political events or situations, and this has an individual, biographical element to it which depends on people's prior relational affiliations and values. Furthermore, while emotion emerges in social relations, these are constantly shifting and therefore emotion is open to continual change, because it is part of emergent relations. Emotions, then, both shape and are shaped by social relations as they shift and change over time.

Note

1. I would like to thank Jason Hughes for suggestions on the wording of this section.

2

Emotions in Historical and Cultural Relations

If emotions are patterns of relationship then one would expect them to vary greatly across different historical periods as social relations change, and between different cultures where we find varied patterns of relationship. Indeed, there is a great deal of evidence gathered by historians, sociologists and anthropologists to say that this is the case. I want to draw on some of that evidence in this chapter, although much of it is highly controversial. Some anthropologists, and certainly many psychologists, still argue that there are 'basic emotions' common to human beings in all historical and cultural contexts, as these have developed through biological evolution prior to the influence of particular societies and cultures. I will begin the chapter by saying something about this debate and then move on to the issue of differences between historical periods and different cultures in the form of their emotional life. While I do not have the space in just one chapter to review all the evidence about emotions in the historical and anthropological literature, I will give a flavour of this by focusing on three different areas of study: first, the emergence of the western style of 'romantic' or 'erotic love' in the 12th century; second, changes in the emotional style of 'refined' or 'civilised' behaviour between the 12th and 18th century in Europe; and third, I will consider the implications of an anthropological study of 'mother love' and responses to child death in a Brazilian shantytown. I will then consider the debate in anthropology about whether the idea of 'emotions' is a western style of thinking based on certain discursive practices. Are there some cultures that do not have an understanding of emotions at all?

Basic Emotions

The idea of basic or primary emotions, as they are sometimes referred to, is that these are states of neurophysiological arousal that have emerged in human evolution, as well as in the evolution of some other animal species, and then become 'hard-wired' into the brain. Once this has occurred these emotions are then produced whenever an appropriate stimulus arouses them. This idea follows in the footsteps of Darwin's work on the emotions, of which I will say more in the next chapter, which understood emotions to be habitual actions occurring in a species under certain conditions that then become biologically ingrained throughout the evolutionary process, passed through the generations by hereditary inheritance of these specific habits (Darwin, 1872/1965). Like the contemporary psychologists who have followed him, Darwin based this idea on commonly observed behavioural patterns, bodily gestures and facial expressions in humans and other animals that are thought to be the *expression* of these basic or primary emotions. Thus, the work of the contemporary psychologist Paul Ekman is based in part on empirical research into the cross-cultural recognition of facial expressions that are understood as communicating basic emotions that all humans in any place or time could recognise and understand (Ekman and Friesen, 1971). From this Ekman went on to outline five basic emotion families that he believed are constants in human experience – anger, fear, enjoyment, sadness and disgust – which have evolved to deal with fundamental life tasks that are common to human societies (Ekman, 1992; Johnson-Laird and Oatley, 1992). Indeed, as Turner (2007) points out, despite the different names that some researchers give to certain emotions, there is some consensus in the field that anger, fear, sadness and happiness are primary emotions, common not only to humans but to other mammals as well.

For Ekman, each basic emotion is not a single affective state but a family of related states that share a common theme, while also displaying variation. So, for example, a child having a temper tantrum in a nursery, two people having an argument in the street, or a driver getting mad and expressing 'road rage' at another driver, would all be associated with the common family emotion of anger. The different variations in the way emotions are expressed can be due to cultural learning and individual life history, but many emotions still can be universally recognised by the common family to which they belong. Categorising the five basic emotions depends not only on each family having characteristic signal responses, like smiling as an expression of enjoyment, but that they each have distinctive responses in the autonomic nervous system and, perhaps also, in the central nervous system, where they are characterised by particular brain activity. It is these characteristic underlying physiological and neurological responses that distinguish the five basic emotions, and possibly more, as separate families of emotion. The basic or primary emotions thesis does claim to account for cultural variability in emotion as well as similarity, as variation is present in emotional expressions. Plutchik (1962, 1980) was one of the first researchers to talk about how primary emotions are mixed to create new emotional experiences, much like an artist mixes primary colours on their palette to produce a vast array of different colours and shades.

One of the problems of the basic emotions thesis, though, is that beyond the very broad consensus on four or five emotions categorised as primary, there is much variation between researchers on which emotions to include in the list as being basic or primary ones. Among a table of 20 different researchers in this field drawn up by Turner (2007: 4–5) there is more difference than consensus on which emotions to include in the list of basics or primes. Some list love, surprise and acceptance, while the majority do not, perhaps because emotions like love or a desire for acceptance are less easily observed in facial or other gestures, or in behaviours. But what this illustrates is that when it comes to compiling a definitive list, the emotions thought of as basic or primary are much harder to identify and agree upon than one would think. In a review of evidence from 30 years of research to test the correlation between emotional expressions and physiological responses – that is, the appearance of specific signal functions with changes in autonomic and central nervous system functions, or self-reports of feeling states – Barrett (2006) has concluded that strong correlations between measureable responses have failed to materialise as expected. This has led her to conclude that attempts to understand emotions as 'natural kinds', which is to say non-arbitrary groupings of instances occurring in the world that are given by nature, are mistaken: there is insufficient evidence to reduce a range of what we regard as emotional expressions or behaviours to specific underlying mechanistic causes that would ensure they belong in the same family. Thus, the natural-kind view of emotion may be the result of an error of arbitrary aggregation. This occurs because we assume that the expression we see on someone else's face or body signals their internal state, which *is* the emotion. Furthermore, because this is due to causal mechanisms, the expression is largely involuntary. A smile is assumed to signal happiness and yet that need not necessarily be the case: people smile when they are not happy or one may smile on recognising a friend in the street, in which case the smile is influenced by the target rather than one's own internal state.

Indeed, as I indicated in Chapter 1, what we take to be the emotion another person is expressing – or the emotion we are feeling – is interpreted as much by the context we are in as by facial or bodily expressions. The anthropologist E. Richard Sorenson was present when Ekman undertook his initial work with the Fore people of New Guinea on the recognition of facial expressions, noting that the protocol of the research was to have a translator-assistant tell each participant in the study an 'emotion story' before they were asked to choose from a range of photographs of faces the one which best expressed the emotion indicated in the story. Sorenson noted it was likely that some choices were influenced by the communication between translator and participant in the telling of these stories. When he showed Ekman's photographs to the Fore without the accompanying stories, they were uncertain, hesitant and confused about the facial expressions in the photographs (Sorenson, 1976). As we shall see in Chapter 4, most facial expressions are ambiguous in themselves, so that when participants in experiments are asked to identify emotions from photographs of facial expressions, they look to the researchers for clues as to what the experiment is about and how they are expected to respond – a social interaction that researchers often assume to be bracketed out under experimental conditions.

Thus the mistake made by proponents of the basic or primary emotions thesis is to think that what today we describe as particular emotions such as anger, joy, or fear are reducible to certain bodily behaviours or facial gestures which *are* in themselves *the emotion*. Furthermore these expressions are biological, in that they are underpinned by changes in autonomic and central nervous system functions that emerged in early evolution, making them pre-social; isolated from the patterns of relationship in which they appear and get interpreted. In this book I will make an argument for the opposite view: in presenting a complex and aesthetic understanding of emotions, I argue that the physiological patterning of bodily responses to situations is inseparable from the application and making of social meanings in that context. It is therefore not neurophysiological patterning and the subsequent bodily expressions that are *the emotion*, but instead these have to be understood in the context of relational patterning and social meaning. As I will show in the following sections, emotions are in part cultural variants that depend on socioeconomic circumstances and how they support or curtail certain relationships, and also how this is felt and understood in local culture.

Romantic and Erotic Love: The Language of Love

Initially it was a surprise to me that love does not feature on more of the lists of basic emotions drawn up by those who propound this thesis, and when it does, as in Ekman's studies (Ekman, 1992), it is understood as an 'emotional attitude' that is not a basic emotion. In other studies love appears as a secondary emotion derived from pleasure, joy or happiness. Yet my surprise quickly faded as I started to think about how we actually define love in western culture, for the very tangibility of love quickly dissipates in the glare of analytical reflection. When we talk of 'love' what we actually refer to are a myriad of different feelings that can be experienced in a variety of relationships, such as those between caregivers and children, between siblings, friends, and lovers. What I had actually been researching was the origins and genealogy of romantic or erotic love in the west. However, I want to stick with this because an exploration of this kind of love illustrates precisely the complexity and historical and cultural variability of emotional experience that is the subject matter of this book.

This section of the chapter is subtitled 'the language of love' because it is clear that the way we talk, write, sing, feel, think, act and create love relationships in the western world today is derived from a language and a set of practices invented in the courts of the nobility in Europe during the 12th-century Enlightenment. Of course, romantic or erotic love has gone through many changes since that time but the culture of what came to be known as 'courtly love' is still with us in many important ways and it shapes the entire way we feel when we are in love. The language of love was created by a group of singers and poets in the 12th century known as the troubadours, a wandering band of entertainers who moved between the courts of the European nobility, addressing their songs in particular to the ladies of the court. The troubadours themselves were drawn from all ranks of society, ranging from great lords to those from the lower ranks of the nobility, parts of the bourgeoisie, clerics and the low born who became errant minstrels (Harvey, 1999). Initially they all came from the region of medieval Europe known as Occitania, which covered the modern-day south of France from just below Poitiers, down across the Pyrenees and stretching east towards the Italian Alps. The first known troubadour hails from this region, William IX, Duke of Aquitaine and grandfather of Eleanor of Aquitaine, who, in her time as both Queen of France and later Queen of England, was to do more than anyone to promote troubadour song in the courts of Europe (Swabey, 2004). Coming from the region they did, the troubadours mainly composed in the *langue d'oc*, a Romance language derived from the Vulgar Latin, similar to Catalan. What was significant about this was that the troubadours composed their lyrics in the vernacular, setting the precedent for all popular songs since which are composed in everyday as opposed to formal language.

Of course, the troubadour tradition not only had its geographical and linguistic context, it also had a social and an economic one too. It emerged at a time when the power of the feudal warlords in Europe was not waning, but was beginning to see the emergence of some rivals, a slight shift in the balance of power which made opportunities for the creation of new cultural forms. An expansion of trade saw the rise in importance of the bourgeois class, and with them grew some of the great trading cities in which the first secular universities were created. From Islamic areas in southern Italy, Sicily and Spain there came Latin translations of Greek and Arabic texts including those by Aristotle, Virgil, Horace and Seneca. Perhaps most important for the idea of romantic love were translations of Ovid's *The Art of Love* and *Cures for Love*, together with Cicero's *De Amicitia* or 'Concerning Friendship'. Along with these came translations of love poetry from the Arabic world which also fed into the ethos of romantic love, together with the myths and stories of the Celtic world. An example of this is Chrétien de Troyes' tale *The Knight of the Cart*, which plays on the romantic theme added to the Welsh myth of King Arthur. The tale elaborates upon the character of Sir Lancelot and his slavish devotion to Queen Guinevere, in order to set up a classic romance in the troubadour style. In this a gallant knight falls in love with the married queen, singing to her his praises in word and/or song of her beauty, nobility and purity. This creates a tension in troubadour lyrics around the dichotomy between reason and desire, and also the idea that the object of true and passionate love is ultimately unattainable. In the *Knight of the Cart* Lancelot abandons his reason to his love for Guinevere and at the end of the tale it is she who controls her passion in the interests of reason (Swabey, 2004).

A central aspect in the development of troubadour love song is the position of women, both in the lyrics and in society as a whole. In the first millennium in feudal Europe women had little or no power in what was essentially a society controlled by warlords. By the early part of the second millennium things had improved only slightly. Marriage was a secular and practical arrangement in which women (as well as young men) had no choice over who they would marry: the idea that a partner should be chosen on the basis of one's feelings for them was completely alien, and, once married, women were subservient to their husbands. Even noble women had little power of their own to exercise. An intelligent, learned, ambitious and noble woman like Eleanor of Aquitaine, who was apparently also incredibly beautiful, attracted suitors largely because of the lands she had inherited, and could exercise power only through her marriages, first to King Louis VII of France and, after divorcing him, to King Henry II of England, and then through her children, particularly Richard I (also known as Richard the Lionheart) who also became King of England. In fact Eleanor was despised for her many qualities and for the fact she had obtained a divorce from Louis VII. However, by the 12th century one avenue for direct power and influence that opened to noble women was to become a patron of scholars or artists, as Eleanor did with the troubadours.

The position of women and the nature of marriage were hugely influential in the style of troubadour song. Because marriages were essentially loveless, love became expressed in terms of adultery, as the poet or singer was writing a love song to a married lady of the court who was unattainable because of the marriage, or he was writing a love song about a knight or nobleman courting a married woman, as Lancelot did with Guinevere. Also, the singer or poet was composing a ballad about the charms of a woman who was often of a much higher social status than him, and once again because of this was beyond his reach. This is why so much of troubadour poetry is about unrequited love, about the joys and pains of admiring and longing for another at a distance. As we will see shortly, this is a tradition we have inherited from the troubadours, as the same sentiments, and even similar modes of expressing them, characterise the popular songs we know today. In the 12th century, though, this placed high born women in a highly ambivalent position, as a woman who succumbed to the adulterous advances of a man would be socially chastised, even ostracised. This meant that in troubadour song women had to be seen to remain chaste and pure despite the amorous advances of their suitor. Thus, in this particular expression of heterosexual love, the woman becomes the object of adoration yet cannot respond. As Swabey (2004) says, troubadour song elevated the status of women at court because they became the focus of lyrical poetry, yet this elevation was only as a silent, chaste and pure object of idealisation.

Still, troubadour love song was revolutionary in its elevation of women at court and the place it allowed them as patrons of artists and entertainers. Despite the fact that elements of troubadour song and poetry were drawn from a variety of different cultural influences, it was the origin of the feelings and ideas we have about love in the west, and because of that it also added something new to the emotion we know as love. The troubadours created the tradition of *fin'amor*, which is heartfelt or true love. The emphasis on learning that had fuelled the 12th-century Enlightenment with the availability of texts from classical Greece had also created a desire for the cultivation of the self and the refinement of manners. As Harvey has said of this type of courtesy:

The matter of good behaviour in the households of the nobility, *cortesia*, was becoming an art form. A man needed tact, charm and discretion; he had to be elegantly dressed, cheerful, urbane, and skilled in managing the sensibilities of other members of the household, including his superiors. Body-language and language itself became vitally important: the careful use of eloquence characterised the courtier, along with an agreeable public mask. But such self-control in company could also be construed as hypocritical dissembling to cover ambition, jealousy, manipulation, greed, and back-stabbing in what could be a very competitive environment: advancement, material comfort and security depended on the smile of his lordship and his recognition of one's services. (Harvey, 1999: 13)

The love songs of the troubadours had to reflect this new style of courtesy, which was also informed by the knightly codes of chivalry. A man had to display tact, charm and discretion in courting a lady, as a rough and tactless approach would show that he lacked the necessary sensibilities for her feelings and was therefore uncouth and not a worthy suitor. The songs therefore elevated the lady to a high, almost unreachable level, singing the praises of her qualities and beauty. As the woman had to be pure and chaste, a religious element also entered these secular songs and poems, again drawn from the chivalrous codes of the Christian knight, in which she was placed on a pedestal as the object of worship and devotion, the troubadour pledging his service to his lady. But these feelings were essentially religious ones of worship, devotion and service to God that were now being expressed towards another human being. Indeed, the religious element lingers on today in our feelings of love, for example in the desire to find a soul-mate, the one 'made' exclusively for us, to be worshiped and cherished.

In the 12th century, though, the contradictions at court outlined in the quotation above meant that the troubadour's songs of love were meant precisely to ingratiate him with the high ranking members of the court, the lords and ladies, and more often than not, unless the troubadour was a gentleman player, he would be in the pay of those people. If the lady of the court was the patron, he would be in her paid service. The unspoken question was posed about the sincerity of these love songs, whether they were sung purely for money and the possibility of social advancement. As Paterson (1999) has shown, this led troubadours like Bernart de Ventadorn to assert that *fin'amor* is true or heartfelt love, in that it is love not corrupted by money or a desire for worldly wealth or social position, and instead is based on the courtly virtues of constancy, delicacy with regard to the feelings of others, sincerity and discretion. If all of this goes together to make a code of love in troubadour song, Paterson also points out that the songs deploy a range of characteristic *topoi* or characteristic ideas, phrases, motifs, stylistic devices and metaphors that form part of the code. For example, Spring is often used as an evocation of the youthful joy of love, and in Spring the birds sing for love just like the troubadour (Paterson, 1999: 33). However, because the lady is unattainable the troubadours' songs swung between the joy and pain, elation and dejection of being in love: the joy in anticipation of mutual pleasure and the delight in the pain of unrequited love.

Yet despite the allusions to religious devotion and the necessity to preserve the chastity of the loved one, troubadour song had clear undercurrents of erotic and sensuous desire. Thus the troubadour Guilhem de Peitieu declared in song, 'God let me live long enough to get my hands under her cloak!' (quoted in Paterson, 1999). Ironically, given the social position of women at the time, it was the female troubadours, or *trobairitz*, who were much more earthy and frank in the sexuality of their songs. One of the most famous *trobairitz*, the Comtessa de Dia, sings 'I should like to hold my knight naked in my arms one evening', and 'When will I have you in my power, and lie with you one evening, and give you an amorous kiss?' (quoted in Sankovitch, 1999: 120–1). As Sankovitch (1999) says about this, here the Comtessa opposes the standard representation of women of the day as holders of moral power – often a power used against the desirous advances of men – to her impatient yearning for sexual power.

From all this we see the form of troubadour song and the tensions inherent in it. There is the extolling of the virtues of courtly manners and refined behaviour which takes into account the sensibilities of the lover being wooed in the act of courtship itself; there is the joy of being in love counterposed with the pain of unrequited love; the woman who is the object of desire is approached with a pseudo-religious sense of devotion and servitude; yet underneath this and occasionally breaking through to the surface is the sexual desire for the other and their body. Not all troubadours displayed exactly the same code of love, if we can call it that, and troubadour song might best be seen as a dialogue between different singers and poets as to the exact nature of true or heartfelt love. And in this debate no issue was more hotly contested than the place and need for self-discipline or *mezura*. The troubadour Bernart de Ventadorn held to the position that it was impossible to retain self-control when in love, while Marcabru thinks that it is of the utmost necessity to be able to moderate the passions in order to avoid the extremes of behaviour that might contravene courtly etiquette (Paterson, 1999). This sets up

the classic tension between reason and passion as expressed in the following extract from Chrétien de Troyes' *The Knight of the Cart*: in this
scene Lancelot is hurrying to try to see the wife of King Arthur, Queen
Guinevere, with whom he is in love, and in his desperate rush he thinks
of jumping into a cart that will get him to her quicker. However, for a
moment he hesitates, because ...

> ... reason, who does not follow Love's command, told him to beware
> of getting in, and admonished and counselled him not to do anything
> for which he might incur disgrace or reproach. Reason, who dared
> tell him this, spoke from the lips, not from the heart; but Love, who
> held sway within his heart, urged and commanded him to climb into
> the cart at once. Because Love ordered and wished it, he jumped in;
> since Love ruled his action, the disgrace did not matter. (quoted in
> Swabey, 2004: 150)

The situation is only resolved when Lancelot sees Guinevere and she
reasons that it would be wise for them to be discreet. Here is an example
of the woman upholding reason in the face of the man's impetuous passion. What is also illustrated above, though, is the metaphoric use of language through which feelings speak: reason speaks from the lips but love
speaks from the heart. There is a very different embodied sense to being
held in the grip of passion than of reason. Love beats in the heart while
reason is in the head, and the person feels torn between two compelling
forces. In the next chapter I will say more about the metaphorical power
of language in emotions, but now it is worth noting that love is felt as
an emotion located in the heart. When love is rejected or unrequited
the lover then feels to suffer from an aching or broken heart, and these
metaphors have been with us since at least the days of the troubadours
900 years ago.

What I am claiming here is not the usual argument in which language
provides us with a vehicle for the expression of emotions that essentially
remain the same in all places and times. This view would have it that
there are basic emotions universal to all humans and only the mode
of expression of those emotions changes, leading to variations in emotion which are spoken of differently in different cultures. Still the basics
are the same, leading to the possibility of translation and cross-cultural
understanding. Instead of this I am arguing that as social relations
change, as they did in the 12th century in Europe with changing power
balances between different groups, new languages are created to express
new feelings. The language of love as written and sung by the troubadours was not a vehicle to express emotions already there waiting to be

articulated; rather, it gave form to new and vaguely emerging feelings. In doing so it formed, shaped, refined, clarified and debated them; it created a dialogue and drew on a new set of practices in courtly manners, through which people could interact, feel and think about themselves and others differently to how they had in the past. The troubadours' songs were among the cultural influences, along with letter writing, that '[suggest] a growing interest in individual identity, in relationships with others, and in the exploration of personal feelings' (Swabey, 2004: 24). But these identities and feelings were not just explored in these cultural genres and practices; they were formed and created through their articulation in song, poem and letter, in the context of the changed relations that presented the opportunity for them to emerge. As Foucault (1988) said of the letters of Cicero and Seneca in the classical age, they were the very technologies and practices that created a new kind of self and self-reflection: we can add to this that they also crystallise new feelings and create new emotions.

While the language of love as written by the troubadours has changed somewhat over the centuries, it nevertheless lives on today in a recognisable form. Although the heyday of the troubadours had passed by the end of the 13th century, their work was recognised by Dante in Italy in the 14th century, had spread to the courts of Spain and Germany (in the latter case through the tradition of *Minnesang*), and reappeared in 19th-century England where there was a new interest in what became known as 'courtly love'. Social relations had also changed over that time in Europe, with the aristocratic courts losing their power to democratically elected governments with the rising power and wealth of the bourgeoisie. By the end of the 12th century the church had begun to recognise and sanctify marriage, and by the time of the rise of bourgeois power in the 18th and 19th century, this class was championing the idea of companionate marriage and friendship in family life. Feelings of romantic or erotic love no longer have to be expressed outside marriage but now are an integral part of married life, along with ideals of friendship in the marriage. In our own time in the early part of the third millennium, erotic and romantic love no longer are the preserve of heterosexual couples. Yet much of the troubadour sensibility of love and their style of expressing it lives on. Take, for example, two songs written centuries apart but almost identical in their style and sentiments: the first, *The Skylark*, is by Bernart de Ventadorn and was written sometime between 1150 and 1180 (I quote here only the first verse).

Now when I see the skylark lift
His wings for joy in dawn's first ray
Then let himself, oblivious, drift

For all his heart is glad and gay,
Ay! Such great envy seizes my thought
To see the rapture others find,
I marvel that desire does not
Consume away this heart of mine. (Kehew, 2005: 75)

The similarity between this song and a song called *Skylark*, written by Hoagy Carmichael and Johnny Mercer in 1942, is striking. Both songs use the metaphor of the skylark as a free bird, able to fly above a landscape to search of a heart's desire – a love lost or not yet found, waiting somewhere to be claimed. As Carmichael and Mercer write, 'Skylark / Have you anything to say to me/Won't you tell me where my love can be.' And both use the metaphor of the heart for the feelings of love and desire; in the first song, by Bernart de Ventadorn, he envies the glad heart of others in love, and worries that his own desire for the same kind of happiness will eat away his heart in sadness. Similarly, in their song, Carmichael and Mercer have the would-be lover ask the skylark to carry his heart with it, to find freedom and happiness in the true love waiting somewhere out there. Both songs express the sadness and heaviness of someone waiting and longing in a state of unrequited love, the key motif of the troubadours' songs.

While some of these forms of expression might seem more dated today, we find very similar feelings in contemporary song lyrics, only they are expressed more directly. Scheff (2011) has found in his study of popular song that a large number still deal with the sentiment of unrequited love. In a survey of top 40 hit records in the US between 1930 and 2000 he found that 25% concerned the subject of heartbreak, more than any other category of song, including songs about the joy of being in love, which were far fewer. As with the troubadours, these songs of heartbreak include songs about falling in love with someone at a distance, someone the subject of the song may not know or dare to talk to, an object of love perpetually out of reach. In recent years there have also been songs with more sexually explicit lyrics, especially in genres such as rap, however as we saw above this is not totally out of keeping with the more raunchy lyrics written by some troubadours. When Scheff spoke to some of his students as part of his research about the place popular songs had in their lives, most reported that such songs had an intense, almost religious, private meaning for them, marking out important events or occasions.

However, Scheff goes on to claim that many of the heartbreak songs in popular music are not about love but about infatuation and lust, especially those about longing for someone from a distance. This leads Scheff to make a distinction between genuine or true love and infatuation or dependency. Infatuation is the idealised fantasy of another person, often based on appearance alone, whereas in the case of pathological dependency the word love simply acts as a denial of that very state, as in the case where people stay in relationships with those who abuse them on the grounds that they are in love with them. Contrasted to these two states, genuine love is a form of belonging in which two people are interdependent, which is to say both are attached to each other and have a mutual attraction and understanding, but neither is overly dependent on the other so that the relationship is lopsided. Here, there is attunement between the two without total dependence or engulfment. The problem with pop songs is that so few are about this kind of genuine love and so, according to Scheff, in the modern world we confuse the term love with other feelings like infatuation and lust.

The longing that is expressed in heartbreak songs and songs of unrequited love is directed to an idealised person or group rather than a real one, and is symptomatic of the alienation of modern society. Lacking a sense of belonging to a community or group in which real and meaningful relationships with others can be formed, people long for relationships that are purely idealised, a longing that gets expressed in popular songs about yearning for love and the heartbreak that persists without it. Certainly, classical sociologists such as Marx and Durkheim would see this as a symptom of alienation or anomie. In Marx's case alienation would ensue from the separation of individuals from the means of production and from each other in the absence of a society based on bonds of mutuality, the desire for such being replaced by an ideology of love in which this desire is directed exclusively to just one other person. For Durkheim, the desire for belonging to something bigger than oneself is the result of anomie and expresses the desire for society, but is replaced in the collective conscience by something else. In Marx and Durkheim's day, this something else was religion: now, Scheff is suggesting, it is idealised romantic infatuation which has become a new form of religion.

However, while there is much truth in this, there is a problem with Scheff's conceptualisation of genuine or true love. That is, to know what genuine love is means that first you must hold the universal standard for the definition of love that is true in all times and places, and this is something no one can do. When we say what constitutes genuine or true love we judge it by some standard of the day, and that is a moving platform constantly shifting throughout history. To claim that non-genuine love is idealised infatuation is to ignore the fact that, since the days of the troubadours in the west and perhaps before them in other cultures, idealisation of the other has been a central part of the idea of erotic or romantic love. The troubadours concocted a heady mix in which desire for someone out of reach is fused with sexual and erotic feelings, a religious devotion and desire to serve, and a sadness of the soul and spirit. However, they also introduced the idea that the more refined courtly manners should play a part in love, meaning that sensitivity both to one's own feelings and those of the other should enter into courtship. This is the basis for the possibility of mutual understanding and attunement between people that Scheff thinks is the basis of genuine love. Yet this is an historical legacy that has been left to us, not only by the troubadours, but by other social classes as they changed the feelings and thoughts about love, as we will see in the next section. But for good and ill the troubadours have shaped the emotion that today we know as love. As social standards change we may want to change our feelings and emotions, but this is hard because they have become educated by a culture that has enveloped us since we were infants and been ingrained in us as habits of feeling and thought which compose the emotions. As Marge Piercy writes in a poem quoted by Scheff, 'To Have Without Holding/ Learning to love differently is hard, It hurts to thwart the reflexes/of grab, of clutch' (quoted in Scheff, 2011: 118). But if these are our reflexes or habits, as I would have it, they are not biological ones: they are habits that have become engrained through historical, biographical, practical and relational embodying.

Civility, Civilisation and Transformations in Emotions

The sociologist Norbert Elias also notes the effect of the medieval codes of courtesy on the art of the troubadours and on *Minnesang* in his works on the civilising process, accounting for the socio-genesis of courtesy and love song in terms of the changes in social relations that I have outlined above (Elias, 1939/2000, 1969/1983). He also makes the same case I am making, that while the troubadours reflected in their songs many of the court conventions of the day and many of the emotional games played at court, nevertheless 'neither this convention nor its expression could have arisen had genuine experiences and feelings of this kind been absent' (Elias, 1939/2000: 250). Furthermore, troubadour love song had a setting and style in which lovers down the centuries have recognised their feelings, as I showed above. However, Elias's primary interest is the way that medieval courtesy was transformed through social changes into the ideas and practices of civility in the absolutist state courts of the Renaissance in Europe (from roughly the 14th to the 18th centuries), and then to the ideas and practices of 'civilisation' that have rooted deeply in bourgeois society from the 18th century onwards. Behind all the breaks and discontinuities of this history in the social relations between classes, factions and groups, and radical shifts in their codes of etiquette and morality, Elias observes a longer term trend towards the internal pacification of society which also had such massive implications for people's social practices that it completely remoulded their personality structure, including their emotions. We will come to this in a moment, but obviously it had a profound impact on all the emotions, including those types of behaviour judged as aggression and the feelings behind them.

For example, Elias points out that the troubadours sang not only love songs, but also songs that commented on the hospitality, or lack of it, that they had received in the courts of various lords and knights, and they composed war songs or *chansons de geste*. One such poem by Bertran de Born, written between 1180 and 1200, goes as follows:

> I tell you ... that neither eating, drinking, nor sleep has as much savour for me as when I hear the cry 'Forwards!' from both sides, and horses without riders shying and whinnying, and the cry 'Help! Help!', and to see the small and the great fall to the grass at the ditches and the dead pierced by the wood of the lances decked with banners. (quoted in Elias, 1939/2000: 162)

It would be unusual for us today to hear such a song, extolling the joy of warfare and the delight in killing and maiming. Indeed, among the modern-day troubadours a style emerged in the 1960s of anti-war and pacifist songs, as exemplified by Bob Dylan and Joan Baez. However, these singers were not in the employ of warlords; rather they were aligned to a generation in the 1960s that was against the military–industrial complex of the day and so the emotions they sang of were very different to the ones expressed by Bertran de Born. In fact, he was one of the minor nobility with a castle at Autafort where much of the conflict among the Plantagenets was fought out (Harvey, 1999). He was born around 1140 into this complex and shifting network of ambitions, alliances and conflicts between local barons, his songs reflecting this situation. As Kehew (2005) points out, Bertran de Born unashamedly revels in the emotions that battle stirs up, combining this side of his personality with a refined poetic sensibility that also allowed him to compose sensitive verses about love. In the following verse, however, Bertran's poetry is once more directed to war as he tells us explicitly what he will do in battle to one of his arch rivals: 'And if there I find the thick bellied Poitevin, They will see of my brand how it cuts, That on his head I will make/Mush, mud, and brains mixed with the joints of his mail' (quoted in Kehew, 2005: 149).

That Bertran de Born like other minstrels of his time could mix such bloodlust with the refined sensitivities needed for love poetry was no surprise to Elias. His point was that the personality structure of the times reflected the social relations in which people lived, where minor nobles like Bertran had to be constantly on their guard against violent attack, meaning that their future was highly uncertain. And yet in the larger and richer courts where women could achieve a small degree of power as patrons of artists and entertainers, new practices of courtesy were shaping at least part of people's emotional lives. This meant that the personality structure of the times among the nobility swung between a readiness for war and victory, then guilt and pity at the savage treatment of the vanquished and prisoners of war, and at court a demand for more courtesy in behaviour with some semblance of sensitivity to the feelings of others, especially in the practices of courtship and the art of love. Thus, as Paden et al. (1986) show, Bertran's poems that exalt the joy in battle are matched by those that express strong love for a beautiful girl. However, there is controversy over the 'overly simplistic' way in which Elias is thought to have read the works of troubadours like Bertran de Born, especially in terms of his war songs (Rosenwein, 2010). It is said that these are not simply an expression of aggressive feelings but are also rallying calls, attempts to boost morale in warfare, and are concerned with physical interaction and male power (Léglu, 1999). As Léglu also shows, though, the ideology of those like Bertran is very much that of the warrior whose role it is to ensure the nobility keep fighting each other, and in this sense aggression and the stirring of aggression is certainly a part of this. Nobles like Bertran were not concerned with creating social stability.

It was not until the advent of the absolutist courts of the Middle Ages, coalescing around the nation-states that we know today across Europe, that greater stability was achieved in the life circumstances of the ruling elites, and greater restraint was applied to all aspects of their behaviour according to new codes of civility. Elias is not claiming that this was a greater *repression* of the basic instincts and drives of humans to war and aggression, which in earlier times were given free reign; rather this is a *different modulation of the habits which had been formed in earlier times*. The modulation of the structure of people's affects now had to be more constant and even; it was expected that moods and emotions would not swing between extremes, as people exerted a new kind of pressure on each other through social competition. As the court became internally pacified people had to advance their cause by currying favour, especially with the king and queen and their inner circle, rather than by waging war. But this involved belonging to cliques, forming alliances, planning one's tactics for advancement and outwitting rivals in courts where civility was the order of the day. In this, 'continuous reflection, foresight, and calculation, self-control, precise and articulate regulation of one's own affects, knowledge of the whole terrain, human and non-human, in which one acts, become more and more indispensable preconditions of social success' (Elias, 1939/2000: 398). The value given to a person now rested on mastery of these social skills, but their success depended on insight into the feelings and thoughts of others, the likely strategies they were forming and the best way to respond to these. Thus the images people formed of others were richer and more nuanced, involving an understanding of the other's inner life that would become what we know today as 'psychological'.

Although life at court became more pacified, war still raged between nation-states, and the treatment of the lower classes and other non-human creatures would be what we see today as barbaric. For example, in the 16th century in France cat burnings took place as public entertainment on Midsummer Day, when a bag of one or two dozen cats would be dropped from a scaffold into a fire underneath, and the crowds would revel in their caterwauling (Elias, 1939/2000). Towards the end of the 18th century in France, the execution of the regicide Damiens involved a drawing and quartering that was so botched, the executioner had to hack off the condemned man's limbs while he was still alive before throwing his torso onto a fire (Foucault, 1975/1979). However, it is interesting that by this time such a punishment, which had been common in society up to then, so shocked the people of France, along with many of the powers across Europe, that it was one of the factors that led to the downfall of the French aristocracy and brought on the revolution. It is not that societies at this time were becoming more enlightened and civilised in some absolute sense, for as both Elias and Foucault show in their different ways, changing feelings and attitudes actually reflected new forms of power relations in society that created new social disciplines – ways of controlling oneself and others.

For Elias, this involved the greater rationalisation of behaviour through planning and foresight and a more constant, as opposed to a harshly repressive, control of immediate impulses. In *The Civilizing Process*, first published in 1939, Elias couches many of his ideas on the changing structure of the human personality in terms of Freudian theory, in which the superego and the ego, which is to say conscience and conscious reflection, come to play a larger part in steering people's behaviour than the impulses of the id or the 'it'. The problem here, though, is that this can make it sound as though Elias is arguing, in Freudian style, that the civilising process attempted to repress the more primal instincts through control by the higher levels of consciousness (Rosenwein, 2010). In his later work, Elias changes the terms of his argument somewhat to understand the way the whole structure of the personality changes under the pressure of social demands, including the circuit of impulses and drives (Elias, 1978, 1987). In warfare today, human acts of violence are more commonly fused with shame and repugnance and are attempted to be hidden. This means that, for Elias, there are no basic instincts, drives, or emotions, biologically inherited by humans that remain untouched by experience and learning, as culture moulds every aspect of the self from the earliest years. The unlearned aspects of human behaviour do not remain untouched by processes of maturation and learning: in fact, in human life, the two go together so there is no dichotomy between biology and social experience; a view that, as we will see in the next chapter, is shared by John Dewey. For humans, language and cultural experience provide the means by which we steer our behaviour, so as a child matures there is no moment at which you could grasp, in a pure state, an unlearned behaviour separate from the social conditioning that influences it. So, for example, unlike Freud (1930/1961) who thought that civilisation involved the largely unsuccessful attempt to repress or sublimate the sexual and destructive instincts of humans, Elias believes that instead 'it is not aggressiveness that triggers conflicts but conflicts that trigger aggressiveness' (Elias, 1988: 178). The battle in civilisations is not between primal instincts and enlightened cultures that attempt to tame them, but between different groups competing for power and prestige.

In 18th-century France, the struggle between competing social classes and groups centred on the very codes of etiquette developed by the ruling elite, which symbolised their sense of civility. As Reddy (2001) points out, the *haute bourgeois* felt themselves excluded from court circles because of the rigidity of the aristocratic system of etiquette, and, like earlier critics of courtesy, they came to see the overly polite and formalised manners of the aristocratic court as nothing more than hypocritical dissembling; a social mask adopted to attain power and status. Certain bourgeois groups began to develop a more open, egalitarian manner that prized frankness and sincerity above politeness in the face of power and rank. They sought emotional refuge in closed groups like the Masonic lodge and the private salon, where members of this class began to develop a more open emotional style in which relationships were based on bonds of affection and trust rather than the overly elaborate manners of the court. The upper middle class also championed the idea of affectionate marriage and friendship in family life that was unknown prior to 1700, and which would change the feelings about love, marriage and the family in the west. Marriage was no longer an arrangement to ensure the reproduction of rank and wealth within certain circles, but was to be based on love between marriage partners, extending to love for their children. Indeed, this social movement got the label of 'sentimentalism' largely because of the emotional style that characterised it, popularised in novels and plays. In these, simple peasants or serving girls were idealised because their lack of pretension and overly mannered style was seen as 'natural' as opposed to the 'false' manners of the ruling class. Nature also becomes sentimentalised and idealised as something that is inherently good, as in the works of Rousseau. Of course, Rousseau does not want to throw away all the advances in society, including the emphasis on reason and foresight in orienting human action: instead, reason must be guided by nature, rather than the other way around, otherwise reason itself can be corrupted. As Reddy says of sentimentalism, it was thought that '[r]ecognition of emotions and expression of them would lead to right action, whether in the realm of art, politics, or private life' (Reddy, 2001: 164).

For Reddy, what sentimentalism failed to understand in its plea for a natural and emotional way of being, was that it too was a system of emotional management in the same way the aristocratic code of civility was. According to him, the problem of all political regimes, which are also 'emotional regimes', is to employ a system by which people can navigate the emotions created within it without being so harsh that they create emotional suffering and cause people to take emotional refuge, as did the upper middle class at the end of the *Ancien Régime*. The rise of sentimentalism was one more nail in the coffin of the French aristocracy, leading to the revolution, but as Elias points out there was also the deadlock in the ruling elite itself which made any kind of serious reform impossible, reform that could have accommodated the middle classes which, through trade and early industrialisation, were growing more powerful (Elias, 1969/1983). Elias also believes that the aristocratic notions of civility were not completely lost after the revolution, as significant enough numbers of the bourgeoisie had been members of the court for the influence of etiquette to pass through the middle classes. This meant that codes of civility and politeness were combined into the notion of 'civilisation' in the 19th century, albeit in an informalised manner (Wouters, 2007), along with the other things the bourgeoisie were so proud of, such as scientific advancements and learning (Elias, 1939/2000). However, we must be careful of taking this at face value, as the term civilisation can also be used to hide violence and oppression

towards groups considered not to be civilised, and can also allow violence to take new forms, such as warfare waged through new technology
at a distance from its physical and psychological consequences (Burkitt,
1996).

In Reddy's view, the start of the 19th century also saw the emergence
of a new system for navigating emotions, which he thinks of as a modern form of Cartesian dualism in which thought watched, observed and
attempted to modulate feeling, yet often felt at such a remove from emotion it was unable to control it. People felt themselves to be split between
reason and emotion, with reason weak in the face of powerful yet dis-
ordered feelings. This is like the dialogue between reason and passion
recounted in the troubadour tale of *The Knight of the Cart*, except now
the opposition between reason and emotion is no longer felt to be a
dialogue as much as an open opposition between two competing and
unstable forces. Paradoxically Reddy believes that this 'double anchored
self' is what has made constitutional reform, the rule of law and civil
society so stable in western nations, in that the dualism we experience
gives us a tolerance towards indeterminacy and lack of resolution, along
with the ability to face uncertainty with intelligence that is a necessity
in any diverse and open society which must constantly be made anew
(Reddy, 2001).

As with Elias's work, Reddy's is a unique attempt to combine history with psychological understanding in order to develop an historical
approach to the study of emotions. This means we cannot accept the
basic emotions thesis and must try to develop an understanding of how
emotions are changed and reformulated to their very roots in history
through different political regimes and figurations of social relations.
The different social practices and cultural artefacts that are produced
in these various emotional regimes are not simple *expressions* of emotions that already exist, but, as I suggested above, are the very instru-
ments through which emotion is created. For Reddy, the use of words
for emotions is neither descriptive nor performative, in that they do not
simply describe something already there or perform an action by their
very utterance: rather, what Reddy calls 'emotives' form what they supposedly refer to. Thus the works of the sentimentalists – their diaries,
letters, books and plays – actually cultivated and elicited the intense
feelings they purportedly described. This is how different emotional
regimes both elicit and control emotions, through the emotives that are
common currency in the culture. Where political regimes fail to provide
individuals with the ability to navigate their feelings and cause intense
suffering, as did the aristocracy in absolutist France, the regime runs
into trouble.

For me, though, one of the problems in Reddy's work is that he bases his ideas of how people are capable of using emotives on modern cognitive psychology. Like some contemporary cognitive psychologists, Reddy sees no difference between cognition and emotion, understanding emotion as a form of cognition. Thus, '[a]n emotion is a range of loosely connected thought material, formulated in varying codes, that has goal-relevant valence and intensity ... that may constitute a schema'; furthermore, the range of different thoughts, such as perception and memory, tends to be activated together but 'when activated, exceeds attention's capacity to translate it into talk in a short time horizon' (Reddy, 2001: 94). This is how we can be aware of feeling something without always being able to immediately say what it is we feel. I will say more about the cognitive view of emotions in Chapter 4, but for now the problem with Reddy's approach is that he sets an historical view of emotions within an ahistorical psychological approach. Cognitive psychology, which is about the way thought material is ordered and sorted by various codes, like a computer deals with information, focuses only on the thought processes of *individuals* divorced from the social context in which they exist. What Elias showed in his historical sociology was the way that the whole personality structure was changed in the Renaissance through to the Enlightenment, so that individuals were forced by social changes to use greater foresight to moderate their feelings and actions when in interaction with others. In other words, *they came to feel that they were largely cognitive beings*, the locus of the self seated in thought (as Descartes famously said, 'I think therefore I am') rather than in feeling. Through cognitive psychology Reddy hopes to find a universally applicable psychological approach to explain the historical difference in emotion between periods, but the two things are incompatible. Cognitive approaches are *individualistic* because cognition is an activity occurring '*within* the individual' (Reddy, 2001: 332), but the question for an historical approach surely must be the changing nature of social relations which reconstruct the human self in its entirety – not only the way we feel, but also the way we think.

To see the problem of navigating emotion in different historical epochs as a question of cognitive strategy, as Reddy does, also downplays the strategies that people form as *groups*, both in the dialogue that goes on within the group and in the relations between that group and other social factions, cliques and classes. In other words, the focus on cognition, in order to give a psychological explanation of emotions, detracts from the historical and social context in which emotions are formed, failing to show the full complexity of emotional experience and its variation.

Love and Death in Brazil

This next section concerns the anthropological work of Nancy Scheper-Hughes and her studies of mother love and child death in Bom Jesus da Mata (a pseudonym) in Brazil from 1964 until the late 1980s (Scheper-Hughes, 1992). What this provides is a contemporary example of how emotions differ between cultures, depending on the social relations within localities, the material resources available to support various forms of relationship, and the moral values and feelings that stem from this within a group. This gives us a more complex view of emotional life of the type I am arguing for here.

Bom Jesus da Mata and the shantytown Alto do Cruzeiro are deeply impoverished localities where the people make a meagre living as sugarcane cutters, but the work is so poorly paid that poverty, hunger and malnutrition are rife. Because of the widespread malnutrition, many infants are born dangerously underweight and infant mortality is high. In the absence of a firm grounding for the expectancy of child survival, maternal thinking, feeling and practice are grounded in a set of assumptions: that babies and infants have no feelings and, thus, do not have the status of 'persons'; and that babies and infants are easily replaceable or that some are born 'wanting' to die. For those of us living in the rich north-western parts of the world many of these attitudes and practices around the lives and deaths of babies seem shocking, even immoral. For us, mother love has come to seem such a natural, almost sacred thing, and the lives of children so precious, that it is hard to believe that in some places this is not so. It is difficult to read the account at the start of Scheper-Hughes's book, drawn from her diary field notes, of a baby born so malnourished that everyone knows it is going to die and the women around it, including the mother, paying little attention to the struggling child, being more engaged with preparing and cooking a chicken. When the child dies there is no grief; the attitude is that it is better that it did not live given the state in which it was born. This is an example of what Scheper-Hughes regards as the 'routinisation' of infant death in a world where this is the most expected outcome for the babies of poor families.

The attitude that Scheper-Hughes encountered time and again in the shantytown was not to weep for the infants that die, but for the ones that live. One mother said of her dying toddler, 'Let him die, then. He's not the only one I have' (Scheper-Hughes, 1992: 407). Mothers can say this because the infant is seen as having no feelings, as not yet being human. The death of older children who have become part of the family and to who the mothers are attached causes intense grief, but this is not the case for babies. In fact, the women will often do little to try to save a struggling and dying baby, as in the example above, preferring instead to invest the meagre family resources, including food, in the older and healthier children. When mothers talked about their dead babies the emotion they expressed was one not of grief but of pity (*pena*), an emotion that didn't lead to grief, only to a resigned, pitying distance. Indeed, the women believed that tears would block a baby's entry into heaven as a symbol of a mother's clinging love for it, and so tears should not be shed over babies and infants.

Scheper-Hughes notes that many anthropologists before her who had studied life in poor parts of Brazil had taken this indifference of mothers to the death of babies to be a defence mechanism against grief, in that women were so numbed by constant bereavement that they inured themselves against it through a practised indifference. Yet Scheper-Hughes has not noted any lasting psychological effects of delayed or suppressed grief in the women she got to know over 25 years of work in the shantytown. Throughout that time she became convinced that the women's feelings of pity, not grief, are what they actually felt, rather than being a defence against their 'real' feelings. The pity these women actually felt for their lost babies stemmed from the way they reasoned about them, as recounted above, so that reason and emotion are not separate from one another. As I will argue here, there is *emotional reason* just as there is intellectual reason. Additionally, Scheper-Hughes was also able to show that the reaction to infant death didn't stem from a general emotional stunting of people in the shantytown – a generally low level of affect as a result of living in the violence of terrible poverty. Instead of this, the people of the shantytown had incredibly rich and open emotional lives, as do most Brazilians, regarding North Americans as emotionally 'wooden'.

For Scheper-Hughes, then, the response of mothers to the loss of babies stems from their emotional and reasoned adjustment to the appalling realities of their lives and from the way they relate to each other, to their infants and to their older children. But just as their emotional responses are socially specific, so are ours. Scheper-Hughes claims that mother love is something derived from the assumptions and values implicit in the modern, western bourgeois family. As I showed in the last section of this chapter, the idea that family relationships should be based on love, affection and friendship was something unheard of in Europe before the bourgeois family became the model for all family life in the 18th and 19th centuries. Added to this, Scheper-Hughes believes that rising material wealth at that time, especially for the bourgeoisie if not for the poor, led to a new reproductive strategy for women, which was to have fewer children – because with rising living standards more survived childhood – and to invest heavily in them, both emotionally and materially. This is now happening in the richer parts of Brazil where similar forms of family life, and similar sentiments towards children, are developing.

What Scheper-Hughes's research shows us, then, is that many of the emotions we think are grounded in nature as basic to all humans everywhere, and to some other animals, are in fact historically and culturally specific. In the 20th century, psychoanalysts like John Bowlby thought that infant and mother attachment was a biological function based on specific innate behaviours such as smiling, cooing, gazing and nuzzling which allowed bonding to take place. If this didn't take place soon after birth it could lead to a 'failure' of bonding between mother and child (Bowlby, 1969). Attachment was taken to be natural because similar patterns of behaviour between mothers and their offspring which lead to bonding are said to be observed not only in humans but in other animals such as birds. Likewise, the same school of British psychoanalysis developed the idea that grief is an emotion that is basic and common to all humans and some other animals as a response to the loss of special attachments, observed in behaviour patterns such as crying or calling out and searching (Parkes, 1972/1975). However, what Scheper-Hughes is suggesting is that these emotions are not biologically given responses to certain events, such as the birth of a mother's child or to loss, because we do not observe them everywhere in human societies and they do not appear automatically as a response to the same events. As we have seen above, in parts of Brazil, mother love and grief took very different forms, and grief was not present at all in the relationship between mothers and their babies.

This has led Scheper-Hughes to claim that mother love 'is far from universal or innate and represents instead an ideological, symbolic representation grounded in the basic material conditions that define women's reproductive lives' (Scheper-Hughes, 1992: 401). However, I disagree with the idea that emotions are the result of ideological or symbolic representations, as they are key aspects of people's lived, embodied, relational lives, albeit aspects that are historically and culturally contingent. In the west, mothers and fathers do invest a lot more in their children, especially emotionally, and the effect of losing a child is not a representation but a devastating emotional loss. Equally with Reddy's idea that emotions are thought material that has goal relevant valence and intensity, and as such are mental representations, this completely misses the feeling of the visceral nature of attachments and losses that mark people's lives in cultures where particular relationships are valued. Emotional navigation is not just a cognitive strategy but is social and cultural and, as Scheper-Hughes showed, dependent upon material circumstances. But emotions are material in another sense, in that they are lived through the human body and involve intense feelings. These have a symbolic dimension and involve thought material, but they cannot be reduced to that alone, as I will show in the next chapter.

This is a problem that can emerge in anthropology as researchers focus on the different linguistic practices that occur between cultures. In Catherine Lutz's fascinating work with the Ifaluk, a people who live on the Micronesian atoll of the same name, she discovered that these people do not have any word in their vocabulary that would translate as 'emotion' (Lutz, 1986). In the absence of such an overarching category, Lutz got a group of the tribes-people to identify some words that were 'about our insides', as in the west emotion words are used to identify internal states. Although 31 words of this nature were identified, it quickly became clear that these were related as much to the *situation* the Ifaluk person was located in as it was to any internal feeling state. This led Lutz to critique the western conceptualisation of emotion as only to do with private, internal states with little reference to the situation, but also the association in the west of emotion with irrationality, danger and the feminine (Lutz, 1988). Lutz then claims that the different discourses found in various cultures actually create the emotions they supposedly describe, as well as establishing a system of domination around them, especially between men and women (Lutz and Abu-Lughod, 1990). In anthropology, a similar debate goes on in the discipline as in others around the nature of emotion, with some arguing that certain basic emotions can be identified cross-culturally (Levy, 1984) while thinkers like Lutz and Abu-Lughod claim that the western conception of emotion is precisely that – western – and, according to Lutz, there are some cultures in which our idea of emotions just would not make sense.

Although I would side much more with the approach of Lutz and Abu-Lughod, given what I have been arguing in this chapter, nevertheless I think that there is a problem with approaches like theirs which seek to align emotions, along with relations of power and domination, to discourses – or sets of linguistic practices – alone. What I have shown here is that as social relations change, due to the shifting power balances between different groups and classes, so do people's feelings change as new patterns of relationship develop between them. People then seek out new forms of articulating these feelings that crystallise, shape and form them through new linguistic and social practices. Yet bodily feelings are still important because, certainly in the west, they tell us about our relations to others and also to ourselves, something I will elaborate in Chapter 5. Furthermore, what we characterise as particular emotions such as 'being in love' are actually complexes of different feelings that can include, certainly in the western world, sexual desire and longing mixed with feelings of friendship and personal attraction, or at the more obsessive end of the spectrum, feelings like worship and devotion.

In the next chapter I will say much more about the centrality of bodily feelings to what we in the west call emotion, as feelings give us a sense of our embodied relation to the world and to others. However, at the end of this chapter my main conclusion is that it is difficult to maintain a theory of basic emotions or emotion families, as if the current names we have for emotions refer to inherited habits of action, expressions and gestures that appear in all cultures. Clearly they do not. Furthermore, the social relations we are embedded in vary greatly across cultures, depending on material resources and power balances between groups. As these relations change, the whole structure of the personality changes, including feelings and emotions. Foresight and planning enters into a different relationship to feeling and impulse, as activity has to be sensitively oriented to different circumstances. Under such conditions emotions cannot be automatic responses to identical life experiences, such as ways of dealing with childbirth, loss, or adult attachments. In changing social and cultural relations humans work on their received habits and practices to change them into new forms of relating to others, and with this new forms of feeling and emotion emerge.

3

Emotions and the Body

At the end of the last chapter I concluded that emotions are best seen as complexes of different feelings and bodily sensations that are organised within local cultures at specific historical times and places and thereby given a meaning. The implication of this is that emotion cannot be reduced to the physical, the social, or the discursive realm, as emotions are complexes of all these things. Which is to say that emotions can only be experienced by living, feeling, speaking human bodies, located at given points in historical and cultural relations: the social practices and communicative interactions within those relations form what we call the emotions. Yet this leaves us with unanswered questions, particularly around the nature of feelings and the role of the body in experiencing emotion. These are the issues that I will explore in this chapter, beginning with bodily feelings and how these are the basis of the emotions. As we saw in Chapter 1, Cromby (2007) has made an analytical distinction in which feelings can be put into three categories, although in practice these overlap. First, there are the embodied components of emotions, like the racing heart when we feel afraid; second, the extra-emotional feelings such as hunger, thirst, or pain; and third, there are the more subtle feelings that arise in social interaction and in interactions within the world more generally. However, in this chapter I will broaden this definition out somewhat, while still sticking to its general outline, in order to try to define different types of embodied feelings and emotions. To understand these I will develop an aesthetic approach to the emotions, which, as I said in Chapter 1, is not about aesthetics in the sense of the theory of the appreciation of art and beauty, but is the study of how humans make and experience meaning, with the body and bodily feelings being central to this process. This aesthetic understanding of feeling and emotion will be based on the work of thinkers like William James, John Dewey and Mark Johnson. However, I will begin with a critical appraisal of the work of Darwin on the emotions, because the work of the pragmatist thinkers James and Dewey developed as a response to it, as a way of keeping the body central to an understanding of emotion while at the same time taking into account individual and social meaning in the experience of emotion.

Emotions, Sensible Feelings and the Body

As I showed in the last chapter, many contemporary psychologists who place the body and its expressions at the centre of the study of emotions follow in the wake of Charles Darwin's classic work on emotion (Darwin, 1872/1965). Darwin was not the first to study the different expressions or bodily manifestations of emotion; his book references a series of previous authors who had catalogued the many different facial expressions and bodily gestures that are seen as expressions of specific emotions. However, following the publication of *The Origin of Species* in 1859, Darwin was the first to claim that these expressions had developed as 'serviceable habits' early in human history which had become, through evolutionary adaption, biologically ingrained instincts that can be observed in humans and some other animals under certain conditions. Although the evolutionary slant on the emotions was new when Darwin published his study in 1872, what was conventional in Darwin's thinking was that the facial expressions and bodily gestures are only the *expression* of emotion, which is itself a state of 'mind'. This can be seen in the central question of Darwin's book, which is 'what are the movements of the features and of the body, which commonly characterize certain states of the mind' (Darwin, 1872/1965: 18). For example, fear expresses itself in vocal cries and in the flight movements which are efforts to hide and escape; however, 'these are just the manifestations that would accompany an actual experience of the evil feared' (Darwin, 1872/1965: 8–9), and that experience is a mental state of fear. However, this means that emotion is essentially a psychological experience with its bodily manifestation an expression of it.

This stance was significantly changed by the American school of pragmatism towards the end of the 19th and into the 20th century, beginning with the work of William James (1884/1971, 1892/1985). Although the pragmatists accepted Darwin's theory of evolution, they began to rework the understanding of the emotions that was based upon it. In particular, William James focused on the *aesthetics* of emotion, which is to say on the bodily *feeling* that is not just an expression of a prior emotional state, but actually forms a central part of the experience of emotion itself. In an aesthetic understanding of experience it is the *felt* qualitative unity of situations that gives meaning to them, including the emotions associated with the situations, prior to linguistic articulation of their meaning or a rational, reflective stance towards them. Bodily feelings then come to orient us in various contexts and give meaning and sense to situations. Feeling is as much a part of the basic ability to perceive the world and be conscious of it as the other senses, such as sight, hearing or touch. This means that feeling is as central to perception and consciousness as the other bodily senses and, as such, it orients us in our relation to the world around us, including the other people in that world.

For James the body acts as a 'sounding-board' which every change of perception or consciousness makes reverberate (James, 1884/1971). James's classic example of this is the feeling of fear one would experience on meeting a hungry bear in the forest. Such an encounter would not first of all excite the mental *idea* or affectation of fear, which then gets expressed in bodily responses like raised heartbeat and sweating, freezing with fear, or turning and running (what has traditionally been called the fight/flight reactions). Rather, the bodily changes follow directly the perception of the exciting fact and the feeling of the bodily sensations *is* the emotion, or as I shall claim here, is an essential part of the emotion. Take away these feelings and our thoughts of fear are nothing but pale shadows of the full experience. To *feel* fear the body has to act as a sounding-board with all the bodily reverberations common to that emotion. This is shown by attempts to imitate an emotion in the absence of its usual instigating factor, in which case emotion is felt to be hollow. Unlike the theories of basic emotions we touched on in the last chapter, James thinks that the varieties of emotion are innumerable as they are changed by social and personal experience. However, he does divide them up into the 'coarser' emotions, such as anger, fear, love, hate, joy, grief, shame and pride – which are associated with strong bodily feelings and reverberations – and the 'subtler' emotions, such as moral, intellectual and aesthetic feelings – which are accompanied by more indistinct bodily feelings (James, 1892/1985). So, even those activities that are largely intellectual also require the bodily sounding-board, because what would reading a book be without getting emotionally involved in a story and feeling for the characters, or in reading a scientific or academic book having the feelings of pleasure, displeasure, agreement, disagreement, or irritation. It is these feelings that bring an embodied sense of meaning to whatever it is we are doing.

However, over the years, criticism has been levelled at James's ideas about emotions, largely because many have confused them with a form of behaviourism that suggests emotion is primarily about the physiological responses to stimuli in the environment, and that the cognitive and psychological aspects of emotions are rendered redundant or at best only epiphenomena (Sartre, 1939/1994). Unfortunately, James did not help himself in this regard, particularly with respect to a rather poorly worded passage in his essay on emotion, often quoted, in which he tries to elaborate his notion that the emotion does not precede its expression. James said that contrary to the common belief that 'we lose our fortune, are sorry and weep; we meet a bear, are frightened and run; we are insulted by a rival, are angry and strike', instead 'we feel sorry because we cry, angry because we strike, afraid because we tremble' (1884/1971: 42–3). What is missing here, say critics, is a psychological understanding of why we are crying, and that particular emotions are not direct upon the instigating perception. I may cry because I am happy rather than sad, the two emotional experiences being qualitatively different.

As Barbalet (1999) points out, though, this criticism is a misunderstanding of James based solely on a reading of his essay on the emotions without putting it into the context of his whole psychological enterprise. For James, thought and feeling go together in what he calls the 'stream of consciousness' that flows on like a river. Furthermore, *the role of feeling in the stream of consciousness is to connect together certain thoughts and relate them to the objective situations that have aroused them, as well as to ourselves as the person who is thinking the thoughts.* For example, fond memories are suffused with feelings of warmth and intimacy that make them mine or part of me. My warmth and affection for treasured possessions or friends speak of my relation to them and the way I regard them as mine (my things, my friends). As James says,

> If there be such things as feelings at all, *then so surely as relations between objects exist* in rerum naturâ, *so surely, and more surely, do feelings exist to which these relations are known.* There is not a conjunction or a preposition, and hardly an adverbial phrase, syntactic form, or inflection of voice, in human speech, that does not express some shading or other of relation which we at some moment actually feel to exist between larger objects of our thought. (James, 1892/1985: 29, emphasis in original)

James goes on to show how the word 'and' not only has a grammatical meaning but stands for a *feeling* of connection between thoughts in the stream of consciousness, one thought following on from the other, or stands for the feeling of connection between objects, events, or people. This feeling of 'and' is also evident in the inflection of voice we use when we say the word, which might subtly change with the different situations in which we use it – for example, if we are waiting for someone to make a connection that we feel is obvious, we may say 'and' with an impatient intonation of feeling. Equally, there is a feeling of hesitancy when we say 'but' as we stop to consider alternatives or oppositions, and a feeling of possibilities when we say the word 'if'. Once again, whenever we speak or read, the bodily sounding-board is present to give feeling and meaning to our utterances, whether these are uttered to others or silently to ourselves in the stream of our thoughts. And these feelings express the *patterns of relationship* we have with ourselves, with the train of our thoughts, with others, or certain events and situations.

Furthermore, because the pragmatist thinkers like James stressed the fundamental importance of *action* in all psychological processes, our thought and feeling are seen to be directed by practical, aesthetic, or ethical interests. That is to say that the stream of consciousness does not direct itself, but is influenced by our practical engagement with the world and with others. As we enter particular situations we are oriented in our action not just by existing circumstances, but by past experience, our own interests, and by what we anticipate as the likely outcome of the situation. This depends upon prior acts of *discrimination* in which we have not only connected objects, people and events, but discriminated between them in terms of mine and not mine, or likes and dislikes, that incline us towards certain things or towards the desired outcome of situations. Thoughts and feelings therefore not only register circumstances present at hand and orient us towards them; they also anticipate the possible outcome of those circumstances. In this case James believes that we have *feelings of tendency* within the stream of consciousness, often so vague we are unable to name them, which direct our thought and action towards particular outcomes or ends (James, 1890/1950a). In this way, thought, feeling, action and movement are all part of the same global phenomenon of bodily being in the world, and they change as the situation we are in unfolds: for example, if our expectations and anticipations are not met we may feel frustration, or perhaps even relief, depending on the circumstances. At other times, our feelings of tendency may be so vague we cannot yet name them, in which case they remain as indistinct inclinations or intuitions that guide our actions, yet ones we could not rationally name or justify if we were asked to do so.

For James, the bodily sounding-board therefore orients, motivates and adapts our actions to particular situations, connecting the sensations of the body to objective situations or to locations in the body. As Denzin (1984) points out, we localise sensations like pain in our bodies and have a separate language to describe it. However, we also connect sensations and feelings to situations to understand their possible meaning. If I get a tightness and an aching across my chest and then suddenly remember that I spent yesterday digging in the garden, I may decide this is the reason for my physical discomfort: if I can't connect it to any objective situation I may start to worry that it is a sign of heart problems. As Cromby (2007) has said, these are extra-emotional feelings of the body that we do not necessarily associate with emotions, although, as I will argue later in this chapter, feelings of pain and hurt are metaphorically projected into some emotional experiences. Also, the feelings of our body can result in what Damasio (2000) has called 'background feelings', like the feeling of wellbeing we have when we sense that our bodies are fit and healthy, pain-free, relaxed and de-stressed. Such background feelings may not be at the forefront of our consciousness but provide the background, aura, or halo in which other thoughts and feelings are bathed. Alternatively, if our bodies are in pain or discomfort because of illness or injury, this can cause feelings of distress, dis-ease, self-pity, or bad temper that are more at the forefront of consciousness and influence our mood. According to Denzin (1984) moods are emotional feelings like wellbeing or bad temper, the reason for which might transcend particular situations and colour people's approach to life more generally. But this then raises the question of what emotions are and how they are composed of feelings, while at the same time often distinguished from different types of feelings.

For James, an emotion is a 'particular complex of feelings' and body sensations 'of which the psychic body of the emotion consists' (James, 1890/1950b: 459). However, this cannot be the final definition of emotion as James is clear that there is no typical bodily expression of emotion, as this differs according to both social and personal experience, so that the varieties of emotion are innumerable (James, 1892/1985, 1894/1994). Thus unlike theorists of basic or primary emotions, and unlike Darwin, all of whom thought specific emotions could be identified by bodily expression or changes in the autonomic and central nervous system, James is claiming that this is not the case at all. Instead, emotion is mainly identified in relation to a 'total situation' which changes according to both personal and social experience (Barbalet, 1999). Thus, James answers the question 'What is the "real" or "typical" expression of anger, or fear?' by saying that the question ...

> ... is seen to have no objective meaning at all. Instead of it we now have the question as to how any given 'expression' of anger or fear may have come to exist: and that is a real question of physiological mechanics on the one hand, and of history on the other. (James, 1892/1985: 249)

An example may help to illustrate what James is saying here, and how I am using his ideas to build my argument that emotions are complexes of bodily sensations and feelings, understood in relation to particular situations against a backdrop of social and personal history. The example I use below is taken from Gustave Flaubert's novel *Madame Bovary*, and comes towards the end of the book when the central character, Emma Bovary, discovers that she can no longer hide from her husband the secret debts she has run up with a string of lovers.[1] Finding that her current lover cannot pay the debts which stand to financially ruin her and her family, also exposing to her husband her illicit affairs and thus destroying her reputation, Flaubert describes the following scene:

> She stood there bewildered, quite oblivious, but for the sound of the blood pounding along her arteries, which she thought she could hear seeping out of her, like a trumpet-call echoing everywhere. The earth beneath her feet was undulating gently, and the furrows looked like enormous brown waves, pounding on the beach. Everything in her head, all her reminiscences, all her ideas, poured out at once, in a single spasm, like a thousand fireworks exploding. She saw her father, Lheureux in his office, their room in town, a different landscape. Terrified, she felt the touch of madness, and managed to take hold of herself again, in some confusion, even so; because she had no memory of the cause of her terrible condition, that is to say the problem of money. She was suffering purely for love, and in remembering him she felt her soul slip from her, just as injured men, in their agony, feel life seeping away, through their bleeding wounds.
>
> ...
>
> Now her situation, like an abyss, came back to her. She was panting, her chest almost bursting. And in a rapture of heroism which was almost joyful, she ran down the hill ... (Flaubert, 1857/2007: 389–90)

The emotional situation described in the scene above illustrates what I have been saying so far about emotions as complexes. First there are the physical sensations without which the bodily sounding-board would not fully experience emotion. These are the feelings of the pounding heart, the blood coursing along her arteries, the panting and breathlessness and the chest almost bursting. Second, there are the feelings that both connect and disconnect her to the situation in which her lover cannot help her, meaning that she faces ruin: bewilderment, confusion, suffering and agony (not physical but emotional agony). Third, there are the metaphorical feelings I will talk about later in this chapter, such as the blood pumping so fast like it was 'seeping out of her', pounding like a 'trumpet-call', the stream

of her consciousness bursting like 'fireworks exploding' in her head, and she could feel her 'soul slip from her' like injured men feel life ebbing away through 'bleeding wounds'. Fourth, the stream of consciousness turns into a flood, pouring forth reminiscences, ideas, images (her father in his office) in a single pulse. Finally, some of these feelings coalesce into the more complex emotional feelings that can be named, such as terror, love, rapture and joy, as they supersede each other in the stream of her experience, just as James described emotions as continuous and merging rather than as static states (James, 1890/1950b). In the intensity of this experience even the perception of time and space begins to distort, as the ground undulates beneath Emma's feet and the furrows in the field look like brown waves, and all her memories return in a single pulse.

Although the scene above describes an emotional crisis, it does help me to illustrate, albeit in a dramatic literary form, what I am saying here about feelings and emotions. Feelings are bodily sensations that result from some change in the organism as it consciously orientates itself to situations and their likely outcomes. Feelings are also to do with the sense we have of relation between different thoughts and the tendencies within the stream of consciousness, connecting up our thoughts and experiences as *ours*, belonging intimately to ourselves. In this way feelings are the vital aspects of experience, the things that make us know we are *alive* and *living* the experiences that happen to us, or living the thoughts that emerge in the stream of consciousness. Thus our thoughts, memories and mental images will also have an affective valence, moving us to feel something as we think, remember, or imagine certain scenarios. Many of these feelings combine temporarily into named emotions, like terror, fear, love, affection, anger, hate, or joy (to name but a few of the many varieties of emotion), before they dissipate and are recombined into other emotions in the stream of experience. But these emotions are always related to a situation and our trajectory towards it, as in Emma Bovary's emotional crisis above: she only knew terror, confusion and love because of the situation she faced and its likely outcome. Without this she would not have felt all that she did, nor would she have been able to know the reason for what she was feeling and be able to name specific feelings and emotions. It is only in the context of the situation that we live emotions and they make sense to us.

Situations and the Emotional Body-Mind

William James's work on feelings and emotions was developed by his fellow pragmatist thinker John Dewey. He agreed with James that emotion is not a psychological phenomenon in itself that gets expressed in move-ment or action, but *is* the bodily feelings that arise in movement or action, like laughing or crying are experienced in the rhythmical discharge of energy (Dewey, 1894/1971). Dewey also took up the aesthetic under-standing of emotion, in that emotion is about the felt qualitative unity of situations that brings meaning to them. However, Dewey thought that James's mistake was to consider acts of perception that excite emotion in particular situations in isolation from other acts and situations, rather than seeing them as coordinated into larger patterns of action that not only have present conditions but also an end point, alongside conditions that people bring from past experience. Furthermore, Dewey thought that aesthetics was not just about sensing the felt qualitative meaning of situations, but also *valuing* them. In any act of meaning-making there is also the creation of value that we *feel* in particular circumstances, and this extends James's idea that feelings are discriminatory. For Dewey, valuing a situation is not so much a psychological act of perception as an action or habit. For example, if I meet a wild bear in the forest, being totally unaccustomed to such situations, I may freeze with fear or turn and run: however, a forest ranger, trained for such situations, may respond differently, knowing what to do when encountering bears. Being more habituated to the situation, his or her feelings may also be different. If I encounter a bear in totally different circumstances, say, being made to dance for money on the streets of a foreign country, I may feel pity or outrage rather than fear. My feelings and emotions will depend on habits developed in past experiences along with the values that I bring to situations; so my feelings and emotions towards the dancing bear would depend on my values about captive animals and their treatment. In this way, Dewey is extending and deepening the notion that emotions are not basic instinctual biological responses, but are sensate bodily feelings that are modified, changed, refined and reconstructed into innumerable varieties by social and personal experience.

The fact that a single act is never to be considered in isolation, but is always part of a larger series of coordinated activities, has another impli-cation for the understanding of emotion. This is because, for an emotion to arise, an activity must be inhibited in some way by the expectation that it is part of a larger whole. In order to know what it is we are feel-ing, we have to pause for a moment to *interpret and value* a situation and to sense where it might be leading (James's 'feeling of tendency'). In fact an emotional scenario may go through a series of different stages as the pattern of relationship subtly changes and people orient themselves within it. To return to the example of Emma Bovary given in the last section, before the onset of her emotional crisis, she expected her lover to give her the money to pay her debts: when he said he could not, the expected course of action was inhibited; she then tried pleading with him, then tried to make him feel guilty, and finally got angry with him in order to try to get the money. Only when it became clear to her that this was not going to happen, and that she faced certain ruin, did her emotional crisis ensue. Here, there were inhibitions and pauses as the act went through different phases and various emotional modulations, the two characters moving through the shifting emotional figuration, interpreting and reinterpreting what was playing out between them.

In addition to the present situation and its possible outcomes, there is always the past and what people bring into the current situation from their past. In this light, for Dewey (1894/1971), emotion is also about *disposition*, the habitual way in which we are disposed to act according to our feelings. In Chapter 1 I wrote about this at some length, particularly in respect of the man on the train who acted violently when he found a woman sitting in one of the seats he thought he and his wife had booked. After a lifetime of violent relationships with others, beginning with his father when he was a young child, and believing others looked down on him, this man was disposed to angry and violent acts. Thus, a disposition is not only a feeling of which we are conscious; it is a practical attitude, of which we may not be fully conscious or in control of, that assumes a readiness to act in a certain way. An emotional disposition is, then, an adjustment of formed habits from the past to the situation we must orient ourselves to in the present moment. We all recognise such emotional dispositions in the people we know, their readiness to respond emotionally to certain situations in particular ways, and how this forms part of what we see as their character or personality.

In terms of what creates dispositions towards certain feelings and emotions, forming the background of our actions, Dewey picks out two key factors. First there are the personal dispositions created in our own biography that I spoke of above, reflecting the pattern of relationships we have had with others throughout our lives; and second, there is the background of social and cultural meanings that gives form and linguistic articulation to feelings and emotions. In terms of this second factor, Dewey thinks that the cultural meanings belonging to a society or a social group of which we are a member are the structural background against which our individual acts, and the flow of our stream of consciousness which registers the immediate quality of situations in sentience or feelings, take on a shape and particular meanings (Dewey, 1929/1958). The background meaning that we are aware of to some degree is what Dewey refers to as 'mind', whereas consciousness is an active and interactive process engaged in particular situations with other people. Here Dewey is saying something similar to Raymond Williams (1977) who talked of structures of feeling, which, as I said in Chapter 1, are formed by meanings and values as they are actively lived and felt through practical consciousness in the immediate moment, whereas the social and cultural meanings they draw upon are fixed forms from the past that only come to life when they are lived as part of practical consciousness in real, particular relationships.

Likewise, for Dewey, the structural framework of mind and meaning, and the fleeting, transitive nature of consciousness and action located in the immediate moment, are connected temporally. The organised system of meaning makes sense of particular situations, while the latter provide the drama of the immediate. This can be seen in terms of the western style of romantic love that I detailed in the last chapter, in which the social meanings and practices of courtesy, civility and politeness have informed the meaning of love, along with feelings such as sexual desire and longing, companionate friendship, devotion and servitude, and the sadness of unrequited love. Yet these form the background to the immediate situations in which we meet someone and fall in love; that is, the immediate moment in which these feelings and emotions are *lived* with all their drama and intensity. And it is in these situations that words like 'I love you' take on the vitality and energy of the relationship in that moment, as if the words had been newly minted on the spot.

Thus, social meanings and personal biography set the background structure and form the habitual direction for interaction in the moment, while the latter provides the novelty and drama in which this is lived. Yet the language in which social meaning is created and through which we can communicate about our own unique experiences is always something of an abstraction from the situations in which we live and in which experience is formed. Dewey is therefore against the idea that there is such a *thing* as *the* emotion of fear, hate, or love, in abstraction. If speech were to exactly reproduce that to which it refers, 'we could never speak of fear, but only of fear-of-this-particular-oncoming-automobile' (Dewey, 1934/1980: 67). And yet without more generalised social meanings emotion would remain *in situ*, in the contexts in which it appears and we could never communicate about emotion above and beyond the situation in which it is experienced. However, we learn the meaning of certain actions or perceptions as indicating emotions within particular situations of interaction with others, just as 'a child is instructed to term certain perceptual situations anger, or fear, or love, by way of informing him as to their consequences' (Dewey, 1929/1958: 304). It is only when action or perceptual awareness 'is taken in some *reference*, to conditions or to consequences or to both, it has, in that contextual reference, the distinctive properties of emotion, sensation, thought or desire' (Dewey, 1929/1958: 304–5). In this sense, an emotion is always '*to* or *from* or *about* something objective ... [it is] implicated in a situation' (Dewey, 1934/1980: 67). In the immediate situation, then, thought, feeling, sensation and other forms of perception run together in the immediate pulse of consciousness, and it is only a split second later, as we reflect on our stream of consciousness, that we pick out certain elements and name them linguistically as thoughts, feelings, or emotions, abstracting them and making them linguistically meaningful for ourselves and others.

This gap between feeling in the immediate moment and language or linguistic utterance is what allows humans to use wit, irony and sarcasm in their vocal intonations, or to give away something of the immediate register of their feelings in unguarded moments. As Bakhtin (1986) has pointed out, the emotion words in a vocabulary, or in his terms a 'speech genre', are neutral in terms of their feeling. Even a word like joy, which in linguistic terms conveys the meaning of happiness, can be used to the contrary depending on the expressive intonation it is given, as when someone says 'oh joy' when facing a less than appealing prospect. Given an intonation that means exactly the opposite of the word, the emotional-evaluative response to the situation is unmistakeable – that what the person is feeling is the antithesis of joy. Similarly, antithesis of meaning can also be expressed verbally or in writing, as in the phrase 'any joy is now only bitterness to me' (Bakhtin, 1986: 87), which conveys the feeling or mood of the person that they are now beyond feeling any joy in their life. In these examples we can see how emotion is a complex in which the feeling and expressive intonation with which words or phrases are said is used as a counterpoint to the linguistic meaning, creating a fuller spectrum to emotions. Emotion, then, is not found in the meaning of words themselves, for there has to be a bodily feeling in the utterance of the words for us to understand the emotion a person is experiencing. As Bakhtin also shows, these feelings have an emotionally-evaluative aspect to them, meaning that feeling evaluates and discriminates through the creation of value. The utterance 'he's dead!' exclaims shock at the news of someone's death, but it can also be tinged with grief or a hint of gladness in the spontaneity of the moment, depending on one's relationship to the newly deceased. Thus, the value expressed in the intonation comes from the feelings that stem from the nature or the pattern of relationship one had with that person, which in the unguarded moment can reveal one's feelings for them despite the requirements of social convention.

Given this, just as we cannot truly extract feeling and emotion from the situation in which it occurs, nor can we abstract it from the body. In

Dewey's terms, humans have a 'body-mind', which is a feeling, thinking body that feels because it can think and value within its activities. This notion of the 'body-mind' was explored in Dewey's later work (Dewey, 1929/1958), the concept indicating his belief that human mental life does not emerge from a 'higher' transcendental realm of 'reason' – a spirit which is opposed to nature and therefore separate from the body and psychophysical life – but rather the mental sphere emerges from, and always remains dependent on, biology and the psychophysical. Dewey created the term 'psychophysical' to get around the tendency in common speech – in English, at least – to identify the physical with the inanimate, so that the term 'psychophysical' describes an active, thinking organism; one in which action and thought are inseparable. Indeed, animate organisms, such as humans, only come to *think* because they are active and their activity demands thought. At this level, thinking and feeling are inseparable, as thinking animals both think and feel their way through activities in the world. However, this is not the same as having 'mind', which is the mental awareness that action and feeling are meaningful, for meaning can only arise within language and culture. The 'mind' emerges from psychophysical experience, yet it is restructured in another level of organisation achieved through social and cultural activities. This is particularly so with the acquisition of language, through which mental processes are reconstructed as movements and feelings are named. As Dewey says:

> Complex and active animals *have*, therefore, feelings which vary abundantly in quality ... bound up in distinctive connections with environmental affairs. They *have* them, but they do not know they have them. Activity is psycho-physical, but not 'mental,' that is, not aware of meanings. As life is a character of events in a peculiar condition of organisation, and 'feeling' is a quality of life-forms marked by complexly mobile and discriminating responses, so 'mind ' is an added property assumed by a feeling creature, when it reaches that organised interaction with other living creatures which is language, communication. Then the qualities of feeling become significant of objective differences in external things and of episodes past and to come. This state of things in which qualitatively different feelings are not just had but are significant of objective differences, is mind. Feelings are no longer just felt. They have and they make *sense*. (Dewey, 1929/1958: 258, emphasis in original)

Although Dewey came to regret the use of the term 'mind', with all its metaphysical connotations, he actually uses it in a way that tries to shed its metaphysical baggage. For Dewey, mind is not a transcendental phenomenon, for, as we can see in the quotation above, it only arises with social meaning and with other capacities and habits humans have invented rather than biologically inherited (Brinkmann, 2011; Putnam, 1999). With the use of language, feelings are objectified as properties of the community, in that we can talk about our feelings and the consequences these may have for the group, but we can also discriminate among them and identify them. Some feelings may be designated as sensation, some as thought, appetite, or desire; others are designated as emotions, which have a particular meaning. Emotions can be of anger, fear, or love; they are directed at the world in general, but in particular at other living creatures, especially human. As Dewey says, our experience is never immediately any one of these things, but only becomes so when it is taken in its contextual reference: only then does it take on the distinctive properties of feeling, emotion, sensation, thought, or desire.

A practical example of how Dewey's ideas help us to understand emotion can be given with reference to loss, bereavement and grieving. At the psychophysical level, elements of what humans call 'grief' can be seen in the bodily movements and actions of other animals, forming the psychophysical aspect of the emotion. The movement and actions that form emotions have been referred to by Dewey (1894/1971) as 'kinaesthetic images' and by Sheets-Johnstone (2009) as a 'kinetic bodily logos', both meaning by these terms the corporeally conscious movements of animals that are attuned to dynamically evolving situations. Examples of the kind of kinaesthetic images observable in grief are the bodily movements of shock and alarm, followed by movements specific to the emotion of grief, such as searching for the loved one (Parkes, 1972/1975). This kind of searching for the one who has been lost has been observed in greylag geese that have been separated from their mate (Lorenz, 1963), but is common across different animal species. So too is the crying out for the one who is lost, also observable among the greylag geese. We also see these kinaesthetic images in human movements among those who are grieving, as the bereaved restlessly search for the one who is lost and cry for them hopelessly even when people know that the person is dead. As Dewey noted, these kinds of bodily movements have a natural rhythm, as in the peaking and ebbing waves of crying and yearning in the bereaved.

But this is where we depart from the realm of the psychophysical and enter the human realm of the body-mind (a step Sheets-Johnstone doesn't take), in that humans know intellectually the distinction between life and death, and that their restless searching and crying for the deceased is futile. This has been turned into numerous poems, ballads and laments that sing of those who are lost and our inability to turn back time to reanimate them into life. In his poem *Sea Drift*, Walt Whitman describes two sea birds he saw as a child nesting on the coast of Paumanok, only for the she-bird perhaps to be killed and not return to the nest. Whitman's poem then describes the he-bird waiting every day for his mate to return and calling for her all night above the sound of the sea. Putting the lyrics to the sea bird's calls, cries and songs, Whitman writes, 'Blow up sea-winds along Paumanok's shore; I wait and I wait till you blow my mate to me' (Whitman, 1892/1975: 276). As an adult writing the poem, Whitman identifies the grief of his own lost and unrequited loves with the call of the bird – 'He pour'd forth the meanings which I of all men know' (Whitman, 1892/1975: 277). But here in poetic language, drawing from laments for lost love dating back to the troubadours and beyond, Whitman formulates in words, and therefore recreates for us all once again, the emotion of grief, something that the bird cannot do. In its calls and searching, Whitman clearly saw the kinaesthetic image of grief, but only he can articulate this in language. In its psychophysical bodily logos, the bird was clearly distressed. However, only humans like Whitman have the words to transform its bodily logos into grief. Clearly humans and some other animals have enough shared psychophysical bodily logos to be able to read each other's kinaesthetic images, but this does not mean that our worlds completely overlap. Although animals have feelings and intelligence, no one can say for sure if they have what we speak of as emotions such as grief.

In addition to this, there are other feelings common to emotions like grief that are unique to humans, such as anger and guilt, and a whole network of personal support and social rituals that guide a person through the grieving process. This is very much a process – a series of various feelings and emotions that take place over specific durations of time – that is dependent upon the individual, their personal history and present circumstances, but also upon the social rituals that prescribe acceptable periods of grief (Parkes, 1972/1975). As people start to emerge from these periods of grief, there is a need to reconstruct lives, habits, relationships and identity, and again this is something that is unique to humans. These social rituals and the way people can articulate their feelings in language means that, for humans, the body-minded experience of emotion is very different from that of other animals. However, the world of linguistic meaning is unique to humans and, as I will argue here, *deepens and extends* the experience of emotion in wholly distinct ways, reconstructing the psychophysical kinaesthetic bodily logos and images. Thus, feelings are not simply felt, they make sense only to the extent that they are meaningful. Furthermore, emotions are not automatic for humans upon a particular stimulus or event, but depend on the value and interpretation people place on the object or situation. As we saw in the last chapter with Scheper-Hughes's study of loss in a Brazilian shantytown, the women did not grieve for their dead babies as little value was placed on a baby's life. It is only with increasing material wealth and different parenting strategies that mothers and fathers invest heavily in fewer children, both financially and emotionally, including unborn and newborn babies. To experience grief, the thing you are grieving for has to be given a high value otherwise your feelings upon the loss of a person or object are of a lesser intensity, just as the women of the shantytown felt pity rather than grief for suffering or dead babies.

In summary, then, the body acts as a sounding-board in all our experiences, as bodily feeling *connects* and sometimes disconnects us from situations, other people and our own thoughts and selves. In this way feeling connects and picks out the pattern of relationship that binds together our experiences in a vital way as they are lived through our bodies. But feelings also *orient* us within situations and create *feelings of tendency* as to their likely, or desired, outcome. It is in these situations that we come to experience certain scenarios as anger, fear, love, joy, or hate, and name them as such, reconstructing our bodily feelings in the process as they are articulated in ways that are socially and culturally meaningful. But feelings are also expressions of *value and discrimination* in that they express our own personal likes and dislikes, tastes and distastes, inclinations and disinclinations, interests and disinterests. As we shall see in Chapter 7, although these are personal they are also social and meaningful and say something about the social groups we are part of, or identify with, as much as they do about our own personal value systems. Behind our body-mind responses to situations there is the entire cultural field and the meanings from it that we impute to particular contexts. It is only through these meanings that we can value the situation and the events or objects within it and then *feel* about it. These feelings then come to guide our actions within that situation, but only insofar as those actions are connected to a wider series of acts that also have significance for us. The clash of integrating these different acts then gives us pause for thought as we ponder our emotions and decide how to act on them.

In the next section I will say more about the connection between feeling, emotion and language, because it is clear from what I have been saying so far that they are intimately connected – in that language can actually reconstruct feelings and make sense of what we call emotions against the background of social meanings – yet at the same time feeling and language are not identical. As I showed with contrary expressions, feelings and words can be juxtaposed in order to create meaning, showing both their difference and their intimate connection. However, without feeling we would never be able to speak, and without speech we would not be able to articulate feelings.

Language, Feeling and Emotion

> The content of the human psyche – a content consisting of thoughts, feelings, desires – is given in a formulation made by consciousness and, consequently, in the formulation of human verbal discourse. Verbal discourse, not in its narrow linguistic sense, but in its broad and concrete sociological sense – that is, the *objective milieu* in which the content of the psyche is presented. It is here that motives of behaviour, arguments, goals and evaluations are composed and given external expression. It is here, too, that arise the conflicts among them (Vološinov, 1927/1976: 83).

What Vološinov is saying in the quotation above is something that I have been trying to outline here, which is that feeling and emotion – along with other aspects of the 'psyche' or of mind and body – are not, as we in the west typically think of them, private experiences that are basically incommunicable. Rather, emotions are about the public experiences we have in social situations located in the world with others. Thus the formulation in which feelings and emotions are given, as well as other aspects of consciousness such as thoughts and desires, is not that of a private language but of verbal discourse in its broadly sociological sense. That is to say, *the sense it makes not just in terms of the grammar of a particular language, but the sense it makes in terms of the pattern of relationship in particular situations of interaction in which that discourse is employed.* This is the objective milieu in which feelings and emotions can make sense to us and to the others we are engaged with and related to. Without the objective situation and verbal discourse, our thoughts, feelings and emotions would be meaningless.

This was what Dewey was also claiming when he said that perceptions only take on meaning in language as we name and think of them as thoughts, sensations, feelings, or emotions. However, what Vološinov is saying above is that our mental life is also changed with the acquisition of language, because consciousness is given in the formulation of human verbal discourse. So, for example, feelings like caution can be given expression in actual situations by utterances like 'look out' or 'be careful'. And when we reflect on situations we can say or think things like 'I was very cautious in that meeting', our feeling taking the shape of caution. These are not necessarily expressions of prior thoughts but flow directly from the situation we are in. This is because language is not primarily a mental phenomenon but a habituation and modulation of the body that is used in social contexts. Thus, as the body feels caution this can be directly articulated in linguistic utterance, so that feelings are deepened, extended and restructured by language. However, the same is true of all conversation as it takes place in social situations. As Vygotsky shows, every conversation and phrase is preceded by a 'speech motive' which is what we are moved to say in the circumstances. Vygotsky goes on to say that,

> This motive is the source of the affective inducements and needs that feed the activity. With every moment the situation that is inherent in oral speech creates the motivation for each turn of speech; it creates the motivation for each segment of conversation or dialogue. ... Thus, oral speech is regulated by the dynamics of the situation. It flows entirely from the situation in accordance with this type of situational-motivational and situational-conditioning process. (Vygotsky, 1934/1987: 203)

It is clear in the above that what motivates speech is not a fully formed mental process or content, but an *affective* one: that is, what one feels one *has* or *wants* to say in that situation or what one is moved to say without thinking. Furthermore, this need or want is not necessarily a psychological content in the form of words or sentences already formulated 'in the head' and repeated verbatim like a script: rather, what one feels impelled or desires to say flows from the situation and says something of what one *feels* that situation to be or how one is moved and affected by its emotive quality.

However, linguistic or discursive expression can also take place silently as we speak to ourselves. This is what James thought happened in the stream of consciousness as some inflection of voice expressed to ourselves some shade of feeling. On entering a situation we are wary of we can say to ourselves 'be careful' or 'watch out', only we do not have to express the words to ourselves in their full phonetic articulation: as Vygotsky argued, we can think in 'word meanings'. That is, we can speak to ourselves silently using the *image of the word* or, more precisely, its meaning, without vocalising it for ourselves phonetically. Instead, we work with the *sense* of the word, or we could say its *feeling*, rather than its precise meaning. As James said, we can feel the verbal inflection of words like 'if', 'and ', or 'but'; we can feel their meaning with the body sounding-board as much as understand them intellectually. For Vygotsky, as with Dewey, meaning is just one aspect of the sense of the word, albeit its most stable or structural aspect, and yet in different contexts in which we use words their sense and feeling can subtly change. I illustrated this earlier by the example of someone who says 'Oh joy' with a certain feeling or intonation that clearly indicates they face an unpleasant prospect. Here, the sense of the word 'joy' is redeployed in a certain context and given an intonation that communicates the opposite of its meaning. The sense of the word has changed. This is similar to someone who says the word 'nice' when they are handed something that is unpleasant.

Thus, the sense or feeling we have for words is something that outstrips their actual meaning. But then we would not have this feeling or sense without the words and the meanings themselves. This is what Vygotsky tries to convey when he says that thought is restructured with the use of speech. There is no such thing as a 'thought' independent of language that then gets 'expressed' in language, somehow being magically translated from one form, the mental, into another, the verbal. After we have begun to master speech as young children, it becomes not only the means of verbal expression but also a means of thinking. Except that when we think, we work with the global *sense* of the word rather than its precise meaning, so that each of our thoughts is not precisely articulated in fully formed sentences. That only begins to happen as we speak, and yet we know our meaning before we speak, located as we are within a situation in which a conversation is occurring and what we say flows from the affective inducements in the dialogue. Thus, what is true of speech is also true of other aspects of perception, including feelings and emotions. Like thought, feeling and emotion do not precede language and speech and then get expressed in them by some act of translation; feeling and emotion are already modulated by word meanings as we come to sense the meaning of verbal discourse. As speech becomes part of the bodily habitude, it retunes the bodily sounding-board so it can pick up the affective valences in conversations and vocal intonations, as well as in kinetic body images, movements, expressions, gestures and actions. These different aspects of our bodily being are not discrete, but part of the global phenomenon of corporeal presence in a world of other corporeal presences conditioned by the sociology of verbal discourse in concrete situations.

However, just because feeling and emotion are now restructured by language and speech that does not mean that feelings are automatically and readily open to linguistic articulation. As James outlined, we may have a feeling of connection or of tendency that is so vague and indistinct that we find it difficult or impossible to verbally articulate it. And as Vygotsky illustrates, thought as a global phenomenon, that is as a striving after meaning which aims to connect and make sense of situations, operates according to sense or sense-making activity, and yet that does not come readily formulated in words. It exists as a sense that something is or might be meaningful but is not yet fully articulated. As Vygotsky puts it, quoting from Uspenskii, 'What I say seems to shape up as thoughts ... but not in language. ... At times the fog clears ... and, like a poet, we think that at any moment the mystery will assume a familiar image' (Uspenskii in Vygotsky, 1934/1987: 280). But this is also true of feelings and emotions: in certain situations or predicaments we may have vague feelings that we cannot fully articulate, so that we strive to understand what we are feeling or why we are feeling that way. But the striving is towards some form of articulation, linguistic or otherwise (perhaps in visual or other images that artists create, attempting to share with others the meanings they have sensed).

Let me summarise what I am saying here. My main point is that with the acquisition of language, perceptions, feelings, thoughts and images become semiotic in that they are meaningful signs that we can *name*. This naming through language does not simply name some content already there, it changes it through the meaning attached to the word. For example, in sight we do not just see blocks of concrete (although even that is a perception that comes with a name) we see houses, factories, warehouses, office blocks, etc. The words infuse our perception and change not only what we see but also what we think. If someone says they live in an apartment we don't need to see it to know what they mean – we think in a word meaning that also creates an image for us. Likewise with feelings and emotions, for they too have a semiotic function; shock, surprise, anger, disgust, hatred, attraction, like and love are not just words but feelings that most people know and regularly experience. We also see and interpret their meaning on the bodies of others as kinaesthetic images, in terms of their movements, gestures and expressions. *These signs and word meanings are not the expression of a prior emotion; they are an element of the complex in which emotion is created.* The words give shape, sense and meaning to feelings and emotions that change as social relations change, and, with them, as forms of language and social practice change; as this occurs new feelings and emotions appear that make sense in the social relations of that particular time and place. Nevertheless, we *use* words with a feeling as we strive to make sense of immediate social situations that we are part of: the strict linguistic or grammatical meaning of words is not the most important thing in the immediate moment of conscious experience, but the sense with which we use the words: the way they come to articulate our sense of being moved in the flow of ongoing interaction as we are affected by the actions, feelings and emotions of ourselves and others.

Although I am in agreement with other social constructionists like Harré, who claims that emotions cannot be studied independently of local moral orders and the emotional vocabulary of a community, I disagree with him when he says that the effects of the bodily sounding-board are only 'leakages' into consciousness that are 'incidental' to the emotion (Harré, 1986: 5). Instead, while the emotional vocabulary is the ultimate *definition* of precisely what emotion is felt in a certain situation, experientially the bodily sounding-board is vital to us *living* that emotion in its context. Furthermore, the sense with which we use words in the immediate situation can also subtly change or play with their meaning, in which case our whole being is involved in the utterance of emotional-evaluative intonations, which then follow an emotional or affective pattern alongside, or juxtaposed with, a grammatical one. Emotion can be expressed verbally but it is the modulation of the entire body that gives the utterance its contextual meaning. In this sense, while discourse and emotion are intimately connected they are not the same. To use an emotion word one does not truly *feel* is a hollow experience; one only feels an emotion, and the feeling comes through in the utterance, when the entire bodily sounding-board reverberates with the experience.

Drawing together what I have said here about language, feeling and emotion, I think there are three key factors to account for in the relation between them. First, that words come to shape, form and restructure feelings and other perceptions as these are linguistically articulated. The words come to be part of the feelings – such as surprise, caution, anxiety, excitement, etc. – because language, like feeling, is one of the modulations and possible uses of the body. Feelings are also combined into larger complexes that we call emotions, just as romantic love is a combination of sexual and personal attraction, longing, desire, joy and, at times, sadness. Second, inner speech (in the form of word meanings) and other perceptions that form part of the stream of consciousness, is an affective response to a situation – as when an argument is carried on with someone in our minds long after the actual exchange of words is over – yet inner speech and other images that form the stream of consciousness can also provoke and instigate feelings and emotions. The sudden appearance of a bad memory can create many of the feelings and emotions that were part of the original situation, along with some new ones, or the recollection of the argument with a friend or colleague can cause one to mentally resume the argument again independently of the external adversary. Third, all of this relates in some way to situations we have actually lived through, or can imagine ourselves in, and it is that relationship, along with its linguistic articulation, that is the reference point for emotion. To say 'I was angry yesterday' does not really tell us much, but to say 'I was angry yesterday when I had that argument with my boss about my pay' tells us so much more, about both the quality of the feeling of anger and its reason.

Before finishing this chapter there is one more important aspect of the body and the part it plays in feeling, emotion and language that I want to consider. This is the role that the body plays in allowing us to both understand meaning and to metaphorically project it onto different experiences. All of this is important for the experience of feeling and emotion because this is often constructed in metaphors, just as nerves are felt as 'butterflies in the stomach' or love is felt in the heart while reason speaks from the head. Again my argument here is that this is not just a metaphorical way of talking, it is a way of *feeling*.

Metaphors, Feelings and Emotions

Although human meaning is usually associated with the products of human culture, and particularly with the language in which meaning is both created and expressed, in recent years Mark Johnson (1987, 2007) has challenged this as a fundamental assumption of the social sciences and philosophy. While discourse creates meaning in the linguistic sense, language and discourse do not contain the *possibility* of meaning, of humans being able to make sense out of their experience in order to express it discursively and to use language spontaneously. In his own aesthetic approach to these issues, Johnson argues for the centrality of the human body in the production and understanding of meaning, claiming that meaning is originally non-propositional and pre-conceptual. For example, the human body is upright and bipedal, so that human children learn early on to walk upright; our eyes are set in the front of the face rather than at the sides, so humans are aware of what is in front of them and constantly sensitive to things behind them or at the sides, on the periphery of vision. This means that a statement like 'all of your future is in front of you' has not only a linguistic meaning for us, it also makes sense in a bodily way, with the future ahead of us and the past behind us, just as the end point is in front of us and the starting point behind us as we walk down a path.

These embodied forms of meaning are what Johnson calls 'image-schematic structures', although they are not images in the pictorial sense, ones that we can visualise. Rather, the image-schematic structures emerge from repetitive, active interrelations between humans and between humans and the world. An image schema, therefore, 'is a dynamic, recurring pattern of organism–environment interactions. As such, it will reveal itself in the contours of our basic sensorimotor experience' (Johnson, 2007: 136), which is to say that we *feel* such image schemata at the level of recurring body movements and postures, rather than having a clear, conscious picture of them we can reflect upon. These schemata are fundamental structures of perception, object manipulation and bodily movement, so that 'we project right and left, front and back, near and far, throughout the horizon of our perceptual interactions' (Johnson, 2007: 137). In addition to this, habits of bodily movement are also present in perception, just as Dewey says that the habit of walking is latent in our perception of distance, even when we are sitting still and looking (Dewey, 1922/1983). However, this has led Sheets-Johnstone (2009) to criticise Johnson's notion of these being image schemata; if this form of perception emerges from habits of body movement and object manipulation, why reify them as image-schemata that then have to be 'embodied'? Why not just call them 'body concepts'?

While I do not want to get into this debate here, and for the sake of argument I will refer to 'body concepts' rather than the more cognitive sounding 'image schemata' or 'schema', Johnson's ideas are useful for me in the understanding of feeling and emotion. First, this is because of how he emphasises that meaningful experiences must be *felt* before they can be understood; however, second, Johnson also shows how body concepts can be *metaphorically projected* onto different fields of experience. Thus, our bodily sense of being balanced in space can also serve our more abstract ideas of balance in the justice and legal system: before finding someone guilty of a crime, we want to hear a balanced case based on the evidence for and against their guilt. This also applies to concepts that can have more emotional connotations, such as 'force'. For example:

> We begin to grasp the meaning of physical force from the day we are born (or even before). We have bodies that are acted upon by 'external' and 'internal' forces such as gravity, light, heat, wind, bodily processes, and the obtrusion of other physical objects. Such interactions constitute our first encounters with forces, and they reveal patterned recurring relations between ourselves and our environment. Such patterns develop as meaning structures through which our world begins to exhibit a measure of coherence, regularity, and intelligibility. (Johnson, 1987: 13)

These patterns of recurring relations reflect not just on forces acting upon us, but we soon realise that we, too, can be sources of force on ourselves, on other people and objects. When we face forces that prevent us from reaching a goal or something desired, we feel frustrated, defeated, or impotent, but when we achieve something that is desired we feel pleasure, powerful, or successful. Also, humans are not just physical forces that act on one another, we also move each other emotionally, or affect one another, as shown in the last sentence with all the different emotional feelings that can be attached to forces working with or against us. As Johnson (1987) remarks, the feeling of what force means could be described as its 'emotive meaning', although this will change in the different contexts in which we encounter force. So, for example, if we feel 'forced' by a manager at work to take on a role we do not want, or by a partner or friend to do something we would rather not do, even if we haven't been forced physically to do something, we nevertheless may experience this as a kind of force. What we call 'emotional blackmail' is something of this order, where we feel forced into actions because someone has played on our emotions for them ('if you really loved me you'd ...'), or on our sense of duty or responsibility ('think of your responsibility to the organisation ...'). As I have been claiming here, the various contexts and the words we use to describe them will also shape the way we feel – for example, the feeling of frustration is different from defeat – yet it is not the words alone that create the meaning or the feeling and emotion. That also requires the contextual bodily sense of the emotion – the feeling of the recurring patterns of relations and actions. Some of the names referring to feelings and emotions refer directly to the recurring patterns of relations and interactions, such as dependency, hostility and trust. And we employ metaphorical projection to describe these feelings, as when we learn we can rely on someone because of repeated patterns of relations and interactions, we come to 'lean' on them.

Metaphors such as these, then, are imaginative in the sense that they involve the metaphorical projection of one domain of experience onto another, so that leaning on a trusted friend *is like* leaning on a sturdy prop. Other feelings themselves are metaphorically experienced, just like sexual desire can be experienced as a 'force' or a 'drive' which compels us to sexual activity or attraction to another person. Many metaphors articulate the way the bodily sounding-board reverberates in emotional experience, such as 'bursting' with pride, 'falling' in love, 'insane' with jealousy, 'boiling' with anger and 'struck down' or 'paralysed' with fear. These metaphors do not just describe the feelings we already have, but deepen, extend and complete the feelings in their articulation; they create them as much as they describe them. For example, love is centred on the heart and, as we saw with examples of troubadour poetry in the last chapter, when we are in love we want our heart of be free to express what we feel; if it is not, we wish our hearts could take wing like the skylark, flying to the object of desire. This is not just a form of talk it is also a form of feeling, in which the organs of our body are metaphorically drawn into the experience of emotion and create what it is to experience that emotion with the full force of the bodily sounding-board, without which the emotion would be hollow. Similarly, I noted in the last chapter how songs of unrequited love frequently refer to this emotion as 'pain' or 'hurt', as if we have been physically injured. A 'broken heart' can be painful, in that we come to feel 'in pain' in a metaphorical sense, yet feel in pain nonetheless. In this way a non-emotional feeling such as pain can become an emotional feeling through metaphorical projection.

A key factor in this understanding of the contribution of metaphor and imagination to the emotions is that they are not to be regarded as romantic flights of fancy that transcend the body and reality; instead, they are forms of imagination that grow out of bodily experience as it underpins meaningful understanding and reason, while at the same time reconstructing bodily feelings within more elaborated cultural and linguistic meanings. In this sense, imagination and metaphorical projection does not separate us from reality but deepens our relationship to it, adding new dimensions of meaningful understanding into reality. Obviously this changes with cultural understandings; a scientist looks at the sun and sees a furnace of nuclear fusion, whereas William Blake looked at the sun and saw God on his chariot surrounded by the heavenly host. However, in both cases, imagination connects humans to reality in a more meaningful way, expanding our understanding of it. This is where I depart from Sartre in his understanding of the emotions, in which emotion was seen as a magical transformation of the world in consciousness itself, without an actual transformation of objective reality (Sartre, 1939/1994). Thus, if someone faints with shock or fright, this is a totally ineffectual way of dealing with the situation; but for Sartre this is not the point of emotion. By fainting, the body as directed by consciousness, unable to change the reality of the shocking situation it encounters, negates reality by changing its own relationship to it. It is a form of escape, denial or negation of reality. Another example would be the way people pull the bed sheets or duvet over their heads at night when they hear a noise on the stairs and fear someone has broken into the house. The bed sheets are no effective protection from what we fear; they are a denial of reality. However, although Sartre's theory may be a suitable explanation of certain types of responses among the negative emotions, like fear, it is less able to account for the more positive emotions. More importantly, though, it is not able to do this as it sees imagination as a way of disconnecting from reality rather than a more meaningful way of connecting to it. Magic transforms the relation to reality according to its own principles, but only in consciousness. However, what I am arguing here is that imagination is, from the beginning, a bodily connection *to* reality, and that magic is just one of its forms. Other aspects of imagination actually help us to transform reality, by inventing tools, creating new meanings and, in so doing, changing social practices, including feelings and emotions. As Johnson shows, at root imagination is a bodily ability to metaphorically transpose one field of experience onto another, one pattern of relating to the world into another pattern, something that has an emotive meaning.

A final example may help us here. The author William Styron has described in emotional terms a severe depressive episode that he went through in his later life, which brought him almost to the point of suicide. Noting how the modern concept of clinical depression was once understood in emotional terms as 'melancholia', Styron feels that the clinical term has emptied depression of all its terrible emotional force. Furthermore, the emotions he felt during his period of depression, or should we say melancholia, can be accurately described in metaphorical terms, as the 'suffocating gloom', the 'immense and aching solitude', the 'dreadful, pouncing seizures of anxiety' and the 'gray drizzle of horror' (Styron, 1990/2004). These are not poetic elaborations of the experience, but the way this actually felt. In addition there is only what Styron can call 'madness', described as a 'brainstorm' when all his thought was turned into mush and any rational thinking about his situation was impossible. Clearly, these emotive and metaphorical terms had the greater power to capture Styron's experience in terms of feeling and emotion, leading him to reject the clinical term of depression.

In conclusion, Styron's experience also helps to draw out the underlying themes of this chapter, that feeling and emotion can only be understood with reference not only to language but also to the situations from which they arise. Once he was through the episode of depression, Styron wanted to know why he had suffered this terrible melancholia. Although he could find no single reason in causal terms, there were a number of different meanings that seemed to provide a reason for his depression. He didn't rule out the possibility that this was in part due to an aberrant biochemical process in the brain, noting that his father had also suffered from depression and therefore there might be a genetic tendency to the condition in his family. However, this didn't seem reason enough, especially as the melancholia had not set in until he was approaching his sixties. Indeed, one possibility that would make the depression more meaningful would be that the tangible sense of darkness that overwhelmed him was the intimation of his own looming mortality. On reading a book about famous figures in history who suffered melancholia and how a common factor was the loss of a parent in early life, Styron also remembered the death of his mother in childhood and how, at such a young age, this was a loss he felt he had not fully grieved.

What Styron is doing here is searching for the meaning of this experience, making sense of it in terms not just of neuroscience (which we will turn to in the next chapter) and clinical depression, but in the human terms of patterns of relationship – in this case broken in early life – and other situations in his life, such as reaching the later stages of his years. The clinical terms were not fully acceptable because they did not capture the fullness of his experience, including the reasons for his feelings and emotions. They could only be properly accounted for in linguistic and metaphorical terms, and in reference to certain situations: in others words, in all the dimensions in which life is lived, and in the complex forms – bodily, thoughtfully, meaningfully, culturally, historically and linguistically – in which feeling and emotion are known to us.

Note

1. I am using this extract from the novel not as a text for a literary analysis, but in terms of the way an author recreates an emotional scenario that connects with readers because it is believable for them, chiming with similarly highly charged emotional experiences they may have had.

4

Emotions and the Body in Neuroscience

Over the last two decades work in neuroscience has become increasingly predominant in the literature on emotions. Although much of this research is disembodied, in the sense that the brain, seen as independent from the rest of the body, is the focus of neuroscience, this disembodied stance has been challenged by Antonio Damasio, a neurologist whose work I will focus on in this chapter for the very reason that it tries to bring the body into neuroscience. When studying the role of the body in emotion it is therefore impossible to ignore this research, and nor should we. Obviously, the brain and the central nervous system are such an integral part of our bodies that their contribution to the production of emotion cannot be ignored. However, in this chapter I deal with the existing research in neuroscience in a highly critical way, not because I want to deny the role of neurophysiology in the emotions – indeed, in developing a complex and embodied stance on the emotions, neurophysiology has an important part to play in this – but because I feel that neuroscience is currently *conceptually* inadequate in the way that it deals with emotions and the body. This is because it has imported models of psychological processes drawn from cognitive-behavioural psychology and computer science that I feel misrepresent the way that human beings relate to their world and to each other. So, as I argue in this chapter, although Damasio's work brings the body into neuroscience, it too falls prey to models of humanity that are highly mechanistic, failing to be a complex understanding of what emotions are all about. Compared to the position I am developing in this book, neuroscience is also asocial and ahistorical, believing that the neural processes and systems that govern the production of emotions are neurologically hard-wired through evolution and therefore universal phenomena. Towards the end of the chapter I suggest some ways forward as to how neuroscience might be used in a more socially and historically informed understanding of emotional experience.

Antonio Damasio on Emotions, Feelings, and Feeling the Feelings

Damasio's work has had a huge impact in popular science, capturing the public imagination with a number of beautifully written books which have led much of the recent research and discussion on the emotions (Damasio, 1994, 2000, 2004). His achievements are rightly recognised because he challenges two highly limiting tenets in neuroscience. The first is the tendency for neuroscientists to study the brain as separate from the body: because neuroscience is so focused on what happens in the brain, it tends to ignore the obvious fact that the brain is an integral part of the body. The second tenet Damasio challenges is the tendency, not just in neuroscience but in much of philosophy, to understand rationality as something separate from the emotions. Since the time of the philosopher René Descartes, whose works were published in the 17th century, western society has tended to view emotions as something separate from rationality; indeed, the 'two' inclinations, the emotional and the rational, are thought to be at odds with one another, regularly fighting for dominance over the influence on human behaviour and conduct. In the European Enlightenment of the 18th century two broad philosophical traditions set up in opposition to one another, one dominated by the figure of Immanuel Kant who thought that reason should still and moderate the passions, while the other, 'romantic' tradition was personified by Jean Jacques Rousseau who (as we saw in Chapter 2) believed that human nature – including the emotions – was inherently good and should always inform and guide rational decision making. It could be said in very generalised terms that since that time the thinking of the western world when it comes to the human condition has centred on a basic dichotomy which assumes that emotions are bodily phenomena while thought and rationality are to do with something disembodied and called 'the mind ', the 'two' being separate phenomena. The radical nature of Damasio's thinking is that he has, in part, challenged this assumption.

I say above that Damasio has challenged this only 'in part' because, following Darwin, he understands the emotions basically as bodily responses. The difference with Enlightenment thought and past neuroscience, however, is that Damasio sees the brain and the body as interconnected. For Damasio, the 'mind' cannot be explained exclusively in terms of brain events, even though it is dependent on them. Instead, the mind emerges from brain–body interactions, thus from the organism as a whole as it acts in the environment. As Damasio says,

> The organism constituted by the brain–body partnership interacts with the environment as an ensemble, the interaction being of neither the body nor the brain alone. But complex organisms such as ours do more than just interact, more than merely generate the spontaneous or reactive external responses known collectively as behaviour. They also generate internal responses, some of which constitute images (visual, auditory, somatosensory, and so on), which I postulate as the basis for mind. (Damasio, 1994: 88–9)

Some of these bodily responses to the environment are emotions in that, for Damasio, 'emotions are actions or movements, many of them public, visible to others as they occur in the face, in the voice, in specific behaviours' (Damasio, 2004: 28). An emotion then is caused by a stimulus in the environment which triggers the public, behavioural response understood as the emotion. Because Damasio thinks this public behavioural response is *the emotion*, he sees himself as working in the tradition of both Darwin and James; although as we saw in the last chapter Darwin actually thought emotion to be a mental phenomenon before it became enacted behaviourally, and James had an aesthetic and socially informed understanding of the bodily emotional responses which, as we will see, is very different to Damasio's. For Damasio, there is a sequence of events in emotional responses in which the 'chain begins with the appearance of the emotionally competent stimulus' (Damasio, 2004: 57), which triggers the basic mechanisms of life regulation that keep the homeostasis of the body in balance; some of these mechanisms, which have evolved to keep the body alive, are the behavioural responses known as emotions. For example, when the proverbial wild bear appears out of the forest, the fear response to run for one's life is a basic mechanism evolved to keep the organism alive. In this light, 'emotional responses are the result of a long history of evolutionary fine-tuning' and are 'part of the bio-regulatory devices with which we come equipped to survive' (Damasio, 2000: 53). However, to say that such emotional responses are purely bodily is wrong, if by that we mean a body without a brain. Of course in all complex animals there is no such thing, as the brain is centrally involved in producing emotional responses. In fight or flight behaviour, for example, a stimulus in the environment, once detected by a component of the brain's limbic system, triggers the enactment of the body state characteristic of the emotion of fear.

The chain of emotional experience for humans does not end here, however. For Damasio, there are three sequences in the chain that results in a conscious emotional experience. These three sequences or stages are constituted by, 'a *state of emotion*, which can be triggered and executed non-consciously; a *state of feeling*, which can be represented non-consciously; and a *state of feeling made conscious*, i.e., known to the organism having both emotion and feeling' (Damasio, 2000: 37, emphasis in original). In Damasio's scheme, a state of emotion is as I have described it above, such as the fear reaction when running from the bear: this can be non-conscious in that, in the immediate moment of the reaction, we may not be consciously aware of feeling fear. A state of feeling 'consists of having mental images arising from the neural patterns which represent the changes in body and brain that make up an emotion'; and finally a state of feeling made conscious (or feeling the feeling) 'occurs only *after* we build the second-order representations necessary for core consciousness' (Damasio, 2000: 280, emphasis in original). These second-order representations are other representations that have been integrated in order to give rise to a proto-self, which is 'a coherent collection of neural patterns which map, moment by moment, the state of the physical structure of the organism in its many dimensions' (Damasio, 2000: 154). In other words, once the image of our own self emerges in our thoughts – that coherent collection of neural patterns which maps the state of the physical structure of the organism – then we know that *we have* emotions and feelings happening to *us*. Thus, an emotion is the transient change in the state of the organism caused by an emotionally competent stimulus; a feeling is the representation of that transient change in the state of the organism 'in terms of neural patterns and ensuing images'; and 'when those images are accompanied, one instant later, by a sense of self in the act of knowing, and when they are enhanced, they become conscious. They are, in the true sense, feelings of feelings' (Damasio, 2000: 282).

To help clarify this let us say that the wild bear appears from the woods, triggers the emotion of fear from my basic neural response system, then as I am running away the feeling of fear emerges with the image of a wild hungry bear that appears in my mind, but the fully conscious feeling of fear emerges an instant later with the image of the wild bear chasing *me*. Only in the latter instance am I fully conscious of feeling afraid, fearing for my very survival with images in my head of what the wild bear would do to me if I was caught by it.

However, for the understanding of emotions I am trying to build here, there are a number of serious problems with Damasio's account. Let me say again, as also Svend Brinkmann (2006) does in his incisive critique of Damasio, that my own critique is largely conceptual as I am not challenging the neurological findings of Damasio, but the way he interprets and conceptualises his findings. As a social scientist, I can see right away that although Damasio has conceptualised the brain and the body as a partnership or ensemble, and sees this in interaction with 'the environment', the latter term seems to denote nothing more than an occasional vague reference to external stimuli, which are haphazard and disconnected events that trigger the survival mechanisms of the body-brain. The conceptual framing of Damasio's understanding of emotions is therefore *behaviouristic* because it centres on what he calls the 'machinery of emotion' (Damasio, 2004: 29), and the circumstances leading to the 'triggering' of this machinery are, in external terms, made up of stimuli in the environment, which seem mainly to be 'objects' or perhaps events. Given Damasio's very distant view of the social world, which hovers somewhere indistinctly in the far off background, rarely are these 'objects' other people with whom we interact. Rather, they are objects in a non-specific 'environment'. More accurately I should say that Damasio's view of emotions is a *cognitive-behavioural* one, because he does account for the mental stimuli that can trigger the machinery of emotion, composed of the imagery generated by the brain. Thus, stimuli that trigger the regulatory mechanisms of the body-brain can be 'external', such as threatening stimuli in the environment, or they can be 'internal' in two different ways: they can be 'triggered from the "visceral" inside' in the way that low blood sugar levels may trigger hunger, or 'from the "mental" inside (realisation that a catastrophe is about to happen)' (Damasio, 1994: 117). The 'mental inside' is composed of the way that the brain manipulates the mental imagery, the process upon which thought rests. In this way, thought can also trigger emotional responses, for the imagery of that looming catastrophe can trigger fear just as much as the perception of the wild bear. This is cognitive-behaviourist because human responses are understood as based upon the complex interaction between thoughts and instinctual behaviour.

There are a number of problems with this, though. As Wetherell (2012) points out in her critique of Damasio, he actually works with a thesis about emotions that is more akin to the idea of 'basic emotions' than to any other approach. That is, certain visible, publicly observable bodily movements, behaviours and expressions are taken to *be* the emotion, whether that is anger, fear, joy, sadness, or disgust, and that these are culturally and historically invariable. In fact, Damasio makes a distinction between 'primary emotions' that are largely innate and are the basis of emotional experience in childhood, and 'secondary emotions' that are experienced in adulthood. While in his early work this seemed to allow for some form of learning and modification of emotions, in his later work Damasio claims that secondary emotions are also mostly preset by biology. Thus, 'notwithstanding the reality that learning and culture alter the expression of emotions and give emotions new meanings, emotions are biologically determined processes, depending on innately set brain devices, laid down by a long evolutionary history' (Damasio, 2000: 51). But I will argue in the last section of this chapter that brain devices are not innately set in any rigid way so that, as the neurologist A.R. Luria (1966) suggested, learning new practices within a culture can actually reshape the functioning of the brain and nervous system within certain limits. This can be linked to the idea that evolution actually selects for plasticity; for the capacity to adjust in response to particular conditions (Jablonka and Lamb, 2005).

However, because Damasio understands emotion as biologically determined processes that result in fixed, universally recognised behaviours which can be named as specific emotions, it is then a question of the neural register of these responses as feelings, followed by a second-order cognitive representation of it as a feeling of the feeling. Only then do we become conscious of feeling the feeling of the bodily emotional response. But this ignores the point made by Dewey that the distinction between feeling and emotion (indeed, the distinction between all forms of conscious perceptions) is basically a situational and linguistic one rather than a cognitive-behavioural one. Normally we refer to a sense of caution in unknown circumstances as a feeling, whereas we would refer to being in love or being joyful as an emotion. It is not that one is purely cognitive while the other is behavioural, because behaviour and the bodily sounding-board play a role in both, as cognition also does: rather, it is a question of how we reflect on our feelings and emotions with respect to the situation from within the nomenclature of our local and global culture.

Furthermore, Damasio's theory ignores the evaluative aspect of emotions that comes from their historical groundings in social and cultural meanings. In James's and Dewey's approach, images in the stream of consciousness or situations in the social world do not trigger automatic, mechanical responses from the body: we *interpret* the meaning of objects or events in their particular social contexts according to the sociocultural values and meanings that we – as individuals with our social background, biography and affiliation to particular values – bring to it. Thus the dancing bear, forced to dance on the streets for money by a cruel owner, elicits very different feelings and emotions than the wild bear in the forest. As Dewey showed, we do not respond automatically to stimuli in the environment because human acts are organised into larger networks of activity that inhibit immediate responses, giving us pause to thoughtfully evaluate the situation before we know exactly what it is we are feeling. He understood that while nature, including the human body and brain, is central to the experience of emotion, that body-brain is nevertheless always acting in a context which it seeks to evaluate through both thought and feeling. In this evaluation, social meaning has moved to the beginning of the act and runs all the way through it, so that Dewey argued that the 'seat' or locus of mind is not to be found in the central nervous system, the brain or its cortex, but in 'the qualities of organic action, so far as these qualities have been conditioned by language' (Dewey, 1929/1958: 291).

The vital place meaningful interpretation has in understanding what emotion or feeling we are experiencing has been established experimentally by Ginsburg and Harrington (1996), who conducted a microanalysis of experimental participants' bodily expressions in responses to videotapes of people describing happy or sad events, along with a videotape of a baby playing in a bath and laughing infectiously. The experiment was designed to test the results of earlier studies on emotions, like Ekman's, in which experimental subjects were shown photographic slides of angry and happy faces, the results of which suggested that the subjects tended to automatically mimic the emotions they saw in the slides, measured by the way their facial muscles began to form into sympathetic reactions. However, Ginsburg and Harrington found that it was by no means as simple as this and that much depended on the instructions that the experimental subjects were given. For example, half of the 30 participants in their experiment were told that the psychologists were studying their emotional reactions to the videotapes, while the other half were given neutral instructions that made no reference to emotions. The participants were themselves videotaped to microanalyse their facial reactions and were also asked to self-report their emotions while viewing the clips. The results were much more complex than the earlier, more simplistic, studies would suggest, with the experimental participants' facial responses being dependent on the instructions they had been given for the experiment and, in some specific cases, the self-reports of emotions differed from what would be assumed from their facial responses. From this they concluded that 'facial displays are contextually contingent, as is the relationship between those displays and reported emotional states' (Ginsburg and Harrington, 1996: 231).

For them, their findings challenge the view that an emotion springs fully blown into being on the appearance of the appropriate or emotionally competent stimulus, as well as the idea that certain bodily expressions are unique to a given emotion. What the microanalysis of their experimental participants showed was that the bodily displays we take as signifying particular emotions take shape over a span of time, even if that is down to milliseconds, and that there are intervals of ambiguity, contradictory expressions (a smile would appear with a grimace) and periods of modification of expression. All of this is dependent on the context and how the subjects interpreted the situation, based in part on the instructions they were given about the experiment and what the experimental team had told them they were studying. The experimental participants looked for cues from the others around them, particularly from the leaders of the experiment when they hadn't been given clear instructions, to try to interpret how they should respond in that situation: their responses were not just mechanical ones to the images they were being shown. Also, there was a degree of difference in the response of different participants to the same situations, suggesting that people's reactions can be cumulative and dependent on earlier emotional responses or on personal history and experience, as William James believed. The implication of these findings is that emotion is not an automatic (mechanical) fully formed response to a stimulus, but that certain facial, vocal and postural displays can indicate to others the nature of the joint activity that is underway, 'the situated line of action' in which people are involved, thus playing an 'important regulatory role in social interaction' (Ginsburg and Harrington, 1996: 252). While Ginsburg and Harrington do not deny that the central nervous system is necessary for emotions, they conclude that this is just one of the constituents of the person–context dynamic system in which emotions occur, forming over durations of time – what I am calling a complex that changes and shifts over time, also changing what we feel.

All of this underlines my argument for the importance of the context and its meaning in constituting emotional experience for the person engaged in it. Furthermore, as I have been claiming here, emotions do not emerge from our body-minds as reactions to a neutral environment, but come from the patterns of relationships we are engaged in, relations that mean something to us. So if I am angry with a colleague because they got a promotion before me or because they made a disparaging comment about something I had written, my response is to do with my own evaluation of my work, my worth, value and ambitions, within a broader competitive career structure, rather than an evolutionary instinctive response. As Daniel Robinson has said, even evolutionary biologists and neuroscientists could not account for these types of tense relationships between people in terms of evolutionary theory or brain function. We do not explain the emotional conflict and tensions between people in a workplace setting, or in a political context like that between Israelis and Palestinians, by their brain functions. We don't do this because the emotional conflict does not originate in the brain and cannot be understood there. This is not to deny that you need a body-brain to feel emotions, rather it is to say that brain functions in themselves are not enough to explain emotion. As Robinson says, 'it is as if one asked what it is that makes that building a dwelling and was told, "The bricks" ' (Robinson, 2004: 290). Contrary to this, the very nature of having to 'account' for particular emotions that arise in relationships ...

> ... rules out the sorts of mechanistic, causal explanations grounded in scientific laws and principles. An 'account' of instances such as human relationships is something of a story or narrative in which one discovers how the participants understand the conditions facing them and how these understandings give rise to certain sentiments, desires and decisions to act. The story told, the listener now can make sense of the events through an essentially empathic and sympathetic process. (Robinson, 2004: 290)

Furthermore, we need this kind of account because in it we see the *reason* why people engaged in a particular relational complex feel the way they do. In this sense there is no emotion without a reason, even if the reason may be obscured by processes of denial or uncertainty, as in cases of confusion or anxiety. But in most cases of emotion we know what we are feeling by evaluating it against a relational situation in which we are engaged, and we start to name the emotion we are feeling once we have identified the reason why we feel that way. This was illustrated at the end of the last chapter in the example of the author William Styron searching for the reasons for the onset of his clinical depression: the explanation that this was due to aberrant brain processes was not sufficient, and instead he looked to both his current life situation and a significant bereavement in his past to find human reason for a very human predicament. That Damasio does not see emotion in this way, sticking instead to mechanical and causal explanations, is ironic given that he wants to develop a unified understanding of the whole process of emotion and reasoning.

Instead, Damasio conceptualises emotional experience as more to do with what happens inside the brain than in the situation that the bodily self and mind is located in. Thus he claims that, 'the brain induces emotions from a remarkably small number of brain sites' (Damasio, 2000: 60), most of which are in the subcortical region. For example, according to Damasio, the amygdala is central in recognising and expressing fear. What seems to qualify this as an emotion is the site of induction in the brain, which makes fear different from a surprise reaction or pain. Feeling surprise or pain therefore seems to be distinguished from feeling an emotion, because pain 'is the consequence of a state of local dysfunction in a living tissue' (Damasio, 2000: 71), and although emotions may result from this, the causes are not the same. However, this assumes that the physical location and physiological changes happening in the body and brain – once we are aware of feeling them – are what cause us to name one set of bodily changes as 'sensations', such as pain, and another set as 'emotions'. Where this leaves what I have been calling feelings, such as surprise, is totally unclear. But to understand why we call certain bodily changes 'pain' while we call others 'feelings' or 'emotions' really necessitates an understanding of the way we use language to articulate these feelings, such as that undertaken by Dewey and by the philosopher Wittgenstein in his study of pain talk. A particular brain location – such as the amygdala and its role in the experience of fear – does not explain why this sensation is *called* an emotion, while an uncomfortable sensation in the visceral inside might be *called* hunger or a local dysfunction in a living body tissue is called pain. As Wittgenstein argued, pain is not a neural representation that we *know* and then feel; I do not know pain, I have it: I am in pain. The words I use for that pain are not descriptions of it but part of its *expression*; which is to say not the expression of an underlying feeling or mental representation, but an expression in terms of being in pain, just as a child cries when it is in pain. Indeed, echoing Dewey, Wittgenstein argues that children learn pain language by replacing the cry with words, so that learning pain language is not learning a way to describe an inner feeling, but is the learning of a new 'pain behaviour' which is now part of the feeling (Wittgenstein, 1958: 89e). Just as we may see pain in someone's body or on their face, we can hear it in their words, as part of the global phenomenon of having or being in pain.

This, then, lead us to challenge Damasio's physiological and neurological distinction between emotions and feelings, and the whole three stage conceptualisation of emotion, feeling, and then feeling the feeling. The reason this needs challenging is not just in terms of semantics but because of the representational conceptualisation of mind which twice removes us from our experiences. What I want to suggest instead is that there is no difference between fear, feeling afraid and feeling the feeling of being afraid: when we are afraid we are afraid, and that is that. This does not mean that people are always aware of their feelings: someone may clearly be nervous before giving a talk and we may observe that by their trembling hands as they handle their papers or their trembling voice as they start to speak. When we ask if they are OK and they say 'fine', that does not mean that at some level they are not aware of their nerves. The verbal denial may be a strategy for dealing with a tense situation or a hope that no one will notice their nervousness, but this does not mean that a feeling is not actually felt. This is more so when it comes to our own emotional states, because while we may be able to observe emotions in others, even if they deny them, we do not observe emotions in ourselves. As Brinkmann says (in Wittgensteinian fashion), 'when I say of someone that she is happy, then I am making a report of something that I have observed, but when I say that *I* am happy, I am not making a report of anything': this is because 'saying that I am happy is an *expression* or *avowal* of my happiness, not a report of inner goings-on' (Brinkmann, 2006: 373–4). Thus, when I am happy I am not reporting on a mental representation of happiness, I am speaking from my whole bodily and mental disposition. Similarly, if I deny my feelings, like the nervous speaker, it does not mean that I am not afraid (and know it). Thus, we do not observe or feel feelings and emotions: if my emotion is of love I do not observe it and its mental images and then feel it, *I am in love*. This does not mean that there are no inner goings-on or imaginings in emotion, for I am arguing here that these are central to emotions, as I did in the last chapter speaking of the role of the stream of consciousness in emotional experience, the images and word meanings involved in feeling and emotion, the interpretation of the situation in which we experience emotion and other feelings, and the metaphors in which hurt, pain and other sensations can become part of emotion. My argument is that these are integral elements in the whole complex construction of fully realised human emotions as we evaluate and express our situation, not some feeling or realisation of an emotion that pre-exists conscious awareness and then has to be realised in first-order and then second-order representations. This is the double removal of humans from their experiences I am speaking of here. There are many elements in the relational complex that creates emotion, and experiencing emotion would undoubtedly be impossible without the neurological systems that scientists like Damasio have identified; but that does not mean, as Damasio said in the quotation above, that 'the brain induces emotions', if by inducing we mean to move, to cause to appear or to happen. What is central to the experience of a particular emotion is an event in our lives connected with the people we are related to and the situations we find ourselves in.

Damasio claims to have experimental evidence of the idea that emotion precedes feeling, the latter only appearing with the neural representation of feeling and its second-order representation as 'feeling the feeling'. However, he does not show contextual awareness in this second-hand report of an experiment, or take into account the self-report of the experimental participant in the evidence he recounts. His evidence stems from experiments done by colleagues on patients with Parkinson's disease, in which the patients have tiny electrodes implanted in their brain stems through which is passed a low intensity, high frequency electrical current which radically improves the symptoms of their Parkinson's. However, in one patient the electrical current passed 2 millimetres below the intended contact point on the left side of the brain stem, which caused the woman to suddenly look sad and then begin to cry. A few moments later she was expressing in words how sad and hopeless she felt. When the electrical current was interrupted, the patient returned to her normal state. According to Damasio what had happened here was that the electrical current had flowed by mistake into the brain stem nuclei that control the types of action that produce sadness. And once the behavioural manifestation of sadness appeared – looking sad and crying – the feelings, thoughts and expressions of sadness followed in their wake. Thus, 'sometime *after* the display of sadness was fully organised and in progress, the patient began to have a *feeling* of sadness' (Damasio, 2004: 69). But does this incident prove that?

One has to assume that because the experiment was not designed to test emotional responses those conducting it were not accurately observing or measuring the train of events. Even if these are roughly as Damasio claims, it is not evidence for his bold conclusion. We normally experience emotions in the natural course of our lives in particular social situations and make sense of them in that context: we do not experience emotions in the settings of a laboratory experiment where our brain is artificially stimulated by an electrical impulse coming from implanted electrodes. Normally we cry for a reason – a friend or relative has died or a loved one has left us – and in the absence of a reason it would be interesting to know how the woman in the experiment actually felt. It is said that a few moments after looking sad and starting to cry she was saying how sad and hopeless she felt. However, the woman does not seem to have been asked any more questions about this experience, probably because she was part of a research project on Parkinson's rather than on emotions. But even if we assume the sequence of events is correct, it does not mean that the physical action is the emotion and the resulting ideas and expressions are the feeling of the emotion. For example, we can cry for both sadness and joy, the physical expression being much the same, while the feelings are very different. This is what Ginsburg and Harrington noted above from their experimental participants, that when they were asked for their self-reports of emotion these were often very different from what an observer might assume from their visible bodily state. Much more careful experimentation would need to be done into this before bold and final conclusions are drawn. For now, though, I would maintain that the distinction between emotion and feeling cannot be experimentally maintained by this single observation, and that it remains an analytical distinction that is not helpful in understanding *the experience* of emotion, in which feeling and emotion are not so distinct and any distinction between them is usually made with reference to a linguistic and situational definition rather than on a neurological or physiological basis.

The problem for Damasio, however, is not only his mechanical account of emotions – that they are caused by a neurological response in the brain to some emotionally competent stimuli – but also that he falls into what Bennett and Hacker have called the 'mereological fallacy' (Bennett and Hacker, 2003). Mereology refers to the nature of part–whole relations, and the mereological fallacy occurs when the whole human being, or person, is treated as if he or she were merely a collection of independent parts. In the case of neuroscience, when psychological and emotional experience is attributed to these 'independent' parts, such as particular brain systems or their interrelationships, it is reduced to a level that only makes sense when attributed to the whole person. Thus, in neuroscience, parts of the brain are seen to induce emotions and not situations and webs of relationships in which living, whole persons are enmeshed, and in which they interact with other persons. Yet, for me, it is only in this context that the appearance and disappearance of emotion has rhyme and reason. If the brain simply induced emotions on the appearance of the competent stimulus, then our emotional and intellectual lives would be without this rhyme and reason, and be as haphazard and meaningless as the appearance and disappearance of the random stimuli.

To be fair to Damasio his neuroscience of emotion has some advantages over previous neurological studies, in that emotions are not reduced to specific brain centres or to certain chemicals, such as serotonin. Instead of this, systems made up of interconnected brain units are thought to be responsible for the induction of emotion, and what determines the contribution of a unit is its place in the system. Chemicals in the brain are important in this systemic functioning but they are only a part of the system, thus their contribution to having an emotion cannot be taken in isolation. Furthermore, there is no single brain site that integrates these operations, meaning that our strong sense of integrated thoughts and mind is created by the concerted action of large-scale systems synchronising neural activity in separate brain regions. However, this does not save Damasio from the mereological fallacy, as this systemic operation is confined to the brain only and does not take into account the person and the various situations and relationships in their life, which is the scene for their emotions. In his theories Damasio may well have reconnected the body and the brain in the production of emotion, but he has disconnected this body-brain from its belonging to a person that has a life within society.

As I have already intimated, a key difficulty with the neuroscience of emotion and the way it disconnects the person from their experiences, is its representational view of the mind. Damasio's view is that 'having a mind means that an organism forms neural representations which can become images' (Damasio, 1994: 90), and, in the induction of emotion, these representations are maps of the changes undergone by the body in its emotional state. Because the brain functions according to the systemic interaction of different sites without a single overarching system of organisation, it is activity in the 'interposed' structures that 'momentarily constructs and stealthily manipulates the images in our minds' (Damasio, 1994: 93). However, Damasio also says that while the formation of these images allows us to feel emotions, we are only aware of these feelings (and images) once we have the idea of a self to whom the feelings are happening: thus, 'neural representations must be correlated with those which, moment by moment, constitute the neural basis for the self' (Damasio, 1994: 99). In other places, Damasio likens this to the generation of the 'movie-in-the-brain' along with 'the sense that there is an owner and observer for that movie' (Damasio, 2000: 11). But this instantly raises the old philosophical problem of the homunculus – or the little person within the person – who is the audience for this movie, watching the thoughts and feelings appearing on the screen and in charge of knowing them. Damasio emphatically denies that he has replicated this old philosophical position by saying that this sense of self is 'a perpetually re-created neurobiological state' (Damasio, 1994: 100) which is constructed, moment by moment, by the same neurological underpinnings that perpetually generate the movie. But apart from saying that the sense of self is a temporary neurological construction, in the same way the mental images we see are, what is the difference between this idea and that of the homunculus? Whether the sense of self is a temporary or a permanent neurological construction along with the movie it is watching, there is still a movie going on in the brain and a self (or homunculus) also in there to watch it.

Once again, this is a problem of the mereological fallacy, where thoughts, feelings, and the sense of self that is aware of them, are all attributed to constructions of different systems of the brain rather than being the product of social interaction, as I shall suggest in the next chapter. It is also the centre of the problem I noted earlier where we are twice removed from our experiences. First, there are images in the brain and then secondly the self who sees them, just as there are feelings and the person who feels them. But in my view it is the person who thinks, feels, imagines, dreams and desires, and does so in the course of their whole life experience and history. To say that the brain constructs images on the basis of changes in body state, albeit given some particular stimuli, is like saying that television programmes and the images on the screen are constructed and induced from within the TV set itself, as is the viewer who watches them. The construction of images in the set is partly true, of course, as the TV does reconstruct images which we could not see without the internal electronic mechanisms by which it does so. But the images have been broadcast from somewhere else, from a television studio in which the programme we are watching has been created. Likewise, the images in our minds are not simply induced by different systems of the brain and observed by other systems; they are induced by the dramatic production that is our life with others.

But this is where the metaphor of the TV set breaks down, as this life drama is not broadcast from a distance and then reconstructed in our brains as neurological representations. As Gibson said about the perception of light, this cannot be understood by old-fashioned, mechanical stimulus–response models, as we do not have sensations of light triggered by discrete stimuli that are then picked up and reconstructed by receivers in the brain, because it is not the type of 'information' transmitted over a channel (Gibson, 1979/1986). Rather, we perceive light as we move through the ambient array of light, sensitively adjusting ourselves to it as we go, just as I am suggesting we attune ourselves to and interpret the emotional scenarios we are part of as they unfold around us. The drama of these scenarios is something with which we are immediately engaged in an embodied, visceral and interpersonal way. We do not see the image of the things that happen to us, the drama of our interpersonal lives, in the way we see a play on the television or a movie on the movie screen – in the neurological sense as played out on the screen of our minds. In fact, we do not 'see' it in that way at all as a picture or a movie: rather we are *in* it and *live* it with all the passion that is in every fibre of our being. The images in our brains that this drama leaves us with, which we may use to think through various situations or scenarios, are often a residue of that life experience, not the construction or representation of it on a mental screen that we are watching. Furthermore, it is we, as selves or persons, who are living this life, not a series of mental images in relation to other mental images, although they too are a product of that same life. We could not experience mental images without a brain, but what is going on in our brain is a product of our lives, not of the brain in isolation from life, or at two stages removed from it.

Brinkmann (2006) suggests that this vision in Damasio's work puts us back into solipsism, in that experience is constituted only in the mind (in the 'mental inside') and therefore is fundamentally private, making any connection with other minds or an 'external' reality dubious. This is true. But more than this, while Damasio has embodied the brain he has dis-embodied humans as corporeal presences in the world that interact with other corporeal presences, human and non-human. While the neural systems in the brain undoubtedly construct the mental images we have and, as I hope to demonstrate in the last section of this chapter, the word meanings in which much of our thinking and feeling is constructed, this does not mean that our experience of the world and each other is seen 'in the mind' as a picture. The idea that we see the world before us like a picture is something that has long been criticised by phenomenological thinkers (Heidegger, 1977); instead, they suggest humans experience the world as a bodily presence *in* that world, a world we have bodily as much as intellectually or mentally.

At this point it is necessary to say that all I have argued so far does not mean that we should discard or ignore neuroscience when it comes to an understanding of the emotions: rather, what we need to discard is the mechanical form of cognitive-behavioural theory that neuroscientists like Damasio tend to use as a conceptual framework through which to understand their experimental findings. Neuroscience could fit into another conceptual framework which doesn't ignore the importance of human meaning, both in a cultural-historical and in a personal sense, when it comes to understanding emotional experience. This approach would look at the meaning and reason why we experience the emotions and feelings that we do, setting this in the context of our various social relations and situations. This would be a complex understanding of emotions in the way I have been describing it here, in that neurobiology would be a component in the relational complex in which emotions arise; a necessary component in that we could not experience emotions without being an embodied central nervous system, but this is not all that human beings are. We are also beings in a social world with a social identity, and what we feel and think is inextricably located in this context. Neurobiology is a constituent part of this complex but not the *origin* of feelings and thoughts.

Neurology and the Body in Social and Emotional Experience

What, then, might an explanation of emotion look like that accounts for neurobiology but doesn't see the brain as the point of origin or site of induction of emotion? In a recent article, Reddy (2009) has argued that the idea of parallel processing in neuroscience is of vital importance for the social sciences, as it helps to explain how human beings generate new meanings and can thus say something new, while working with the meanings, discourses and language that they have inherited from their culture. For the philosopher Michel Foucault, not only did discursive practices systematically form the objects of which they spoke, they also formed, within the rules that underlay the discursive system, the agents who could speak (Foucault, 1969/1989). This meant it was never easy for these agents to say anything new, as their powers of agency and speech were always contained within discourse. For Reddy, the idea of parallel processing in neuroscience shows how, through 'top-down' and 'cascade' processing (see Bar et al., 2006; Yee and Sedivy, 2006), the fleeting recognition of an object or the start of the sound of a word can, in milliseconds, lead people to anticipate the meaning of the object or word. This is because the results of high level processing – is what I'm seeing the branches of a tree or the antlers of a deer? – are sent back down the chain to speed up the lower level processing of the perception of edges, shapes (the forked pattern that might be branches or antlers), phonemes, morphemes and words. Thus, as Vygotsky said about the production of speech, we may first of all think with the 'image' of a word, one that contains the meaning of what we want to say, and from this produce a whole, fully formed sentence, knowing what we want to say before we actually say it (Vygotsky, 1934/1987). In parallel processing, the word first appears in the form of its image, which is then anticipated by higher levels of processing in terms of what the person wants to say (and, as we saw in the last chapter, Vygotsky is clear that what people want to say is related to the situation they are in at the time and their relationship to it, not to some purely 'internal' image, sensation or feeling): this is then passed down the system to speed up the production of more words that can fully complete a sentence in verbal speech that expresses the meaning of what we want to say. This is how we can speak in fully formed sentences to others without in advance working out for ourselves every word we are going to say. It also explains in neurological terms how we can *feel* our way through social activities and dialogues with only a general inclination of what we want to do or say, rather than having a fully formed plan or script pre-prepared for a relational scenario. In this way, how we feel comes to orient how we act and speak in particular situations.

For Reddy, this explains how each person is a creative language user who can say something new. Little is yet known about how the different levels of speech production in the brain 'speak' to each other in order to work in such a cascading way, as each level seems to use a different form of encoding, and little is also known about how different systems 'speak' to each other, such as speech recognition and visual perception. In experiments it has been shown that no sooner is a word pronounced than a subject's eyes are moving towards the corresponding visual object depicted on a chart. But this gives experimental confirmation to what philosophers have known for decades: that different forms of perception can be transposed into one another. For example, Merleau-Ponty recognised a process that he called 'structuration' in which what we see can be transposed into words, and what we hear or speak can be transposed into images (Merleau-Ponty, 1964/1968). Structuration works because vision can be understood as structured like a language; that is to say, it has a pattern and form, or 'grammar', which can be transposed into the patterns and forms of speech; likewise, speech patterns can be transposed into the patterns of visual imagery. In fact Werblin and Roska say that as we read, grasp objects, or walk about, our visual perceptions 'form a fundamental "visual language", with its own phrasing and grammar that embodied the neural vocabulary of vision' (Werblin and Roska, 2007: 75). As Johnson (1987, 2007) showed, this process is at the basis of meaning-making, in that basic bodily perceptions, such as a sense of balance, can be transposed (or 'structurated') into verbally articulated value systems, in the way that 'balance' has become a principle behind systems of justice and law, or 'vision' can be extended beyond the realm of perception to indicate forward thinking in someone's ideas.

All of this supports much of what I said in the last chapter about the way in which images, metaphors and imagination play a large part in emotional experience. Metaphors like breaking or sinking hearts, or isolation and solitude, can actually be felt in the body through the images they create. And just as visual grammar can be transposed into linguistically grammatical descriptions of what we see, so too can our emotional reason be transposed into consciously thoughtful reason. In fact, as Duncan and Barrett say, there 'is no such thing as "non-affective thought" ' (Duncan and Barrett, 2007: 1184–5). Like Damasio they argue that no brain areas can be designated as specifically 'cognitive' or 'emotive' ('affective'), so that 'affect is instantiated by a widely distributed, functional network that includes both subcortical regions (typically called "affective") and anterior frontal regions (traditionally called "cognitive")' (Duncan and Barrett, 2007: 1186). This means that parts of the brain once thought to deal with cognition (the processes of thinking) and those thought to deal with affect (emotion) are in fact involved in both thinking and feeling. Thus when we perceive objects we not only see them, we also evaluate them. When making choices we do not make purely rational judgements based on principles of reason, we choose on the basis of 'affective working memory' of the things we value, like, or dislike. Indeed, Duncan and

Barrett conclude that affect is a necessary condition for ordinary conscious experience because it gives all that we perceive and think of a first-person, 'about me' quality without which our perceptions and thoughts would not be ours. (I will illustrate this more in the next chapter.) In explaining how we sometimes experience perception of an object and its affective meaning as separate phenomena, Duncan and Barrett follow Dewey in claiming that they are not ontologically separate phenomena in concrete experience, but a distinction between them can be made in reflection upon this experience. So it is only in reflection after the fact of an experience that we can make a distinction between perception and affect, or between thought and feeling.

However, unlike Dewey, Duncan and Barrett have a representational theory of mind and want to show that affect is actually a form of cognition: thus, 'affect makes important contributions to both *sensory and cognitive processing*' (Duncan and Barrett, 2007: 1184, my emphasis). But the idea of affect playing a role in cognitive and sensory *processing* takes the metaphor of the mind as computer to suggest that cognition receives input and transforms it by various operations into information that is understandable or can be used as the basis of knowledge. In terms of cognition, this understandable information comes in the form of 'representations' through which we can sort sensory data into an ordered form that creates intelligible images or ideas of the world around us. Thus affective reactions are the means by which 'information about the external world is translated into an internal code or representation', and the term 'affect' itself, rather than 'emotion', is used to denote 'any state that *represents* how an object or situation impacts a person' (Duncan and Barrett, 2007: 1185, my emphasis).

In a similar way, Damasio drew on a cognitive-behavioural conceptual framework to understand emotions, in which the brain constructed neural maps on the basis of bodily states and manipulated mental images in order to form mental representations. In some cases these representations were of the bodily states of emotion, and the second-order representations formed the feelings of which we could become conscious. The drawbacks of this computational way of understanding human thought and action have been spelled out at length by Dreyfus (Dreyfus, 1992; Dreyfus and Dreyfus, 1986). From my perspective here, the problem with it is that humans not only process information, they also use that information to *interpret* the world around them and to give it meaning, and they do so collectively. Thus, computational models of information processing are always limited when applied to human thinking and feeling. Many of the articles referred to above also employ similar models and metaphors to the ones Damasio used, particularly representational models of thought which lead to metaphors of watching 'movies' in the eyes or brain. I have already critiqued these models and metaphors above for removing humans from the scenes and relationships of their dramatic emotional encounters, instead theorising the body-brain in isolation from the situations and dramas of emotional experience. This removes us from the first-person, immediate experience we feel and think about.

The representational theories of mind are inadequate because they replicate an old dualistic metaphysics and epistemology in philosophy and science, in which mental representations were understood as symbolic constructs 'inside' the mind or brain which then refer in some uncertain way to a reality 'outside' the organism. The perspective I have been putting forward here – using a variety of different theorists like James, Dewey, Merleau-Ponty, Johnson and Sheets-Johnstone – is to understand thought, feeling and emotion as based on bodily interactions with the world and other people. If we then think of these corporeal actions and interactions as forming what Sheets-Johnstone (2009) called 'body concepts', which lead to the formation of symbolically and linguistically articulated thoughts, this kind of dualism can be circumvented, as thought is not separated from bodily activity in the world. In this type of understanding, we are not removed from bodily experience in a world and encased within a mind that can only represent the world we live in. Instead we are engaged with the world in a direct, active, corporeal way, and our thinking and feeling rests upon this. Thinking, feeling and emoting are not then forms of cognition that are different from perceiving and acting. For neurology this means that processes of thinking or cognition should not be seen as purely internal information processing devices based in brain systems and functioning, which produce representations in the form of neural images, concepts, or propositional constructs. Instead, neural patterns must be based on active experience in and of the world in which we live. As Johnson has said, rejecting his earlier view that image schemata were representations, 'neural activation patterns are merely recurring structures of experiences actual and possible, retained in the organism as synaptic weights' (Johnson, 2007: 159). Furthermore, these are not experienced as inner representations because they are based not just on vision but on all other bodily forms of active perception in the world. Thus,

> When you see a cup sitting on the table in front of you, you are not just having a *visual* experience. In addition to the activation of neuronal clusters in parts of your visual cortices, you are experiencing that cup as something you could reach for, grasp, pick up, and raise to your lips to quench your thirst. The cup affords not just a visual form; it also affords pick-up-ability. (Johnson, 2007: 160)

The fact that much of what is said above relies upon prior experience means that, as Luria (1966) showed, neural networks are open to setting and resetting through learning, practice and enculturation. However, as Reddy points out, this does not mean that perception or emotion is completely 'constructed' by learned responses: as he puts it, a 'wide array of processing strategies are open to conscious adjustment, to contextual variation, and to shaping by repetition and practice' (Reddy, 2009: 21). Thus, as James said, while persons and selves emerge from the interaction of history, community and nervous system, such selves are 'loosely constructed' and thus are various and creative (James, 1892/1985). In terms of emotion this also means, as James showed, that our emotional responses are not preset by biology or standardised by culture, but within this are shaped by personal experience and so come in a variety of forms; ones we can all recognise, but which are individualised and personalised nonetheless.

Before finishing this chapter, I want to comment on another important development in neuroscience that relates to the emotions, which is the study of 'mirror neurons' (Iacoboni and Dapretto, 2006). These are so called because they are activated 'both when subjects *perceive* a bodily movement and when they *make* that same movement' (Reddy, 2009: 19, emphasis in original). This is important for the emotions because it seems that when others make bodily movements or gestures that communicate feelings or emotions, such as smiling or frowning for example, we tend to copy or mimic those movements and gestures in our own body. When someone smiles at us we tend to smile back, reciprocating the friendly gesture and feeling. This is something that even young infants do when adults smile at them, a reciprocal gesture that has long puzzled psychologists as it happens in infants so young they cannot yet know what their own smile looks like, let alone have learned what it means. Thus, the mirror neurons seem to be centrally involved with the perception of emotion in others, which forms the foundation for empathy and emotional understanding as children grow and learn. While this appears to explain our innate ability to reciprocally respond to the gestures of others, we must be careful about over-extending the application of the idea of 'mirror neurons'. Although they would explain the innate tendency of young children to recognise and empathise with bodily emotional displays, as adults we do not always respond in kind to the emotional gestures of others. As Ginsburg and Harrington (1996) found, we interpret the gestures and facial displays of others not solely by a focus on the face or body, but by the context in which they appear. When passing a colleague that you like in the corridor you may both reciprocally smile at one another, but if someone smiles broadly after thrashing you at tennis you may be less inclined to smile back, and if you force a smile it may be through gritted teeth.

So even accounting for the importance of mirror neurons and other neurological factors that are essential to the ability to experience emotions and feelings, the meaning and evaluation of the context is still of central import to an understanding of the exact emotion we are feeling and the reason for us doing so. Neurology is part of, but not the source of, the complex process by which humans emotionally interpret and adapt themselves to the situations in which they act and interact with others. In doing this humans do not act like machines, instead they sensitively, intelligently and, one would hope, empathically adjust themselves to the specific emotional context as they go. The mental imagery we form is a vital aspect of emotional experience and we need a brain to take part in the construction of this imagery. But without a culture in which much of this imagery can be shared, and without the vital bodily engagement in the situations that provide the drama of our lives and the *reason* why we feel what we do, our emotional lives would not only be meaningless and empty: emotional life would not even exist.

5

Emotion, Reason and Self-reflection

Although in the last chapter I was critical of the conceptual framework used by a neuroscientist like Damasio, one of the key advances he has made is to challenge the western assumption that reason and emotion are two separate and conflicting forces. Since the Enlightenment, Reason (and I deliberately use a capital 'R' here) has come to mean the transcendental capacity for pure logical thought, a capacity that is disembodied and has to be unemotional. In the main, emotion has come to be understood as an irrational force that only clouds our attempts to use Reason. In traditional understandings of western civilisation, emotion is seen as a potentially destructive force, largely because it is thought to be irrational. It therefore has the power to unleash chaos and destruction and we can only be saved from the irrational force of emotion by Reason. The outlines of this argument can be found from Sigmund Freud's *Civilisation and its Discontents* to the more recent work of Daniel Goleman in *Emotional Intelligence*. In the latter, Goleman argues that when passion overwhelms reason the emotions run out of control, undermining civility and safety. The irrational has overcome the rational. The issue then becomes how to bring intelligence to the emotions so that, as Aristotle showed, the passions can have wisdom when well exercised – that is, when they are controlled by intelligence (Goleman, 1996). Although Goleman does take on board Damasio's notion that emotions guide our moment to moment decisions, he still reads this as the 'thinking brain' having to take the executive role in this process.

But what contemporary neuroscience tells us is something more radical than this, showing that there isn't a 'thinking brain' and an 'emotional brain', as once thought, as the brain systems used for rational thought and emotional understanding are very often the same ones. In the last chapter I criticised Damasio's mechanistic, cognitive-behavioural conceptualisation of the emotions, but his work on rationality and emotion has something important to say. What many of his neurological case studies show is that if the centres of the brain that deal with emotions are damaged, then rational thought is damaged also. When people lose the capacity for certain emotions their decision making can become reckless, irresponsible and downright dangerous to others. They can also become feckless, unpredictable and unreliable. These patients are still functioning rationally, but their rationality lacks what I called in the last chapter 'emotional reason'. That is, they do not consider the effect that their actions will have on others and also on themselves: that irresponsibility and unreliability will make them unemployable and deeply hurt the ones they love and care about, perhaps destroying their most important relationships. Without emotional reason there is no empathy with the feelings of others, nor any care about one's own fortunes. Reckless behaviour will endanger the self as well as others and can jeopardise one's safety and security.

What this emphasises is that rational behaviour has to have emotional reason as well as intellectual reason. This does not simply mean correct emotional management, whereby the passions are intelligently managed and controlled (Goleman, 1996). It means that reason has to be infused with emotion. Otherwise we face the old conundrum that can no longer be sustained: how to have rationality control the emotions, or to hold them in balance, as if these were opposing phenomena or forces that have to be tamed or harmonised. In actual fact, our thoughts and feelings about the situations we encounter are part of the same process of engagement and reflection with and upon our social world. In this sense, feelings, emotions and thoughts (rational or otherwise) arise from the same source and remain part of our relational engagement with the world and with others. Furthermore, as I will outline throughout this chapter, the self is at the centre of our relational engagement with the world and with others, and at the heart of the self are emotional self-feelings that come from our openness to others in the social world. As was stated in the last chapter, there are no perceptions of the world that are not based on the self – as in 'I' see, hear, feel or think – and because the self is emotional, so too are these perceptions emotional at their core. There is no neutral, non-personal, unemotional way of engaging with the world, and so emotion has to be at the very heart of rationality, as well as all other ways of perceiving and thinking about the world.

Feeling, Reflection and the Situation

As Dewey (1934/1980) pointed out, feeling and thought are both intrinsic in any situation as we immediately encounter it. Any situation we are in causes us to evaluate it and that, in turn, leads to both thoughts and feelings. We come to make distinctions between thought and feeling after the fact, as we *reflect* upon the situation we have encountered. Yet in the immediate moment of evaluation and action, there is no separation between thought and feeling, as perception, thought and action are infused with emotion. Thought and feeling, then, are not really separate at all, as they go hand in hand: what we think and feel can only be distinguished after the fact. Indeed, the demand that we try to work out solutions to problem situations without recourse to our feelings may be a very recent western phenomenon emerging from philosophical traditions in which Reason – as a purely intellectual activity – is given dominance. But if there is no Reason as a transcendental phenomenon that is separate from any given situation of experience, or from emotion and the body, then reason (with a small 'r') comes from the situations we encounter and involves both our thoughts and feelings. Indeed, as the pragmatist philosopher C. S. Peirce (1902/1966) has suggested, originally consciousness is the awareness of feelings about situations.

For Dewey (1929/1958), consciousness at this basic, or psychophysical, level is awareness or perception of the immediate qualities of situations registered in sentience or feelings. At the level of body-mind, consciousness is the awareness of these things in terms of meaningful evaluations of situations, objects, people, or actions. It is meaning, therefore, that is substantive and persistent: a constant background and foreground that makes sense of the things that happen to us in terms of a meaningful framework that links past, present and future. This meaningful framework is only possible because humans are social and cultural beings that can interact and communicate, 'storing' knowledge and understanding by means of symbols, signs and language. At the same time, we are also psychophysical beings with a consciousness that is focal and transitive, aware of a series of 'here and nows' that cannot always be conveyed exactly in speech.

As I noted in Chapter 3, however, the more structural, meaningful framework of mind and the fleeting and transitive nature of consciousness are temporally connected: the organised system of meanings that comes from the past makes sense of particular here and now situations and scenarios, while the latter provide the drama of the immediate. The system of meanings creates a habitual direction of conscious thought, an expectation of the way things may work out, while the immediate situation gives us surprise and novelty. Thus, at any one time we may not be aware of the organised system of meanings that provides the habitual background of thought; this only fully comes into conscious awareness in situations where we are surprised by a novel or unexpected set of circumstances: it is then we are forced into reflection to analyse the grounds of our thought, to try to make sense of occurrences, and in the process to reconstruct our meaningful understanding of the world. For Dewey, this reconstruction is where reflective thought is needed and where consciousness gains its purpose, otherwise we proceed in our thinking by habit.

What elsewhere I have called a *field of perception* is created by this constant background of meaningful consciousness (Burkitt, 2013), but this is not just a general phenomenon, as Dewey points out, in terms of the awareness of meanings and values common to particular social groups. This field of perception is also individualised as it is made up of personal, biographical materials that make the world meaningful for *us* in our own way. This also has an emotional content, as I will suggest throughout this chapter, as at the centre of this field of perception is our own sense of self, our particular *my-feeling,* created in the way that we imagine others see us. This is emotional because it is dependent on our relations to others and the emotional content of those relations. I will come to this shortly. For now it is worth remembering what Duncan and Barrett (2007) showed in the last chapter, that to reflect we need a self in order to do that, so perceptions, experience, ideas and feelings are *mine.* However, instead of their cognitive, representational view of how this occurs, I want to suggest that the sense of self we have in all our perceptions is an embodied and interactive achievement. This also goes against Damasio's idea that the sense of self emerges from a coherent collection of neural patterns occurring in the brain. Rather, in my view, the sense of self we can reflect upon is, of necessity, a social creation.

To return for now to the idea of reflection, for Dewey (1910) reflective thought is that which seeks and examines the ground or basis that supports thinking. Beliefs are ideas that need no ground or justification, but these can only become the object of reflective thought if for some reason people begin to doubt what they believe. In reflection, we believe something not on its own grounds but through something else that stands as a warrant, which could be other corroborating ideas or empirical evidence. This process happens by inference, which is a jump or leap that carries us over to the idea of another thing that helps us clarify new ideas or meanings. These must make sense of new facts or novelties we encounter in particular situations and which make us doubt our accepted, unreflective beliefs. This whole process has a two-way movement in reflection whereby we go from the given, partial or confused data before us to some possible new meaning or idea that could explain them – which is *inductive* thinking – and then back from this meaning or idea to the facts before us in order to connect them or make sense of them – which is *deductive* thinking. Only when inference reaches a satisfactory conclusion by processes of induction and deduction, can we say we have attained the goal of meaning. In this way we also form concepts about the world, something that is the focus of cognitive science which, as we have seen, employs computational or information processing models to explain this phenomenon.

However, what Dewey shows is that the process of reflection is not a purely rational or logical one – in terms of transcendental notions of Reason – in that there are no sharp lines of demarcation between different types of thought. Reflection not only involves inference, induction and deduction, it also involves feeling, imagination and intuition, the last understood not simply as a 'bolt from the blue' type of thinking, but as based on intelligent selection and judgement. As far as imagination is concerned, this is not conceptualised as thinking that is purely fanciful and unreal, but is seen as thinking that supplements and deepens observation. Thus, imagination is a method of expanding and deepening what is real. In this light, C.S. Peirce (1903/1934) has added another aspect to the process of reasoning that sits with deduction and induction, which he calls *abduction,* this being the process of forming an explanatory hypothesis, the very thing Dewey claimed we must do through inference. Indeed, Peirce also refers to this as 'abductive inference' which involves imagination, because, in the puzzling or difficult situation as we reflect on possible solutions, the 'abductive suggestion comes to us like a flash' (Peirce, 1903/1934: 113). In actuality, different elements of the new hypothesis might have been in our minds before, only now, under problematic conditions, we put together ideas we previously hadn't dreamed of putting together. This is not reason in the strict sense, as no logical formulation can be given for the abductive inference; however, the abduction needs no reason as it merely offers suggestion. It then must be tested through deduction, in which the hypothesis allows us to explain new facts that have appeared to us, or simply allows us to reach a satisfactory conclusion in theory. Despite the fact that abduction cannot be explained logically, 'every single item of scientific theory which stands established today has been due to Abduction' (Peirce, 1903/1934: 106).

In his reading of Peirce's ideas on logic and abduction, Scheff (1990) has claimed that feeling is central to the very process of inferential problem solving, which happens by what he calls *total association.* This is the forming of mental connections that is done through feeling and can be arbitrary, inventive and playful, yet also matches up to strict classificatory logic. All the great problem solvers, from chess players to physicists, are masters at using this kind of total association. It is this that makes it possible for us to apply the general, meaningful principles that exist in our culture to particular and unique situations, in the way that Dewey described, because we can *feel* what is creatively applicable to that situation without having to perform long and complex logical calculations in our minds. We take what we *feel* to be appropriate to that instance from the vast array of possible cultural meanings that could apply to it, or we creatively adapt pieces of what we already know in the abductive way that Peirce suggested. Indeed, even in situations of highly logical problem solving, this kind of total association comes into play through imagination, feeling and intuition. As Albert Einstein once told Max Wertheimer, he never thought in logical symbols or mathematical equations but in images, feelings, and even musical architectures (Wertheimer, 1959).

So even at this abstract level, rational thinking has to possess emotional as well as intellectual reason, or else it simply cannot operate. Rationally sorting and classifying all the data we are exposed to (as in computational models of thought or in artificial intelligence models), or potentially could have access to, in order to make 'purely' logical judgements without the quick steps of total association, would be cumbersome and immensely time-consuming. Humans do not think and feel that way, and so total association comes into play in which we employ inference and abduction, using feeling and imagination to make judgements and take decisions. In a study I undertook with colleagues some years ago, this was how we observed nurses making decisions on busy hospital wards, especially in accident and emergency departments where decisions about patient care had to be taken rapidly in life or death situations. Nurses would 'read the signs' on the patients' bodies and from their whole demeanour in context, using what is often described in the nursing literature as intuition, which is actually the use of total association drawn from the nurses' experience and education and how that makes them feel about a particular patient in a particular situation (Burkitt et al., 2001). It was on this basis that rapid decisions would be taken about patient care.

Most of the time, then, we think and feel in the way that Dewey suggested – through habitual dispositions rather than in reflective modes of contemplation, that is until we hit a problem. These habits, when they are functioning usefully, are for the most part subconscious, in that we do not reflect upon them or perhaps even consider them, yet they form the basis for the immediate selection and rejection of various options in the situations we are part of. In other words, they form the subconscious strata for our background feelings and overt actions. Alongside these preconscious habits and feelings there is also the realm of the unconscious, which, for Dewey, is not to be found internally to the human psyche, as in the Freudian idea of the unconscious as an 'inner universe', but rather in the hidden potentialities in objects or situations which are not made explicit. Thus, any situation or object that is overt is also 'charged with possible consequences that are hidden; the most overt act has factors which are not explicit' (Dewey, 1929/1958: 21). This means that not all consequences of action can be foreseen, nor can all aspects of a situation be made known as part of processes of reflection and decision. All human experience and thoughtful reflection are then created on a basis that is not known and not reflective. Dewey remarks how it is that philosophy tends to treat this basis of experience and thought – the unconscious and subconscious, the non-reflected and the lower reaches of imagination and dreamlike imagery – as pathological and in need of explanation, when really it is conscious reflection that is the remarkable moment. Furthermore, conscious reflection is not something other than the subconscious and unconscious, but emerges from within it when a problem occurs and then takes it as its object. The 'reasoning' person, then, is one who makes their inferences, feelings and imaginative abduction articulate in words and meanings. Equally, dream-life is not detached from the objects of reflective waking-life, but takes them as the stuff of which dreams are made, charged with the residues that usually remain implicit in them rather than being explicitly articulated. This means that we should not mistake the imaginative and the imaginary, the latter usually being taken to mean something unreal or fictional: rather, imagination is intimately connected to the real, supplementing and deepening our understanding of it.

In waking-life there is no cause to make explicit the taken-for-granted background of meaning that allows for communication and the exchange of ideas, unless it is no longer working and people end up at cross-purposes. What is then implicit has to be made explicit between all involved and the meanings reconstructed, if possible, so that interaction can carry on. In this process, what was unconscious has to be made conscious through articulation before it can slip back below the horizon of awareness once more. There is, then, in all thinking the constant interplay between the reflective and unreflective, the conscious and the unconscious, as explicit thinking and reflective action always occurs within the boundaries of the implied and the habitual. This is what Shusterman (2008), following Dewey in particular, refers to as 'somaesthetic consciousness', which is the reflective consciousness of the self that is experiencing the sensations of its own body. Reflectivity increases the control of our habits and improves the use of the self, in turn increasing the mindfulness of our bodies, feelings and habitual actions, so we are aware of them and can change them. However, this is extremely difficult and is not something we can do through reflection and willpower alone.

Reflection has to be strengthened through the practice of bodily techniques such as meditation (the practice of sitting, breathing and focusing the mind and body), or for Dewey through the practice of the Alexander Technique (the inhibition of habitual movements and postures in order to correct them), or for Shusterman the use of Feldenkrais practice which induces relaxation and flexibility of the body. All these techniques to some extent reinforce the connection between body and mind, habit and reflection, feeling and thought, and create practices through which they can be better integrated. However, as Bakhtin shows, others can also interrupt, inhibit and shift us from our habitual actions and stances, an understanding of which is at times missing from American pragmatism with its focus on individual reflective introspection (Emerson, 1993).

I will return to the issue of habit later in this chapter: however, in the next section I will focus on the nature of reflection, arguing that this is not a cognitive phenomenon in the sense of building mental representations of the self, but is a dialogic and polyphonic creation that forms and changes within the complex, unfinished social relations in which the self interacts with others. As I said in Chapter 1, self and emotions are not to be regarded as substances that interact in fixed and causally mechanical ways: instead, they are the products of their fluid and ongoing social relations. Furthermore, self and emotion are formed not only in the dialogue between people in interaction, but also in the dialogic relation we have to our own selves, in which miscommunication and misunderstanding can occur. The dialogue with our own self can also reflect and refract in particular circumstances the ideologies and generalised positions held within past forms of society and culture.

Reflection and the Dialogic Self

Alongside Dewey, other pragmatist thinkers emphasised that the nature of reflective thinking is not purely cognitive, in the sense of being about the processing of information, but is actually *dialogical* in that when we reflect on a problem in action, and when we need to undertake the process of the reconstruction of meaningful action, we engage in a dialogue with the others with whom we are interacting, and we also dialogue with our own self: an ability we develop on the basis of the social conversations we have with others. This means that reflective thinking is relational and emotional at its heart. All pragmatist thinkers, especially William James, C.H. Cooley and G.H. Mead, stressed that without social relations and dialogues with others, individuals would have no sense of self. For G.H. Mead (1913/1964; Reck, 1964) when we think in a reflective fashion we are actually having a conversation with the organised attitudes and standpoints of others, or we are conversing with the image of our own self organised by our past activity and life experience. What I will call here the 'reflective dialogue' is, then, a process in which we silently converse with ourselves in words or word meanings to think through a problem in the same way we would talk it through with another. In Mead's terms when we do this, one part of our own self assumes the role of the speaker and thinker, which he calls the 'I' and which never fully gets into the reflective gaze, while another part of our self assumes the role of the one who hears and is seen (thus having an image), which he calls the 'me'. But the 'me' is also composed of the organised sets of attitudes of others to which the 'I' responds. In social situations of action, the 'me' as a socially organised set of attitudes calls for a certain response, but the way we respond as 'I' is uncertain in advance (Mead, 1934). This is because we can act impulsively based on our own past life experience or upon the unique demands and drama of the present situation to which we imaginatively respond. When we reflect on our self in the situation after it is over, we associate the 'I' with our impulsive responses and the 'me' with the image of our self those responses may have created in the eyes of others. Yet the self is always a composition of both the 'I' and the 'me' taken together in reflection.

This is what happens when we reflect: there is no absolute division of roles inside the self, like a homunculus or little person whose job it is to watch a movie being generated by the brain, although of course the brain is centrally involved in reflection. Rather, the self is a temporal social construction: it is a matter of the person I am in this moment looking back on the person I was a moment ago (or longer as the case may be) and assuming a slightly different role – the listener instead of the speaker, the one reflecting on what was thought or felt instead of being the thinker or feeler. But then in the next moment this same self can assume another role, plunged back into engagement with the immediate moment of experience, thinking, feeling and responding to self or others. In this way what we think and feel is not just a matter of the stream of consciousness, as James pointed out, but also of the stream of experience that is going on as we interact with others. All the time the self is subtly changing as it moves through these moments of experience: unifying and dividing, talking and listening, feeling and empathising with the feelings of others, thinking and imagining, then thinking about those thoughts and feelings (reflecting). The same self does all these things in different moments of experience through the flow of time and in interaction with itself and others. It is present in a world of others and then (and only then) can it be present to itself. There is no little person inside the brain watching a movie generated by the brain, which is connected to a body but not to a social world in which it is located.

Furthermore, what we understand as rationality or reason is integral to this reflective dialogue. In particular it is integral to the ability to see ourselves as others see us, as if we are viewing ourselves from the perspective of another. In highly organised or complex societies this means we can assume the standpoint of what Mead called the 'generalised other', or of particular groups in which we assume a general standpoint or viewpoint. In fact, what we call rational thinking is actually impersonal thinking, in that it is not solely tied to one particular person's thinking or feeling. It is a general standard of thought, belonging to no one in particular, and instead follows certain rules that in a particular culture or locality are deemed to order thoughts into a logical pattern. However, the impersonal attitude we adopt in our thinking from the viewpoint of a generalised other is just one of several standpoints, roles and moments we can assume in the stream of consciousness and action. It is but one of the stances or voices that can be taken in the process of dialogical thinking. As Mead said:

> Our thinking is an inner conversation in which we may be taking roles of specific acquaintances over against ourselves, but usually it is with what I have termed the 'generalised other' that we converse, and so attain the levels of abstract thinking, and that impersonality, that so-called objectivity we cherish. (Mead, 1924/1964: 288)

Although I support what Mead is saying here, I do wonder about his passing comment that it is 'usually' with the generalised other we converse, as our thinking is often preoccupied with dialogues with others with whom we are acquainted. Elsewhere I have argued for the importance of otherness within the self, in that from the earliest years our sense of self is intertwined with the voices of others which have their own autonomy, intruding into our self-consciousness and our responses to others often in unwanted, unplanned, unwilled and surprising ways (Burkitt, 2010a). Not all the voices with which we have a reflective dialogue, that shape our consciousness and prime our readiness for action, have the position of 'I': because the sense of 'me' has otherness enveloped into it, many of the voices in our reflective dialogues, to which 'I' respond, have the position of 'other' with their own vocal autonomy.

This dialogical consciousness, in which reflection occurs within the stream of consciousness from different standpoints and perspectives, such as I, me, we, you and they, where we both think and identify with some of these positions and against others, is emotional in varying degrees. Indeed as C.H. Cooley (1922/1983) has pointed out, the 'I' is not only a linguistic marker, a personal pronoun that signifies a particular position in conversation, or an aspect of the self that emerges only in reflection, it is also a deeply felt entity. Central to the formation of the self are feelings of self power that give the term 'I' its *emotional animus* whenever we perceive, think and speak. The *sense* of 'I' has an emotional force behind it which is the 'my-feeling', and if this were not the case then 'I' would be a purely linguistic expression devoid of all life and feeling. An example of the emotional force of 'I' is how children who have mastered expressions such as 'I', 'me' and 'mine' often use them with almost exaggerated feeling – in the sense of, 'that toy is *mine*' – so that the *emotional animus* in the act is unmistakeable. This also applies to perception and ideas so that they too can be named 'I' or 'mine', something that emerges throughout life in all kinds of forms, perhaps most noticeably in heated arguments where we clearly assert what '*I think*' over and against others. This emotional animus that stems from self power is the source of our sense of personal agency and volition, and is also a central emotion in the agency of thought, as certain ideas are claimed as 'mine' and we can work to develop these thoughts alongside others.

In terms of perception, through child development the 'my-feeling' becomes incorporated with muscular, visual and other sensations, so that expressions like 'I see', 'I hear', 'I feel', come as second nature to us. So the body and aspects of the body get drawn into this, although the sense of self is not the same as the body. When we say 'I' we usually connect this to opinions, claims, perception, feelings of various kinds, purposes and desires. But the 'my-feeling' is connected to power because it is associated with the self as being a cause; of having agency and an effect on others and the world around us. In infancy the first thoughts children have associated with self-feeling are attempts to control objects, such as their own limbs and playthings. Then the child attempts to control the actions of the persons close to them, especially caregivers, so that the circle of power widens and gradually differentiates until it forms the complex sets of mature ambition. As children, though, these kinds of actions eventually connect to the first person pronoun 'I' when the child begins to learn language. However, it is still linked to practical action as well, so that children love to have adults watch them performing various tasks and to praise them for their achievements. This demonstrates the earliest correlation of self-feeling with the purposeful activity we call agency.

Like the other pragmatist thinkers, though, Cooley is not advocating a form of individualism where everything in social life refers back to the basic building block of the individual. Indeed, in language, 'I' only has a meaning when it is taken in reference to the other personal pronouns – 'you', 'we' and 'they' – so that 'what we call "me", "mine", or "myself" is, then, not something separate from the general life, but the most interesting part of it, a part whose interest arises from the very fact that it is both general and individual' (Cooley, 1922/1983: 181). Indeed, the whole nature of our self-feeling as it develops and differentiates is inseparable from the way that others respond to us and the significance we *imagine* that response to have, something that Cooley calls the 'looking-glass self'. Thus my-feeling does not develop as a purely individual phenomenon, because how we come to see and feel about our self is inseparable from how we imagine that others see us and feel about us. Thus, the organisation of social attitudes that people take towards us is not only part of our *objective* sense of self, in Mead's terms part of the 'me', but is also fundamental to the sense of 'I', the subjective self. This has to be the case because these are separate aspects of the self only in reflection; in the time of a life as it is lived ontologically, these are flowing, merging and separating aspects of the self.

Other thinkers have put this idea in a slightly different fashion. For Bakhtin (1920–1923/1990) and Merleau-Ponty (1960/1964) human individuals are inadequate on their own and unable to catch sight of themselves in their own individual field of vision. Infants and young children have perceptions of the world around them centred on their own bodies and the internal feeling of bodily sensations; but on their own they would have no way of being able to stand outside of themselves and see themselves from other perspectives unless they can imagine the way they appear to others (or as Mead would have said, take the role of the other in respect of themselves). Young children start to develop this image of their own self not only in terms of the way others act, look, speak and respond to them, but by the way in which these actions communicate how others *feel* about them – the way in which they are valued and judged. In this way, the actions and thoughts of children not only express power through the attempts to draw people and things near and make them their own: their actions and thoughts also show vulnerability in terms of their individual incompleteness and openness to others. Needing to be completed from the outside we are all open – and remain so to some degree for the rest of our lives – to the opinions and valuations of others about us. Because of this, how we come to feel about ourselves – the my-feeling – is never separate from the way that others feel about us, as expressed in their actions, looks, gestures, words and vocal intonations, or from the way we *interpret* and *imagine* they feel about us.

Bakhtin (1963/1984) thinks that this type of reflective consciousness, in which people imagine themselves as reflected in the mirrors of other people's consciousnesses, is peculiar to people living in the western world from the late 19th century onwards, or at least is heightened at this time, and is captured particularly in the novels of Dostoevsky. In these novels the characters find their own self-image as it is reflected back through others' evaluations of them, and also as these images, evaluations and judgements about themselves are debated in their own reflective dialogues, or what Bakhtin calls 'microdialogue'. In this form of modern consciousness, the emotional and evaluative tones of others that are spoken about us infuse our own feelings about ourselves and our actions, emotionally shading our self-feeling. Indeed, their words give form to our own originally indistinct sensations; by giving them a name these sensations are converted into feelings that are more distinct and communicable to others. They also define us as individuals, making us feel something about our self as a distinct presence to ourselves and to others. This becomes central to the reflective dialogue so that, for example, someone who has been told by another that they are beautiful or ugly finds that it is only 'in relation to the other that I can speak about myself in an affectionate-diminutive form, in order to express the *other's* actual relationship towards me or the relationship I wish he would show towards me' (Bakhtin, 1920–3/1990: 50). These reflective dialogues therefore refract within them the feelings and emotions that are present in our relations to others, or that we imagine or wish were present in them.

However, the word of another does not instantly condemn or elevate us, as we can also take into account the evaluation of a third person or seek an even more objective opinion in the morality of the social group we identify with. In this way, Bakhtin's dialogical understanding of consciousness is very much like Mead's, in that we can dialogue in consciousness between different perspectives on our self, some of which are personal while others are more impersonal. From the more impersonal standpoints we can take more rational, moral or generalised views of ourselves and our actions. These positions would be what Mead has called the generalised other, and is what Bakhtin refers to as the 'supra-person' or the 'supra-I', 'the witness and the judge *of the whole* human being' (1986: 137, emphasis in original). This seems to suggest that if we doubt or dispute the partial judgements of other situated people who we think may be biased we can appeal to a higher court constituted by more impartial judgements that see us as a whole. Thus,

> Everything that pertains to me enters my consciousness, beginning with my name, from the external world through the mouths of others (my mother, and so forth), with their intonation, in their emotional and value-assigning tonality. I realise myself initially through

others: from them I receive words, forms, and tonalities for the formation of my initial idea of myself. The elements of infantilism in self-awareness ('Could mama really love such a ...') sometimes remain until the end of life (perception and the idea of one's self, one's body, face, and past in tender tones). Just as the body is formed initially in the mother's womb (body), a person's consciousness awakens wrapped in another's consciousness. Only later does one become subsumed by neutral words and categories, that is, one is defined as a person irrespective of *I* and *other*. (Bakhtin, 1986: 138, emphasis in original)

The way we feel about ourselves, then, sometimes for an entire lifetime, begins to be formed early in life through the words, emotional tones and evaluations of others. The tones are especially important here because they register even before we can speak or understand language and stay with us in the form of feelings about ourselves and others that have an existence and a meaning not simply corresponding to the literal meaning of words. Whether positive or negative the sedimentation of relationships and dialogue – the emotional and value-assigning tonality of others' voices – structure, infuse and colour the dialogue we have with ourselves as well as our field of perception (Burkitt, 2013). It is also something that can be sensed by others, not only in the way we act but in our whole demeanour and expressions, as a kind of aura or atmosphere given off from the core of our being. Despite this, the words and intonations of others never completely define us in terms of who we are – our own self-image or self-feeling – as throughout our lives other words will be spoken about us that can redefine us, or we can speak and act to redefine ourselves (as Mead showed, we can act in ways that transcend the current social definition of our self).

From the earliest years, then, the words, intonations and evaluations of others inform our own self-feeling and our field of perception in both positive and negative ways. Eventually we find ways of speaking that seem to be close to our own voice, although this can never be completely separated from the words of others and our emotional connection to them. Yet the formation of our own voice and relatively stable viewpoint on our own self emerge only slowly and uncertainly. The process can be fraught with difficulty, in that Bakhtin shows how we can become divided selves with a divided voice and viewpoints on ourselves. That is because consciousness of self is perceived against the background of the consciousness of others and from what we pick up of this in their vocal intonations. These often reveal underlying ideological positions held more generally in society that contain prejudicial viewpoints about us, and we can dialogue with these also in terms of answering what 'they' might say. For Bakhtin, this is indicated in Dostoevsky's novel *Poor Folk*, in which a poor man hears someone say in conversation that the most important virtue in a citizen is to earn money. While the poor man recognises the statement was made in jest, he also knows the morality behind it: that the good citizen should not be a burden to others. In a reflective dialogue with himself, the poor man then answers back; 'Well I'm not a burden to anyone. My crust of bread is my own ... earned by my toil and put to lawful and irreproachable use' (Dostoevsky in Bakhtin, 1963/1984: 207). The poor man's crust of bread is earned by being a copying clerk and he is also aware of what 'they' say about having such an occupation, 'that I don't do much by copying'; however, 'What harm is there in copying, after all? "He's a copying clerk," they say, but what is there discreditable in that? ... So I see now that I am indispensable, and that it's no use to worry a man with nonsense' (Dostoevsky in Bakhtin, 1963/1984: 207).

As Bakhtin points out about the extract above, as the poor man holds this reflective dialogue with himself he polemically exaggerates the others' accusatory tones, and as these tones intensify so does his own defensive counter-accent. Indeed, this becomes so exaggerated at the end of the microdialogue that the poor man's tone becomes grandiose and almost omnipotent ('I see now that I am indispensable'). There are two points I want to make about this: first, that the emotional animus in this dialogue is coloured by the dialogue itself, by the positions of accusation and self-vindication. The poor man knows he is looked down upon by social superiors and that the work he does is seen as menial; furthermore, the poor are often morally upbraided in dominant ideological positions for not being able to support themselves financially. This makes the poor man feel degraded and ashamed. But then he starts to assert himself in his own voice, to answer back such critics in tones of pride that he has no shame, indeed no need to be ashamed: he earns his living, and though his wages may be meagre he earns his crust and supports himself; swelling now with pride and reaching grandiose heights, he even starts to convince himself he is indispensable. This leads to my second point, which is that although the background of this reflective dialogue may be the generalised tones of ideological positions in society, such as attitudes towards the poor and the lower classes, the microdialogue was actually sparked by a passing comment made by someone in an actual dialogue and is filled with the tones of the particular people and voices that the poor man will have heard many times in his life expressing such opinions and sentiments. His field of perception is informed by these voices and intonations that morally and emotionally evaluate him, that put him in an inferior position, and yet the poor man has his defence which can be mounted from a counter-position. He can put in some words in his defence that can make him feel more worthy, indispensable even.

I noted a similar situation in Chapter 1 with the example of the young man on a train who acted violently towards a woman who he felt was looking down on him. In recounting the situation and revealing something of his own reflective dialogue, the man said he felt the woman had acted like a stuck-up snob and was demeaning him. His retaliation to this perception was a violent act that in his eyes restored his status.

Thus it is the specific intonation of individuals in words or gestures that play a role in bringing ideological signs to life through their emotional-evaluative positions, and these infuse and inform our field of perception. As I noted in Chapter 3, for Bakhtin language is empty of emotion until words are uttered in speech, at which point words become infused with intonation. This intonation contains *feeling*: an evaluation of a person, object, situation, or idea that can be expressed through the body by vocal inflection and other bodily or facial gestures. It is the emotional-evaluative dialogue between self and others that animates language, in both social dialogues and in reflective dialogues, through the embodied intonations and dispositions people bring to their lived relationships. Indeed, these intonations and dispositions are themselves expressions of our field of perception and embodied sense of the world. However, some of these voices and ideological positions can be hidden, so that we are not necessarily aware of them in everyday speech. As Bakhtin says of the microdialogue of the poor man, his 'affirmation of self sounds like a continuous hidden polemic or hidden dialogue with some other person on the theme of himself' (Bakhtin, 1963/1984: 207). Thus, in affirming ourselves we are not always open to acknowledging the voices of doubt, uncertainty, or even shame, which initially place us in the position of needing to affirm ourselves. As I have indicated elsewhere, this can lead us to think about divided selves and the dialogical unconscious, in the sense of hidden or unacknowledged voices that *structure* our action and speech, so that vulnerability or doubt about the self is the structure that drives us to affirm ourselves, even though it is the affirmation and sense of pride that fills the *content* of our speech and action (Burkitt, 2010a, 2010b). This also accords with Dewey's idea that the unconscious is what is implicit in situations or conversations as opposed to what is explicit. Thus, others looking from the outside may not see or intuit the degradation that lies behind the self-affirmation of the proud person. Such emotional dispositions are the product of a complex tonality of social and reflective dialogues that result in individual embodied fields of perception that are polyphonic and often conflicted and divided.

Emotion, Evaluation and the *Habitus*

At this point I want to take a brief interlude to consider the work of Pierre Bourdieu, who also had much to say about the aesthetic appreciation and perception of values – resulting in feelings and emotions – and the way they are connected to social class, linking to the example above of the poor man who was perceived of lower value due to his social position. However, for Bourdieu, the appreciation of social values is not a reflective act, but occurs through the *habitus* – a series of bodily dispositions that act as structuring structures, orienting the body in social space, which are formative of tastes in terms of 'the capacity to discern aesthetic values'. Through these bodily dispositions the social is made second nature by the process of socialisation, in which people are brought up in a cultural *habitus* that instils practical categories of perception, forming the basis of bodily choices and actions, thus being 'turned into muscular patterns and bodily automatisms' (Bourdieu, 1979/1984: 474). Thus we do not make cognitive choices in particular situations – say when choosing our food in a supermarket – but rather practical choices that are based on visceral tastes and distastes, likes and disgusts. But the group's most vital interests are embedded in these tastes and create cultural capital, just as consuming certain goods shows good taste and sophistication, or tastes considered as cheap and vulgar. Social capital is also displayed bodily as we enter social situations, so that those who have the capital of the highest value enter the scene with ease and grace shown in their manners, bearing and gestures, giving off a sense of being self-assured or self-confident. On entering a social scene the body is like a 'memory jogger', composed of ...

> ... those complexes of gestures, postures and words – simple interjections or favourite clichés – which only have to be slipped into, like a theatrical costume, to awaken, by the evocative power of bodily mimesis, a universe of ready-made feelings and experiences. (Bourdieu, 1979/1984: 474)

However, while the above sounds like what I am arguing for here – in that socialisation is referred to as a complex of gestures, postures, habits and words – this is not exactly the case. Rather, I am arguing that the body comes into situations not only with ready-made feelings and experiences in its muscular patterns, but the body is also essential in *making* (rather than simply experiencing) meaning. Thus, if we follow Dewey (1922/1983) in his ideas about habits, these are only mechanical reproductions of routine actions in the worst forms of repetitive work found in industrial societies, mechanical repetition being so alienating and soul destroying for those subjected to it. Under more free and open social conditions, habit readies us for action and is the effective 'will' behind all our actions but, once in a fluid and open situation, bodily habit intelligently and sensitively follows and responds to the unfolding patterns of relations of which it is part. In addition to this, there is also the possibility of reflection upon and intelligent control of the habits, which Dewey admits are hard to execute, but are by no means impossible to do so. This illustrates, though, that the body is anything but an automaton – a moving mechanical device that imitates a human being by operating according to a predetermined set of codes, realised unconsciously. Instead, the body must adapt itself intelligently to changing circumstances, partly through habit, partly reflectively, thus working at different levels of somaesthetic consciousness, ranging from the non-conscious and the non-reflective, to the semi-aware, to the fully mindful. Bourdieu (1980/1990) does say that reflexivity occurs when habit breaks down, but again this is different from the view that reflectivity is present in the flow of all interactions, as people encounter problems, inhibitions, surprise and drama in the actions and words of others.

Furthermore, reflective consciousness is, as I am arguing here, polyphonic, made up not just of different words but of expressive tonalities. Because of this polyphony, it is always possible to put in a counter-word, an opposite meaning, or a word about oneself that counteracts the dominant valuations of one's self, as with the case above of the poor man. Habits of self-denigration or shame can be countered with feelings of pride, especially if the individual is backed by a social movement that is working to increase the value of the lower classes or the excluded. As Mead showed, there can then be a 'dialogue of impulses' (Joas, 1980/1985), not in the sense of biological impulses, but the socially formed impulses to feelings and responses such as shame and pride. Those who are made timid and shy by a lack of education – a lack of social value – can hide themselves away and make themselves invisible in a room, or they can realise the source of their shyness as a lack of a social value and try to remedy it, through getting an education for example. Thus, the *habitus* and the social values *implicit* in it, can remain at a low level of reflective consciousness for individuals (Burkitt, 2010b), or through reflective dialogue it can be made more *explicit*, debated in reflective or social dialogues and acted upon. In this way a complex – an amalgamation of relations within a situation, one's bodily habits that ready us for action in that scenario, along with the polyphonic dialogues within and between individuals – sets up a moving and potentially fluid series of interconnections one has to respond to. Thus any variation, discordance, interruption, or disconnection in a complex inhibits bodily habit and brings on reflection. As Bakhtin claimed in terms of dialogue, a compassionate response to others is to interrupt their habits so that they may become aware of them, rendering them open to change (Emerson, 1991), something a good therapist can do.

As to the emotions, Bourdieu says that the 'body believes in what it plays at: it weeps if it mimes grief' (Bourdieu, 1980/1990: 73). In some ways Bourdieu is arguing here along similar lines to me, in that he does not want to think of feelings and emotions as cognitive representations but as part of practical activity that enacts the past. Furthermore, he is saying that the values that are embodied in feelings and emotions are not just instilled by interpersonal relations, as Cooley would have it, but in the field of relations between capitals and the divisions and distinctions between social groups that they mark out, which intervene between individuals and the social world. The categories contained in the field of relations between capitals form the basis of the individual's perceptions of values and thus shape the way they value themselves, not their relation to particular others. However, the mistake made here by Bourdieu is failing to understand that those social values are communicated to people by particular others who will refract, and perhaps to some degree deflect, social values. For example, a lower-class child that is loved and valued by its parents perhaps has some shield against the lower value placed on it by the wider society. Whatever the child and its parents may feel, this is not simply the product of mimesis, of imitation ingrained in every muscle and fibre of bodily being: it also exists in the tones and voices of a reflective consciousness, there at some level of somaesthetic awareness, and other counter-tones and voices can redress this and answer back in other voices, other tones, other values. Without this, Bourdieu's portrait of emotion is as one-dimensionally behavioural as the crudest readings of William James's essay on emotion. Thus, while Bourdieu is right to show the social values inherent in our senses, perceptions, feelings and emotions, he is wrong to turn these into the products of a body that is a mimetic automaton without the power of reflective consciousness to change its habits (or *habitus)*. While reflective consciousness will always be limited to some degree by the power of bodily habits, consciousness and the learning of new bodily practices can change to some extent the ingrained nature of our dispositions.

Self, Reflection and Emotion

The key thing I have been arguing so far is that reflection on self and world is not divorced from emotion and our emotional relations to others and the self. When we reflect on ourselves we reflect through the words of others and the emotional-evaluative tones they have expressed towards us; these intonations make us feel something about ourselves. This may not be the exact feeling the other communicated towards us, so that if their view of us is disdainful we may swell up with pride in response, yet even so the disparaging remark is still implicit in our emotional response and view of our own self. These emotional-evaluative stances pervade every element of our perception of ourselves, of others and of the world around us. They are at the base of our self-feeling, or my-feeling, and the way we feel about the world we live in. At the heart of all reflection, then, are these emotional-evaluative tones, including those that have become so integral to us as a person that we do not reflect on them anymore. Like the eye, they are the emotional lens through which we see the world but which may not itself feature in our vision.

When I speak of reflection, then, I mean something slightly different from sociologists like Giddens (1984, 1991) and Archer (2000, 2003) who talk about reflexivity. For Giddens, reflexivity is the constant monitoring of action necessitated by the reflexive institutions of modernity, by which he means institutions that require knowledgeable agents to continually reproduce them through their actions. For Archer, reflexivity (although not something different from self-reflection) is a constant deliberation on the array of choices before us in the social structure. For both thinkers, though, reflexivity is something other than the emotional, unconscious and the habitual: it is a conscious, knowledgeable and, therefore, rationalistic form of making choices in a world where constant choice has become a necessity (see Burkitt, 2012, for a more detailed critique of the concept of reflexivity). In Giddens's view, potentially destabilising emotions are kept at bay by the unconscious functioning as a tension management system, clearing the ground for reflexivity to work without hindrance, basing choice on knowledge rather than prejudice. For Archer, deliberation on action is based on the internal conversation, and part of the job of this reflexive dialogue is to order and prioritise our concerns. We experience emotion when we live up to these concerns and feel good about ourselves, or when we breach them and come to feel bad about ourselves and what we have done. Yet emotion is not seen at the heart of reflection itself, as in Cooley's idea of my-feeling. Here, the way we feel about ourselves is integral to the way we reflect on ourselves, as well as on our actions and the choices we make. This means that reflection is not just about monitoring action or deliberating on choice, reflection is also *aesthetic* in that it is to do with the creation and interpretation of meaning. Through reflection, we seek to interpret the emotional-evaluative meaning imputed to our actions, or to ourselves, by others with whom we are related, or we seek to interpret our own feelings about ourselves and our actions.

Denzin (1984) theorises how interpretation occurs, along with the relation between reflective and unreflective thought, in terms of Peirce's notion of firstness, secondness and thirdness. Firstness refers to becoming aware of a feeling or thought occurring in the stream of experience or in the stream of consciousness (in terms of an image or word meaning) that suddenly engulfs us but which we do not yet reflect upon; secondness is the recognition of that thought or feeling as being part of our own consciousness, as being *mine*; and thirdness places the awareness (firstness) and recognition (secondness) 'into an interpreted context of emotional memory' (Denzin, 1984: 70), which is to say we reflect upon and interpret what that feeling or thought *means* for us; why it has arisen and what it is telling us about our embodied relation to a particular situation or event. Reflection is not something that is ever-present or constant in our experience, like an all-seeing eye that monitors and deliberates on all our experiences, thoughts, or feelings. Rather, reflection is a temporal and intermittent occurrence as we pass from one mode of being into another, such as being absorbed by an experience, feeling, or thought and then afterwards reflecting on that experience as an observer and interpreting its meaning in the light of past experience. But this means that not all of experience and not all of the stream of consciousness is reflective and transparent.

For example, Barthes (1977/1990) shows how the love we feel for another person can stay at the level of what he calls the 'image-repertoire', which is the images that keep turning over in consciousness about the loved one and define our adoration of them. This might be a broken tooth, a glance, the way they hold a cigarette. We can *reflect* on these images that define our love, and we know we are in love with this person, but this never turns into *reflexivity*: I know I love so-and-so, but I can't say why I love that person and not another. The deep reflexivity, knowing *why* I love this person and not another, is missing. All I know is that I am in love and the loved one is adorable. Perhaps this is because we look for the reason for being in love with this person in their body or personality, or we look inside ourselves and our desires, rather than to the relation between us. As Barthes says, 'I am searching the other's body, as if the mechanical cause of my desire were in the adverse body (I am like those children who take a clock apart in order to find out what time it is)' (Barthes, 1977/1990: 71). Thus reflection only turns into reflexivity when we have some knowledge that clarifies or enlightens us as to the nature of our feelings, although reflection and reflexivity can never be separated in any absolute sense (Burkitt, 2012).

Not only do theorists of reflexivity fail to account for the fact that it is partial and limited, they also parcel off habit into the unconscious, non-reflexive aspect of activity and do not understand, as did Dewey, that reflection and non-conscious habit are intimately connected. Thus, not only is emotion at the heart of self-reflection, it can also be the basis for the habitual forms of activity we engage in and that we come to reflect upon only under certain circumstances, where activity is interrupted or does not produce the desired effect. This is how emotion can come upon us unbidden, disrupting our conscious attempts at self-control, because it is not always part of consciously monitored or chosen action. For example, for Todes (2001) habit is directed in that it is a set of actions that unconsciously come into play in certain circumstances when we anticipate something is about to happen or to come upon us. Habit is anticipation of something to come and *poise* is our ability to deal with it – the level of skill we possess habitually to deal with whatever we face in certain situations. When we fail to deal with what the situation presents us with, we lose poise and are thrown off balance. To be poised is to be self-possessed by being in touch with ourselves and our present circumstances and to have some degree of control over them. To lose touch with oneself or one's circumstances is to lose self-possession and poise, to be thrown off balance.

In terms of emotion, we saw in Chapter 1 how Buytendijk (1965/1974) understood emotion as a loss of poise, for example when the fear of the prospect of an examination overwhelms us and we lose all memory and controlled thinking and start to panic. I do not think this is true of all experiences of emotion but it is true of those where we are affected to such a degree that we lose poise – the ease, grace, skilful movement and action by which we orient ourselves in the present circumstance and show ourselves to have a degree of mastery of it. A classic example here would be situations where we are overwhelmed by feelings of embarrassment as we start to lose the ease and grace by which we deal with our situation and suffer from heightened self-consciousness, imagining everyone has seen our predicament and is looking at us in our discomfort and distress. Thus, the beginning of bodily disorder and personal impotence (as we fumble and start to blush) is a sign that evokes shyness, fear and embarrassment in the field of the social encounter. This may only be on the periphery of the encounter and others may not notice it or place as much importance on it as we do, yet in our imagination our *faux pas* is in the spotlight and we are embarrassed.

This kind of experience is temporal as the loss of poise is momentary and circumstantial. This is expanded on by Heidegger (1927/1962), although he relates this to what he calls 'mood' as well as affect, whereas

I am using the term emotion to apply to experiences like embarrassment, fear and anxiety. Nevertheless, Heidegger sees experiences like fear and anxiety as temporal in the ontic sense that we experience them in every-day terms as fleeting occurrences, even though ontologically they bring us back to something. In fear, for example, we fear something that is yet to come, like the dreaded examination, yet this experience also lets something come back to us; perhaps how we have dealt with such situations in the past. With fear we forget ourselves, or as Todes would say lose touch with ourselves, so that the situation we fear overwhelms us. The self disappears as we lose poise and our circumstances flood in and engulf us. Any possibility of reflective control or getting a grip is gone. We also lose touch with and control over the environment we are in and this too overwhelms us, as in the extreme example of a panic attack. In this situation we are disoriented and without poise.

In anxiety, for Heidegger, we do not lose touch with the world around us but it loses all significance for us and we, in turn, lose our involvement with it. The sense of our own self is not lost but instead is heightened, except we now experience it as uncanny. Our sense of self seems unreal and without foundation. However, similar arguments can be applied to all emotions. Falling in love is a 'falling', a loss of balance and poise as we become lost in the image of another person. Indeed, there are degrees of self-awareness, poise and control (or the lack of it), orientation and disorientation, in all emotional experience. In terms of love Cooley talks about two inclinations – which are not necessarily separate but can be competing tendencies – that determine our approach to the loved one: the one inclination is marked by self power and is a desire to appro-priate the loved one or thing into one's own sphere, perhaps even into one's own self, and control it, while the other shows 'that disinterested and contemplative love that tends to obliterate the sense of a divergent individuality' (Cooley, 1922/1983: 187). The one inclination impels us to individuate life and all that is around us, the other to receive life. The balance of these two inclinations in any one person will depend on their past experience and the type of relationships they have had with the significant people in their lives, involving how these enable them to open up to life and experience or desire to control and individuate it. All emo-tion, then, involves the anticipation of the future and the bringing back to us of what went before. It also involves varying degrees of reflection and self-reflection, alongside different degrees of self-control and control of the situation.

What I have claimed in this chapter is that people can become engulfed in subjective emotional experience to the extent that they lose all sense of self or the sense of its reality. However, even in reflective consciousness we are reflecting upon, and in turn from the position of, a self that is emotional at its core. This is composed not just of the my-feeling that is the emotional animus within the sense of being 'I', but also of the reflective dialogues where in our imagination we engage with the voices, intonations and emotional evaluations of others. It is these reflective dialogues that are the core of our being and characterise each one of us as an individual, depending on our own personal biography and life experience composed of the relationships between self and others. However, as I showed at the start of the chapter, even the type of rational thinking based on the more impersonal style of relating to others and the world contains trace elements of feeling, emotion and imagination. Rationality is not separate from emotion, as rationality without emotion becomes distorted to the extent that it is no longer recognisable as reason. But this means there is no completely impersonal, unemotional standpoint on self or world from which we can reflect: only the relatively impersonal and more evenly balanced emotional standpoints, based on cultural standards, from which we can employ our emotional reason.

6

Emotional Labour and Feeling Rules

Since the publication of Arlie Russell Hochschild's seminal book, *The Managed Heart*, about the use of the emotions in working life, particularly in the commercial service industries, a whole series of publications have followed in its wake about the increasing importance of emotional labour in different sectors of the economy. Indeed, as Can-Seng Ooi and Richard Ek (2010) have recently said, Hochschild's concept of 'emotional labour' has become so influential it is impossible to do an exhaustive overview of the concept because it has dispersed into a myriad of different research streams on innumerable sectors of the economy and has also been adopted in many different academic disciplines. However, this is not my purpose here; I do not intend to review the many different ways in which the concept of emotional labour has been used and applied, but rather to analyse Hochschild's contribution to the theoretical understanding of emotion and how this emerged out of her study of flight attendants working in the airline industry in the 1970s. It was this particular study of a form of emotional labour that led to Hochschild's theory of emotion, yet the study of this very particular service industry has, in my view, led to a distorted understanding of emotion. Following on from this I want to see if my alternative, relational understanding of emotion can be applied to how emotion is integrally involved in working lives, using a study of nurses employed in the National Health Service in the UK. I will then go on to consider the use of emotion in the wider contemporary economy in the west.

Emotional Labour and Feeling Rules at Work

Hochschild's (1983) theory of emotion was developed alongside her study of flight attendants working for Delta Airlines in the 1970s. What concerned Hochschild was the way in which flight attendants in the airline industry were not just expected to do physical labour (pushing the drinks and meals trolley up and down the aisles of the aircraft, making sure bags are properly stowed away, etc.) and mental labour (counting passengers on the plane, making sure security and safety procedures are followed and understood, etc.), but in addition they were expected to do what she called 'emotional labour'. That is in general terms the actions by which flight attendants make passengers feel safe and at home on the aircraft and ensure them a pleasant journey so that they will fly again with the same airline. Indeed, flight attendants had originally been called 'air hostesses', partly because most working in the job were women, but also because the women's job was to act as hostesses on the plane, behaving towards the passengers in the way that women were traditionally expected to when hosting guests in their home. This involved supplying the passengers with food and drink, and also acting towards them in a friendly, helpful and welcoming manner. Hochschild called this 'emotional labour' because flight attendants were expected to put on the right demeanour for their passengers; always being pleasant meant smiling and assuming a friendly and reassuring voice. It also meant calming any unpleasant or distressed passengers, so that the flight attendant must always keep calm herself, maintaining an even and accommodating emotional disposition in line with the company's rules on behaviour which regulated the interaction with passengers.

What made this even more difficult was that, in the 1970s, airlines competed with each other for customers by accentuating the sexual attractiveness of the mainly female flight crew who worked as attendants in the aircraft cabins. This meant that many men who flew with the airlines saw flight attendants as 'fair game' in sexual terms, or because they were paying for the flight passengers of all sexes could become demanding of the attendants, not returning the politeness and courtesy that they expected attendants to show to them at all times. This made the emotional labour of flight attendants all the more demanding. Additionally, the main job of a flight attendant is to ensure safety in the cabin and to get people safely off the plane in an emergency, if possible. However, because of the image fostered of a physically attractive 'hostess', many flight attendants felt that they and their job were trivialised. Indeed, even today people often use the pejorative term 'trolley dolly' to refer to flight attendants of both sexes, indicating that they are seen as merely decorative items in the cabin rather than a crew member with an extremely important job to do. One of the reasons the airlines do not accentuate the seriousness of the job is that it would draw passengers' attention to the dangers of flying, and part of the job of flight attendants is to distract attention away from those dangers. But this means doing a lot of emotional labour. As one flight attendant put it, 'Even though I'm a very honest person, I have learned not to allow my face to mirror my alarm or my fright' (Hochschild, 1983: 107).

At the same time, if a passenger is distressed or difficult the flight attendants must be patient and suppress any frustration or anger towards the passenger. So there is constant work going on by these service workers to maintain the 'right' emotions – according to the rules of the airline and the general standards of the industry – and to suppress the wrong ones. This should also be regarded as labour, according to Hochschild, because the emotional labour is being done for a wage, in return for exchange value (money) rather than use value, the latter being the emotional exchanges of mutual support and interaction that go on in the rest of life outside employment. In fact, Hochschild makes a key distinction here between emotional labour and emotion work; the former is what I have just been describing where people are expected to manage their emotions in paid work, whereas the latter is the kind of emotion work that goes on in all areas of life. For example, a mother may suppress her anger at her misbehaving child, trying instead to be kind and patient, and a son may try to suppress feelings of resentment and hostility to his father, instead trying to be respectful and well mannered. This is emotion work because it is the work that we all do in the normal exchanges of life in order to make our relations with others civil and well regulated. As Hochschild says, 'managing feeling is an art fundamental to civilised living, and I assume that in broad terms the cost is usually worth the fundamental benefit' (1983: 21), which is to say that the effort is worth the payback in terms of a civilised life.

The title of Hochschild's book should now be clear in that we all manage our hearts – our feelings and emotions – and do so in the course of everyday civilised interaction. However, the problem occurs when this process gets commercialised and there is the 'transmutation' of this 'emotional system' into the world of paid labour, where emotion management falls under the sway of large corporations, their profit motive and their various management systems that attempt to hook up the management of emotions to the company's rules and regulations. Thus the 'feeling rules' that accompany most social situations, regulating what emotions people should and should not display under the circumstances, which are usually tied to wider social values, now become feeling rules attached to a company and the performance that it expects of its employees at work. This can become a problem for workers because not only is their physical and mental labour extracted for a wage, as Karl Marx showed, but now their emotional labour is also extracted in paid work.

It is not that this is intrinsically a problem of exploitation or alienation, as many people can enjoy their work and the skills and capacities they learn and practise in connection with it: but it is a problem if work is speeded up or if increasingly undue demands are made of workers. It is then that exploitation and alienation creep in. Especially, this can occur in respect of emotional labour if the performance extracted from workers according to the feeling rules of the job means they have to overwork to suppress their own 'genuine' feelings. For example, if demands are made that flight attendants are to be pleasant with passengers under all conditions, particularly if the passengers are being rude and disrespectful, then attendants may feel they are being made to put on a 'false self' and required to perform emotions they do not genuinely feel. In these circumstances workers become alienated from their own self and feelings in their work.

It is not hard to see why Hochschild's work has been so influential. Not only is it a brilliant book based on original research, it also introduced a whole new idea and field of study through the concept of emotional labour, just at the time in the early 1980s when the service sector was increasing in importance to western economies, with more and more people becoming employed in service industries. However, there are problems in Hochschild's conceptual framework. Throughout there is huge confusion about the transmutation of the system of emotional management from the 'private' to the 'public' sphere, creating the impression that emotion work had previously been confined to a private sphere of life until its increasing commercialisation in the mid-20th century. But this way of describing things entirely equates the public sphere with the commercial sector, contrasting the latter with the realm of private life. In passing remarks it seems that Hochschild defines the private world as including relationships like marriage, family and friendships and distinguishes this from the public world of commercialised work. The problem is that this is poorly defined and misleading as a 'private' sphere seems to be totally separated from the 'public' sphere, with emotion belonging naturally in the private. Yet, the private world of family and friendship is, even as Hochschild defines it, fully social as it involves relationships. As we saw in Chapter 2, so-called 'private' emotions like love and grief are socially formed, often through social practices constructed in the public sphere of social activity. Indeed Wouters (1989a, 1989b), drawing on the work of Elias, has criticised Hochschild for ignoring the social and historical spaces in which more finely managed emotion emerged as central to the art of civilisation. Furthermore, this is not pretence or affectation, the actions of a 'false self', as the drive for more civilised emotion comes from a greater mutual identification and empathy between people of all types. Indeed, this emphasis on being more 'other-directed' actually creates more relaxed or informalised social codes in which people are encouraged to express themselves with a more finely tuned balance of tactfulness *and* directness, even among those working in service industries (Wouters, 1989a). Instead, Hochschild creates a poorly drawn and ill-defined line between private and public life, and between a private and public self.

This reflects in the entire way that Hochschild theorises the management of emotion and in the largely dramaturgical perspective it rests upon. The dramaturgical approach was developed by Erving Goffman (1959/1990), who introduced the idea that social 'actors' were literally that: performers who were putting on an act for their fellow actors on the social stage. Thus, following Goffman, thinkers like Hochschild understand the world as like a stage on which social actors perform their roles according to prescribed scripts and rules for different social situations. The goal of these actors and teams of performers is to create the required impression on the audience within fairly ritualised social encounters. An example given by Goffman is of waiters working in a restaurant, where 'front stage' in the dining area they are expected to perform in given ways, being polite and helpful to the diners, while 'back stage' in the kitchen they can behave in more informal ways with their fellow workers and say what they like about the customers. So 'front stage' the waiters have to be polite and helpful to even the most unpleasant or exacting diners, while 'back stage' they can let their face slip, complain and be rude about the customers.

While all of us can see the truth value in this approach, perhaps having experienced situations like this from both sides of the fence, even Goffman has to warn of the limitations of it. As he says, 'All the world is not, of course, a stage, but the crucial ways in which it isn't are not easy to specify' (Goffman, 1959/1990: 78). Despite this Goffman does say that the world is *not* like a stage in that, unlike stage actors, everyday actors do not have a fully written script for the drama they are performing in and do not know in advance what they are going to do. They are, though, just like actors in that while they are aware of the many different standards and rules by which their performances may be judged, nevertheless 'quasi performers, individuals are concerned not with the moral issue of realising these standards, but with the amoral issue of engineering a convincing impression that the standards are being realised' (Goffman, 1959/1990: 243). As performers, actors are 'merchants of morality', concerned with managing the *impression* that they are moral agents and maximising the value of their personal stock as such, rather than in actually realising any moral outcomes that are of deep value to them. But this fosters the view of the self as an essentially amoral social strategist (Danziger, 1997), simply concerned with the right impression management, and a self that, in doing this, is also inherently deceitful as it must make fundamentally amoral concerns appear to be moral. That is the outcome of a good performance. This means that Goffman understands the 'actor's artistry as a kind of deceit' (Wilshire, 1982: 291), in that the self shown to others is a false self, one that is socially and morally concerned, while the true or hidden self is asocial and amoral. In social performances, then, the self always becomes alienated from itself by the very artificial nature of the social product it manufactures. The alienated self occurs because there is a fundamental split created between what one is or feels inside and the demands of society, the requirements of social exchanges and their various 'feeling rules', a process of 'matching inner experience to a cultural dictionary' (Hochschild, 1998: 6). However, this approach makes the self into something partially, if not fundamentally, asocial.

The dramaturgical metaphor of social life is limited, however, because in everyday life our interactions do not occur in 'stage-time', which would be the time of a staged play or film, but in what Wilshire (1982) calls 'world-time', a time that vastly exceeds and yet also encompasses the time of the immediately present social encounter. This means that some of our roles will be important and relatively permanent ones that we cannot simply cast off in a limited time frame, binding us into relatively enduring social relations in which our actions have important consequences for ourselves and others. Being a good father or mother, brother or sister, son or daughter, or a good friend, is something that can be deeply important for us and others, both socially and morally, having lasting consequences on our relationships and quality of life. Furthermore, as Cooley and Mead pointed out, in such interactional contexts where we develop as selves, what we appear to be to others (and how we imagine that appearance in their eyes) is central to who we actually become as a person. Although one can instantly see the advantage of Goffman's style of dramaturgical approach to Hochschild's study of the management of emotional performances by flight attendants in aircraft cabins, where friendly and civil social relations have to be created and maintained for the duration of a flight, there are serious negative consequences in extending this theory of emotion to the emotion work of everyday relations.

Hochschild does recognise the restrictions of a Goffman-style dramaturgical analysis in terms of her study, accusing Goffman of seeing social actors as engaging in mainly 'surface acting' as opposed to 'deep acting'. These terms are derived from the work of the drama teacher Constantin

Stanislavsky (Konstantin Stanislavskiĭ), the originator of the 'method' school of acting, who thought that surface acting was the manipulation of gestures or expressions to simulate an emotion, while deep acting was a real feeling that is self-induced through memory, imagination, or immersion in a situation (Stanislavsky, 1937). Stanislavsky would encourage actors to use 'emotion memory' in preparation for playing a part, in order to remember how they had felt in a situation like, or similar to, the one being faced by the character they were playing. The actor, then, does not just put on the surface appearance of an emotion; he or she induces the actual feeling from deep inside themselves by the use of memory and imagination. For Hochschild, this is what the flight attendants she studied did in putting on an emotionally managed performance for their passengers. Through deep acting they actually induced the emotions required of them by the feeling rules governing their job, and did so through memory and imagination. For example, Hochschild refers to one flight attendant who actually imagined the cabin as her second home and difficult passengers as those people who are not as comfortable there as she was. The flight attendant explained, 'Part of being professional is to make people on board feel comfortable. They're in a strange place. It's my second home. They aren't as comfortable as I am. I'm the hostess. My job is really to make them enjoy the flight' (Hochschild, 1983: 107).

This deep acting was done in order not to make the performance of flight attendants appear faked to the passengers, but instead to make it into a genuine expression of feeling. Many of the flight attendants expressed the view that what passengers wanted were 'real people', and they were critical of those who engaged merely in surface acting, coming across as 'phoney'. At the same time, many of the flight attendants also recognised times when they had barely been able to suppress their anger at an extremely rude and unfeeling passenger, and had got revenge by 'accidentally' spilling a drink on them, or had engaged in surface acting because of the pressures of work. Hochschild describes this as an act of resistance by some cabin crew, not so much against the passengers, but against the airline company when it had speeded up the pace of work, giving the crew less turnaround time at airports. Under these circumstances, when flight attendants were stressed and tired, some would barely bother to act at all for the passengers, resenting what the company was doing to their working conditions. However, it is under these conditions that Hochschild feels that service workers like flight attendants can come to feel alienated from their 'true' selves and 'true feeling', when those who engage in emotional labour are simply surface acting, aware of putting on a facade of the 'right' emotions for the public. As more workers across the service sector of economies are subject to this type of labour, the more people long to connect to their 'real' self in order to feel 'real' or genuine emotion.

Although one can see the explanatory value of Hochschild's account in the way that service workers such as flight attendants are expected to conduct their emotional labour and how they resist it, especially under management control, problems occur when this explanation is extended to the whole of emotional life. When Hochschild applies her theory of the emotions, produced by the deep acting of emotion work in order to manage feeling, to life outside the commercial sphere of service industries, it runs into trouble. Hochschild has this to say about everyday deep acting:

> In our daily lives, offstage as it were, we also develop feeling for the parts we play; and along with the workaday props of the kitchen table or office restroom mirror we also use deep acting, emotion memory, and the sense of 'as if this were true' in the course of trying to feel what we sense we ought to feel or want to feel. (Hochschild, 1983: 42–3)

The difficulty here is that in all areas of life, emotion work is seen to operate by the process of deep acting, whereby we proceed 'as if this were true'. But in the world-time of our relatively lasting relationships to family, friends, and even perhaps some colleagues, what is to say that our relationships and feelings are not true, that they do not emanate from selves with real and important connections to others? Hochschild's work has been infected by Goffman's notion that an essentially asocial and amoral self has to work to manipulate asocial and amoral feelings into ones that will be acceptable according to the feeling rules of social situations. As Hochschild says, 'Goffman does not assume that the individual is effortlessly, pliantly social' (Hochschild, 1983: 214). This is why emotion work is *work*, because we are always working to try to induce what we ought to feel, according to feeling rules, or what we want to feel. *The essential problem is that, in adopting the metaphors of performance and emotion work, applying this to all of life, Hochschild turns all socially expressed affect into affectation. Affect, which is to be affected by a relationship or situation in a deep and involuntary way, can be experienced only by the private self, while the social or public self is engaged in affectation – in staging a self-induced performance according to the required feeling rules.*

An outcome of this split between private and public self – with the according division between genuine and affected feelings – is that emotion is seen to belong essentially to the private self, and this influences the way emotion is theorised. When asking the question 'What is an emotion?' Hochschild answers: 'Emotion, I suggest, is a biologically given sense, and our most important one. Like other senses – hearing, touch and smell – it is a means by which we know about our relation to the world, and therefore it is crucial to the survival of human beings in group life' (1983: 219). This definition of emotion is, as Hochschild points out, close to that of Darwin's, in that emotion is seen as a biological response that readies us for bodily action, whether that is actual or imagined action. She goes on to say:

> Thus when we manage an emotion, we are partly managing a bodily preparation for a consciously or unconsciously anticipated deed. That is why emotion work is *work*, and why estrangement from emotion is estrangement *from* something of importance and weight. (Hochschild, 1983: 220, emphasis in original)

While statements like this would seem to place Hochschild firmly in the tradition of thinking that posits basic emotions that are biologically given, she denies this and claims that emotion cannot be separated from the situation and from the rules and micro-acts that are part of it. Thus 'the act of management is inseparable from the experience that is managed' (Hochschild, 1983: 206), a statement that seems to indicate that the act of managing emotion changes the very experience of it. This occurs because the bodily preparation for action is also related to cognition, as we are preparing for a consciously or unconsciously anticipated deed. All acts of emotional management must therefore also anticipate the feeling rules of particular social situations, and this has to be at least a partially conscious preparation. In this, Hochschild follows Freud's idea that while emotions are biologically based, they also provide a 'signal function' to consciousness. Through cognition, this signal function involves a reality that is newly grasped against the background of our prior expectations. In turn these prior expectations also rest on the existence of a prior self that, through experience, has come to expect certain things to happen in particular situations. For example, someone who learns that someone very close to them has just died will experience the feeling of shock, but *against* the background of prior expectations: that the key people in our lives are always there for us. What then occurs is denial, as in the experience of 'this can't be happening to *me*' and 'they *must* be alive'.

If this idea were framed in terms of the habitual orientation to action in certain situations that I have been arguing for throughout this book, which can under certain conditions be subject to reflection, then there may be potential in it. The difficulty is that Hochschild does not develop an understanding of habit like that created by Dewey. Instead, she tries to use *all* the different traditions of emotion theory in her account, including those that follow the biological (or, as she calls it, organismic) model, Freudian theory and the interactionists like Dewey, Gerth and Mills, and, particularly, Goffman. Yet this is confusing as these models are not always compatible, as I have been showing throughout this book, and so it is not always clear exactly what Hochschild is arguing for. So, for example, she argues that the interactionists show us what gets *done to* emotion and feeling in social situations through emotion management, while from Darwin's evolutionary biology we learn what exactly it is that gets managed – a biological sense. Then Hochschild goes on to argue that this asocial, unmalleable aspect of emotion that we try to manage is also social. But this makes no sense. If, as I am arguing here, the psychophysical responses, rhythms and sensations of the body are transformed in various societies and cultures, as well as in individual experience, into what we in the west call feelings and emotions, then these are not reducible to a biological origin, but must be understood as part of a broader bio-socio-cultural development. Feelings and emotions are therefore also changeable across societies and historical epochs and cannot be unmalleable. Hochschild's appeal to Freud does not help her here either, as Freud also posited an instinctual basis for emotion and human action that civilisations have to struggle against.

It is hard then to work out what Hochschild is arguing for: is emotion basically biological, asocial and unmalleable, or is it, at root, social and malleable? Arguing against Freud's idea that emotion is motored by instinct, Hochschild tries to pinpoint where and how culture impinges on feeling, identifying many points: 'at the point of recognising a feeling, at labelling a feeling, at appraising a feeling, at managing a feeling and expressing a feeling' (Hochschild, 1998: 11). Again, though, feeling seems to exist independently until it gets recognised by cognition, labelled, appraised, managed and then expressed. Although Hochschild doesn't distinguish between feeling and emotion, she does seem to follow Dewey part of the way to understand feeling as a naming of perception, but not to follow him all the way to what I am arguing for here: that in the bodily act of speaking we fundamentally reconstruct what we feel through language, not simply name a prior feeling. If, as I am suggesting, language and culture condition feeling and emotion from the beginning of life, and distinguish between them, then emotion has to be considered as a meaningful reconstruction of bodily sensations that is fundamentally social and not biological in an asocial sense. Thus, linguistic social practices give form to sensation and perception as particular feelings or emotions.

In total, what seems to be occurring in Hochschild's theory of emotion is that emotion is equated with a biological bodily sense in a situation which is then registered by cognition as a 'signal function', at which point conscious work can be done on that basic impulse to transform it into something socially presentable according to the feeling rules of the situation. But then, as in Goffman's work, the social self becomes an alienated self, or false self, because as Hochschild said above, estrangement from emotion is estrangement from something of vital importance and of weight: the signal function that has ensured survival. Following Freud, emotion is also understood as potentially destructive of society, involving aggressive or omnipotent feelings, and to be social these have to be replaced with other feelings by a false self. Thus, 'the false or unclaimed self is what enables one to offer the discretion, the kindness, and the generosity that Noble Savages tend to lack. It is a *healthy* false self' (Hochschild, 1983: 195, emphasis in original). Healthy, maybe, but false nevertheless.

There is an assumption here that any social inclinations cannot be natural, because sociality is an artificial state, much like the conditions in an aircraft cabin where sociability has to be constantly manufactured through emotion management. But as Cooley (1922/1983) showed, children can express feelings of self power, of appropriation and omnipotence, while still retaining the capacity to empathise with others and imagine how they are seen by them and how their actions affect them. Indeed, as I illustrated in the last chapter, the way others see us is not separate from, but fundamental to, our own sense of self as it develops, so that my-feeling is never divorced from feelings for others. For example, when Cooley talks about acts of kindness and altruism, these are not the acts of a false self given to an alien other under artificial social conditions; they are the genuine interactions between real, interrelated people. Cooley refuses the division between self and other motives, so that actions done for others are in some way 'self-sacrifice', whereby something fundamental of the self has to be given up in order to achieve it, whether that is one's 'true' emotions or 'real' self. Rather, I give to *my* friend, *my* family, *my* neighbourhood, *my* community, *my* country, or a general humanity that I identify with. These are acts full of self and self-feeling, but that does not make them selfish and asocial. But Cooley can see things this way because he understands emotions to be woven into the fabric of social relations and interactions rather than emerging from outside them as biological senses which must then be suppressed and worked on for the survival of civilised society. However this is not the case for Hochschild: a social self is a false self and performances of emotion staged according to feeling rules are the requirement of an alienated self concerned with impression management, even if the emotion produced is achieved through deep acting.

These basic dichotomies run throughout Hochschild's book, especially in constant references to spontaneous and managed feeling, where performing or affecting emotion is seen as a barrier to spontaneous feeling. Thus, another reason why Hochschild is drawn to Goffman's work is that he is interested in the 'affective deviant', the asocial person who does not feel what he or she ought to and struggles against the rules of social exchange, trying to avoid paying the 'social taxes' of mutual exchange (Hochschild, 1983: 215). So the flight attendant in Hochschild's study who contrived to 'accidentally' spill a drink on an awkward passenger was an 'affective deviant', not playing by the company rules. But are these responses any the less social than the ones that correspond to 'feeling rules', therefore to be classed as 'deviant'? I would suggest instead that contradictory or conflicting feelings are the result of contradictions in social life. Indeed, Stacey (2011) has shown that in all organisations there is contradiction, paradox and dilemma, and I think this better illuminates the relationship between the airline attendant and the uncivil passenger. One impulse in social life when we are confronted with someone who is being rude and unpleasant is to answer that person in kind, or at least to ignore them; however, in this context, the company rules said that attendants must remain pleasant and friendly to passengers under all circumstances, creating what Mead called a conflict of impulses. These can be debated in dialogical, polyphonic consciousness, the two impulses being articulated in two different voices or tones, two contradictory feelings.

This is where the relational and dialogical approach to emotions that I am advocating becomes important, because it is not the situation itself that governs what we feel, but our own *relationship* to that situation and the people in it. This may create a clash of relational loyalties or of situational demands, which place contradictory expectations upon us and cause emotional confusion or dilemmas. The following example of this is taken from an extract in one of Hochschild's interviews with a 48-year-old woman who felt guilty that she was relieved when her father died:

> The death of my father brought a mixture of grief and relief. Taking care of him and my mother required that I move them out of their own home, rent an apartment, and start housekeeping for them while my own family, my husband and three teenagers, were home. This was my first long separation from my husband and children.

My nerves were raw; my dad seemed never to sleep except in the daytime, while my only time for sleeping was at night. I didn't give much thought about what I should feel, but I felt bad, and guilty to be relieved and sorry at the same time. I handled my feelings by simply asking my dead father for forgiveness and by accepting the fact that I was weak. (Hochschild, 1983: 65)

Hochschild interprets this as a case of 'misgrieving', in the sense that the woman's reaction was not according to the feeling rules of her culture, that relatives should feel sad when a loved one dies. This, and other cases like it, are a result of the 'astonishingly exacting standards we draw from culture to impose on feeling' (Hochschild, 1983: 68). But in order to avoid this dichotomy of culture versus feeling, and instead to suggest a notion of *cultures of feeling*, let's look at this example another way. Perhaps this woman was torn between two cultural demands: the demand to be a good daughter and look after her elderly parents, and the demand to be a good wife and mother, staying at home to care for her husband and teenage children. Leaving them to care for her parents cannot have been an easy choice and her 'raw nerves', anger and resentment may not have been directed only at her elderly parents, who she obviously cared about. She is caught in a cultural contradiction and her feelings could be the result of that. Although Hochschild remarks on the gendered nature of much emotion work, strangely she doesn't remark on gender here (and in the chapter on gender in *The Managed Heart* she notes the extra demands for emotional management placed on women and thus the greater danger of them developing a 'false self' than men). It would have been interesting to know what this woman's husband and teenage children were doing to help their wife and mother in such circumstances, and what their responses were when she was spending less time with them. Could she also have been angry at them? The interviewee remarks in the last sentence of her statement above that she felt weak in this situation, perhaps because she had ignored her own wishes and needs – her my-feeling in all of this, such as a desire to be with her own family – to meet the needs of others in an act of self-sacrifice. When her father died she must have been relieved not only by his death but also at the resolution of the massively contradictory social demands that had been placed upon her and the fact that no one seemed to be meeting her needs.

So what I am suggesting here is that it is a mistake to see such cases as 'misfeeling' on the occasions when exacting cultural standards are *imposed* on feeling. Rather, it is the social clash of different cultural expectations and the way they intersect personal relationships that *create the situation* in which such complex and ambivalent feelings arise in the first place. This woman was *affected* by her situation and felt guilty that because of it she was feeling some of the things she was. No doubt she did have to work to suppress some of her negative feelings, to try to stay patient with demanding elderly parents whose waking and sleeping patterns were totally out of sync with hers; and no doubt there would be some *affectation* of emotion here, perhaps even attempts to affect grief at the end of it all, when what she felt was relief. But all of this has its *emotional reason* when set within the relational complex in which she found herself, with its contradictory cultural demands and expectations. In fact none of her feelings and emotions are understandable outside of her social situation.

What I am claiming, then, is that being genuinely affected by others or by a situation – which is to say *moved* by it to feel something that is not overly reflected on or consciously managed – is as much a part of social life as the occasional need to engage in affectation to create the appearance of feeling what one thinks one ought to feel in that context. Thus being affected, perhaps even in a way one doesn't want to be affected, feeling what one doesn't want to feel, is not essentially a private or asocial experience but is fully social and relational. Indeed, the need to use affectation to create emotion on occasions, even by deep acting, is often because of contradictory and paradoxical social situations that place competing demands on us, making us feel contradictory or ambivalent emotions. Furthermore, in relationships with others one is always affected in some ways by the other, by what they say or do, and this can be involuntary in the sense that we are not always entirely in control of our emotions. This raises the issue of *poise* in emotional experience that I talked of in the last chapter, in that the need to retain self-control over the situation and over emotion is to do with the fear of the situation overwhelming us and throwing us off balance, with a concomitant loss of self. In this view, we are not performers in social life but social beings with varying degrees of control over our own self and actions, deeply affected by the relationships and situations we are bound into in world-time, as they have a profound effect on the course of our lives. We are all caught in the balance of affect and affection, of involuntary feeling and reflective control, in a dialogue (sometimes reflective, sometimes not) of impulses, feelings, emotions and social expectations.

However, despite my critique of Hochschild's theory of *emotion work*, there is still debate about the value of her idea of the alienation, in the Marxist sense of the term, of *emotional labour* in the contemporary service industry, and her ideas remain highly influential in the study of this type of employment (Bolton, 2009; Brook, 2009). I will touch on this debate below as I discuss my own reassessment of the idea of emotional labour through a study of nursing in the UK's National Health Service (NHS). More importantly, though, I want to gauge if my own theory of emotion can lead to a better understanding of emotional labour than Hochschild's.

Emotional Labour in Nursing

There has been much debate over the years about whether Hochschild's concept of emotional labour can be applied to professions like nursing, as her original study of emotional labour with flight attendants was designed to study the *transmutation* of feeling that occurs when the management of emotion is *commercialised*. The problem with studying nursing practice is that nursing is a profession with core values in which commercial exchange is not to the fore. Hochschild is unclear herself on whether professionals like 'the social worker, the day-care provider, the doctor' can be counted as emotional labourers, because although they 'try to affect the emotional states of others, they do not work with an emotion supervisor immediately on hand. Rather, they supervise their own emotional labour by considering informal professional norms and client expectations' (Hochschild, 1983: 153). This is a strange claim, as flight attendants did not work with an emotion supervisor immediately on hand, although the company rules on engaging with passengers were quite explicit about forms of behaviour. Also, throughout her book Hochschild refers to professionals like doctors and nurses as doing emotional labour, which clouds the exact definition of the term. Some, like Brook, argue that emotional labour should be treated like all labour in that, being exchanged for a wage, it is, as Hochschild pointed out, open to exploitation and alienation as partially commoditised labour power, and thus 'it is a contradictory experience where workers are able to use the indeterminacy of the labour process to alleviate and/or oppose their day-to-day alienating existence at the frontier of control' (Brook, 2009: 546). In other words, emotional labour can be both satisfying and alienating, and where it is alienating through excessive management control workers can collectively oppose that control.

For Bolton (2005), though, the term emotional labour as Hochschild conceived it is too broad, appropriately describing some but not all practices in the workplace, where there is a wide array of emotional relations. As an alternative, Bolton suggests that emotional labour should be thought of as just one dimension in a topology of emotion management within the workplace. Through studies of work practices, she felt emotional performance in the workplace was not just about 'pecuniary' emotion management, carried out according to feeling rules that operated to commercialised principles: there was also 'prescriptive' emotion management which operates according to professional feeling rules, and 'presentational' and 'philanthropic' emotional management that is carried out according to social feeling rules. Thus, workers like nurses do emotion work that is not solely shaped by commercialised feeling rules, though some nurses in the NHS in the UK do comment on the creeping nature of commercialisation in the service, including intensified work routines, which leave them feeling like supermarket checkout operatives. Yet much of their emotion work still arises from professional values rather than commercial ones, so there is a difference between 'labours of love and labour power' (Bolton, 2009: 557), a distinction that the concept of emotional labour does not make. Bolton therefore tries to replace Hochschild's dichotomies of private and public, false and real selves, with a topography that attempts to capture the complexity of working life in which emotion emerges for a variety of reasons and motivations.

However, Bolton still takes on board Hochschild's concept of the management of emotion according to feeling rules, along with its dramaturgical framework, as do most researchers working with the concept of emotional labour. Can we see this another way, though, in accordance with the relational approach I am suggesting here? For me, the key to a profession like nursing is the *core values* that characterise it and which dictate the kind of relationships that are created with patients or clients. In a study of nursing that I was involved in a number of years ago, my colleagues and I identified 'caring' as a core value of the profession (Burkitt et al., 2001). However, this is a core value in the sense that it is not enacted by a 'merchant of morality' for dramaturgical effect, but by a practitioner committed to the act of caring as central to nursing practice and the relationship with patients. As Bolton pointed out, this is a value that informs the emotional labour of a nurse over and above, although not entirely separate from, the provision of labour power for a wage.

Caring is also a value which is central to the formation of professional relationships with patients, yet these relationships must always be 'appropriate' in that they are caring but not too close. That is, they must always stay within the bounds of a professional relationship so that the nurse as carer does not get too personally involved with patients. This sometimes creates paradoxical or conflicting demands and a balance must then be struck in the relationship between involvement and detachment for the professional nurse to keep his or her poise. There has to be the right involvement with patients in order to understand their needs and provide care, and yet there has to be enough detachment to prevent the relationship from becoming personal rather than professional, interfering with the nurse's work. At all times nurses have a job to do and caring is a central part of that job while not transgressing its boundaries. To build this caring relationship there has to be a degree of 'emotional attunement', in Scheff's (1990) terms, as empathic communication is necessary for nurses to interpret what is wrong with the patient so that they can provide the necessary care. As I showed in the last chapter, cognitive judgements are not separate from feelings and emotions, so that the latter are not just about trying to affect the emotional state of others. Emotional attunement is necessary in order to 'read' or interpret the situation correctly, making as accurate an assessment as possible on-the-spot, especially in emergency situations where quick judgements and decisions are required. In this way, not all emotional labour is performance for an audience in order to manage impressions. Rather, emotion is central to doing the job at all levels, and, in terms of building the necessary relationship with patients and their families, the balance of emotion is central in this. Achieving that balance is much of what the 'work' in emotional labour is all about, rather than the management of impressions, in that balance is central to the poise needed by professionals to maintain the right kinds of relationships and to do their jobs effectively.

However, what we also found in our study was that nurses were often more conscious of 'performing' the required emotions when they were under stress, particularly when resources were scarce and they felt they hadn't the time to adequately form a caring relationship with their patients. Even though our study of nursing was done in the UK in the late 1990s when privatisation and commercialisation of the public health service was not as advanced as it is today, nevertheless there was the inevitable squeeze on resources often felt in public health services free at the point of use, where resources have to be rationed in some way or another. Structural constraints such as cutbacks in staff or speed-up of the work process were a feature of the NHS during the time of our study, giving nurses less time to spend with patients than they would ideally like to have had. This is the point at which exploitation and alienation can enter into the labour process for people in the caring professions, when they feel the core values of those professions are threatened by structural constraints, or when cutbacks start to affect their levels of pay or benefits, threatening their profession in another way. Here we see the contradictory nature of emotional labour at the frontier of control over the work process that both Bolton and Brook referred to in their different ways.

What interested us in our study, however, was the way in which nurses dealt with these contradictory and stressful situations in their work and the strategies they adopted to cope with them. Here, it was *the situation* that nurses were often concerned with managing, not simply their own *individual* emotions, given that the situation could have a huge impact on the way they were *affected*, dealing with the emotional and psychological impact of illness on themselves, the patient and the patient's family. In addition, nurses had to deal with relations to other professions, especially with doctors on the wards, where there was a marked power relationship between them, with nurses often feeling that they were put in a less powerful position. Along with the structural constraints, such pressures meant that nurses did sometimes feel that they were performing by affecting emotion for others, either through deep or surface acting. But this was far from all there was to it. Attempting to control emotion is also an attempt to control both the relationship with the patient and family, and to control the flow of information in a situation. To do this, space and place became important for the nurses in our study, as the control of space was vital to control not only the expression of emotion, but also the flow of information. As Peter Freund (1998) has said, space is a master metaphor in the study of emotion, as spatial contexts and situations are important for sustaining and establishing boundaries and regulating the flow of information.

Thus nurses who found themselves continually in interaction with others on wards would have to seek out 'private' places if they had been deeply affected by a situation and needed to cry. This would often be the toilet or sluice where nurses would find a space to let go of their distress or grief. It is interesting that nurses choose such places, for these are where potentially dangerous and contaminating substances are washed away. Metaphorically, emotions like extreme distress and grief could also be seen as contaminating, as they might affect other colleagues or patients and threaten the order of hospital wards. As I want to show here, management of emotion is not just an individual act but involves *the collective management of the situation* in which people become affected. Place is then used to manage and contain emotion and the flow of information it communicates, especially when that emotion just *has* to be expressed. As one nurse put it, 'There's nowhere private for the nurses to go, nowhere which is your own, where we can go if we want to have a cry. You end up rushing to the toilet if you want to cry.' Here we see how distress is not an originally private emotion, as the distress this nurse felt emerged from a traumatic experience in a very public place (a hospital ward) when something upsetting had happened to a patient she was caring for; but due to professional standards, a very private place had to be found to give vent to the emotion that was overwhelming her.

Another way of dealing with emotional situations in emergencies was through a division of labour, where one nurse would be dealing with the family while others were working on the patient in a different place:

> But you have to remember as well that we know while we are doing that there is someone dealing with the emotion with the relative. And that, you know for a fact that that's being dealt with and it's being dealt with well. So you are not thinking, "Oh the poor mother what is she thinking now?" Somebody is dealing with that aspect of the trauma, so you can get on and do what needs to be done without having to think of the emotional things at the time. (Burkitt et al., 2001: 73)

Situations like this are not just about performance, then, in the sense of staging, but about controlling affect in situations through the use of space and the division of labour. Someone deals with the emotion surrounding the situation so that others can remain unaffected by it and get on with the business of saving a life. However, for those nurses who are the ones left to deal with the emotion in face-to-face situations with patients or relatives, managing what emotion is shown on the body or face is important as it defines the contingencies of the relationship and controls the flow of information. A spontaneous look of distress or concern by a nurse may send out the wrong signal or have the wrong affect, alarming a patient or relative when the nurse wants to keep them calm and together. The nurse dealing with the mother whose child is with the trauma team wants to communicate that all is being dealt with professionally, and that the child is in the best possible hands. There is also a professional relationship to maintain here, so that the nurse needs to look cool and calm under pressure or in difficult circumstances.

This kind of demeanour is not always understood by nurses as a performance that is 'put on' for an audience. We discussed the concept of performance with one nurse from a surgical ward who did not recognise this as an appropriate way of explaining the way she went about her job. She felt that her calm and unflappable approach was not just a professional performance but was part of the emotional disposition she had developed throughout her life, which she brought into her work. For her, this emotional disposition had been learned from her parents who were also rarely seen to panic, approaching everything in a laid-back manner. Although she said she often felt anxious and panicked 'inside', the coping strategy she had learned meant that this did not register in her appearance or expressions. Interestingly, she did not see this calm demeanour as a performance that masked another 'true' or 'deeper' self; instead, she saw it as much a part of herself as the anxiety that her disposition did not allow her to express. Because this way of being emotional, in this case cool and calm, had been developed from the earliest years of life, she felt it was not a performance – even one drawn from deep acting – but an integral part of her own self. In acting this way, this particular nurse felt she retained her poise and stayed in touch with herself.

There are also times when nurses feel they don't have to suppress their feelings in order to control information but can let the patient see what is going on to get things into perspective, especially if a patient's condition is not that serious. Here, nurses strive for that balance of tact and directness that Wouters thought so important in more informalised societies where people do not always have to put on a show. One nurse in the accident and emergency department put it this way:

> 'Is it wrong to tell them, "You are making a big fuss over nothing. We've just had somebody in here that has died and I'm afraid that is the reason you have had to wait your turn?" I don't think it is wrong, no. Sometimes it benefits to voice your opinion, you are not giving away any confidential information to them. I don't see why we shouldn't let them know what is going on in the real world ... I think you've got to help them put it into perspective.' (Burkitt et al., 2001: 75)

Another nurse in the accident and emergency department backed up this more direct approach to patients, also showing awareness of how the nurses' emotional approach can affect the patient too, stopping situations from becoming overly emotional. As he put it, 'we're not your caring, brow-mopping nurses', going on to say that he avoided 'nursey' talk in order to normalise what can be highly charged emotional situations:

> 'Patients are very, very anxious and they don't want prissy nurses coming along and talking nursey talk to them ... talking in low voices. They want normal people. And you want to make their experience in here as normal a part of their life as you can. I talk to the patients here like someone who I've met in the pub or in the street, I don't relate to them any differently here. Because they are people I think they need a normal conversation.' (Burkitt et al., 2001: 79)

This more direct approach was typical in the accident and emergency department we studied, but not in the hospice where we also conducted research, illustrating that different communities of practice in different settings developed their own emotional culture and ways of dealing with patients and relatives. In the hospice a more empathic and less matter-of-fact approach was taken, perhaps also reflecting the greater time staff had to talk to patients and families and build up a relationship with them. Again, though, *this is not so much a question of the individual management of emotion,* with individual nurses suppressing and inducing particular emotions, *as it is a question of a team using the place in which they work to create a situation with its own emotional culture. What is being managed, then, is not an individual emotional system but a situation.* In the hospice, the team had created a collective way of dealing with emotion when a patient had died, discussing particular deaths and how they felt about them and if they thought they could have done anything better. *Here, teams are managing not just a process of affectation but the process of being affected and how to deal with this.*

This emotional culture and situation also extend to patients and relatives so that there can be a sharing of affect. In the hospice this culture comes across strongly along with the way in which affect is shared between staff, patients and relatives. As one nurse put it:

'We'll you see, we say we'll laugh with them but we'll cry with them as well. You know what I mean? There'll be as much laughter as there are tears really here. Because people say, "isn't it all doom and gloom," so we say it isn't doom and gloom at all.' (Burkitt et al., 2001: 79)

There is, of course, an element of the management of individual emotion in nursing care not unlike that suggested by Hochschild. This is especially evident when nurses have to deliver bad news to a patient's family or friends, which necessitates a rapid invocation of empathy and a summoning up of emotional strength. As one nurse described it, 'I've got to psyche myself up before I open the door ... I just take a deep breath and think what am I going to face this time. ... And you never know until you open that door what reaction you are going to get.' However, the encounter that eventually happens in the room with the family or friends is not purely performative, and to see it as such is superficial. As Theodosius, among others, has said, there is a therapeutic element in a nurse's emotional labour that helps a patient deal with the sense of vulnerability or damaged self that illness brings, and dealing with this is necessary in the process of healing or recovery of a sense of wellbeing. In the example of the nurse I just described having to break bad news about a patient, there is a therapeutic role to play in helping family or friends deal with shock and loss. Therapeutic emotional labour, then, 'requires the nurse to bring something that is integral to herself into the relationship with the patient' (Theodosius, 2008: 156), and this cannot be done through performance, even by deep acting.

Another important point made by Theodosius is that emotions cannot be so successfully managed as Hochschild suggests, as in her study of nursing Theodosius found many instances where nurses didn't manage their emotions well, especially when patients or fellow health care professionals were critical of them or their standards of care. She says that 'emotions are not that easily managed and because they reflect aspects of the self that are considered integral, they have consequences' (Theodosius, 2008: 155). This links to the critique of Goffman, in that the consequences of the work nurses do effect the welfare and lives of patients, their families, and, ultimately, the nurses themselves and their colleagues. It binds the nurse into world-time where actions and relationships are consequential for real, living (and dying) people. Nurses who found it hard to control their emotions of anger or upset when patients' families or friends questioned the care they gave, were so affected, not just because such accusations or complaints might damage their career, but because such questions mattered to them*selves*. As we noted (Burkitt et al., 2001), the values of the profession are not something that is just out there in the professional body, floating in the ether, it is embodied in the very identity of *being a nurse*. The value of 'caring' is part of the identity of being a nurse, so that when someone questions a nurse's standards of care they are questioning his or her very identity, certainly if the nurse is committed to what they do and to their profession. As I illustrated in the last chapter, the emotional-evaluative stance of others influences the way we see and feel about our own self, and this is as true of professional identities as it is of everyday ones.

This is something Theodosius tries to take account of through a dialogical understanding of the way that nurses become emotional, which is very similar to the account I am suggesting here, except she adopts Archer's (2003) theory of reflexive dialogues in which the 'internal conversation' is with the self's own personal order of concerns. However, as we found in the study I was involved in, the values, rules and concerns of nursing are not just personal, although in many cases they become so; they are made part of the self as the person *becomes a nurse* through mutual identification with role models in the profession, and by identifying with the 'imaginary community' of nursing that is embodied in professional standards, ethics and values (Burkitt et al., 2001). What was of interest to us was the relationship between this imaginary community of nursing and the various communities of practice that developed in actual practice settings, where these values were refracted and developed into specific cultures, including the emotional culture of the ward and its management. Thus, as people become nurses within these communities, being a nurse becomes a *my-feeling* that matters to the person and elicits the full range of emotions in relation to others encountered at work. Working as a nurse is a contradictory experience in which alienation and exploitation as a wage labourer are always possible, including alienation from one's emotional labour. However, this is a contradictory experience precisely because nursing is a profession undertaken primarily out of an emotional animus: that the people who take up the profession care about it and the people they look after.

Flexible Capitalism and Emotional Reflexivity

In recent years the debate around emotion at work has shifted away from the concept of emotional labour to what Jason Hughes (2005, 2010) has called 'emotional reflexivity'. As noted in the last chapter, in Giddens's (1984) notion of reflexivity, this is something that occurs as agents in late-modernity are increasingly having to recursively order their social practices according to the knowledge they have about the social world, rather than using taken-for-granted patterns of custom or tradition. Reflexivity demands that we monitor our own actions knowledgably and adjust them to the institutions of modernity as they develop and constantly place new demands on us. However, the recent discussions about emotional reflexivity have drawn on the work of Goleman on emotional intelligence and its application to the workplace (Goleman, 1996, 1998). This is largely because Goleman has brought together strands of thinking from neuroscience and psychology to re-imagine emotions as being open to rational and intelligent control. Moreover, he has explicitly applied his idea that success in life might depend more on emotional intelligence than on IQ in the modern corporation and how its success, as well as the success of individuals within it, depends on the intelligent use of emotion. Others have pointed out why this is so important in contemporary capitalist societies, governed by the principles of neoliberal economics, where the pursuit of ever-expanding profits drives companies into new markets and into new innovations, not just in terms of products but also in terms of working practices (Gregg, 2010). In this uncertain world, corporations and their employees have to be flexible and able to deal with change. The literature on emotional intelligence is highly seductive in this environment.

As Hughes (2005) has noted, in the flexible workplace employees have to become more intelligent, adaptive and reflexive. For Goleman (1996), bringing intelligence to emotions means being able to know our own emotions, manage them effectively and motivate ourselves to perform tasks, but it also means having the interpersonal competencies to recognise emotions in others and, thus, being able to handle relationships better. Although on the surface this may seem like a continuation of Hochschild's ideas about managing emotions through emotional work and labour, for Goleman emotional intelligence means more than being able to suppress and induce emotions according to feeling rules. Instead, we should become more emotionally open and honest but always with a mind to other people, thus expressing ourselves in an empathic way that is also *appropriate*. While Goleman doesn't explain exactly what he means by 'appropriate', it seems to mean in general terms the balance of directness and tact that Wouters noted was the ideal in modern societies. In this view, emotions become a *resource* to be used for personal and corporate success. For example, combining emotional honesty with empathy, someone can be challenging and direct while still ensuring good relationships and avoiding conflict. This is because they are aware of their feelings, using them intelligently, knowing their possible effect on others and expressing them accordingly. To be emotionally intelligent means to unlearn 'defensive habits of conversation', so that instead of arguing, opposing parties 'agree to mutually explore the assumptions that undergird their points of view' (Goleman, 1998: 292). However, this also means that such emotional competencies, effective in team-building and managing change, cannot be scripted in advance according to known and commonly accepted feeling rules; instead, employees have to be given discretion in order to intelligently use their feelings in particular circumstances. Acting according to an emotional script could not, by definition, be emotionally intelligent.

For Hughes, though, who draws on both Elias and Foucault to analyse these trends, the interesting thing about Goleman's approach is that in calling for an *informalisation* of emotional controls at work he simultaneously *intensifies* control in new ways. For example, emotional intelligence requires emotional honesty while simultaneously seeing emotions as projects to be managed; it advocates for emotion not to be scripted, but instead wants a reflexive monitoring and negotiation of emotional life at work. Thus '*emotional reflexivity* involves *both* a relaxation and an intensification of emotional controls' (Hughes, 2010: 45, emphasis in original).

For Illouz (2007), what she describes as 'emotional capitalism' – a culture in which emotional and economic discourses and practices mutually shape each other – can be liberating when applied to the workforce. She traces emotions entering the discourses and practices of workplaces to Elton Mayo's famous 'Hawthorne experiments' in which it was found that productivity increased in the Hawthorne factory when greater attention was paid to workers' feelings. The informalisation this led to in relations between managers and workers Illouz takes to be real and not just ideological. Goleman's ideas about emotional intelligence in the workplace are not, then, a revolution in the way we relate to others at work, but the culmination of nearly a century of knowledge and practice which has made this emotional style a social capital. However, what Hughes (2010) draws attention to, using Foucault's later writings on power, is that emotional intelligence and reflexivity is not a diminution or equalising of the 'old' form of power employed in class relations, but a *new style of power altogether*. As Foucault argued, power no longer presents itself in the form of control by repression but rather as control by *stimulation*: power stimulates, incites and induces, governing the actions of individuals not by force but by shaping the field of action in advance (Foucault, 1982).

This applies to emotional intelligence in that it already delineates the field of action where productivity and profits can be increased through the creation of cooperative and communicative working relationships. However, this is not done through *external* social controls, such as laying down rules and regulations, but by what Foucault calls 'techniques of the self' whereby techniques, such as communicative competencies, are used by people to fashion new relationships to themselves and others. Techniques of the self use these communicative competencies in practices of truth-telling and self-disclosure whereby people feel they are 'revealing' hidden aspects of themselves, but are actually creating them in the enactment of these very practices. This can be seen in emotional intelligence (EI) as 'knowing and managing one's emotions, and managing and motivating oneself, and the more general quest to find one's true self ... is enshrined in Goleman's model of EI' (Hughes, 2010: 48).

However, as I showed in the section of this chapter on the nursing profession, it is not always possible for people to successfully manage their emotions so that they always appear in a form we or our employers would like. People can be deeply affected by an emotional situation and the onset of an emotion is not always realised in the higher levels of consciousness and, thus, open to reflective deliberation and control. Indeed, this is not always desirable, especially where people have to make quick decisions in emergency situations and rely on 'intuition'. Also, there is always the possibility of resistance to company rules or feeling rules, adopting them in a way that is ironic or not too taxing, such as people taking up the inducement to 'get on with people' simply as polite detachment (Gregg, 2010). As Yun has put it, reporting on a study of service workers, 'governmentality is not accepted wholesale and without question, but instead, is accommodated within a range of individual social desires and interests, with which it interacts in a complex and dynamic manner' (Yun, 2010: 313). From the employers' point of view, if governmentality fails or meets levels of resistance deemed unacceptable there are always the 'old' style levers of power to fall back on, such as disciplinary proceedings and firing.

In this chapter, then, I have critiqued Hochschild's theory of the emotions in that although a dramaturgical approach to emotions may be revealing when studying emotional relationships for the duration of an airplane flight, there are serious issues taking it beyond commercial interactions into the realm of everyday life. Hochschild's theory drives a wedge between the private and the public, self and others, and makes all socially acceptable affects into affectations – instances of emotions, biological and cognitive, having feeling rules imposed on them and being transformed into something else by deep or surface acting. Yet many of our emotional moments with others do not conform to feeling rules and are not well managed in the terms they set out, as we can be deeply affected and moved by others and their emotional predicaments. In contemporary western society, both at work and play, expectations are emerging that demand a complex mixture of both tact and honesty in our emotional responses to others. Emotion is about embodied meaning-making that shows pattern and order through iteration and habitual dispositions to emotional situations, yet it also opens us up to the fluid, indeterminate and shifting possibilities of the present moment that contains drama and novelty and to which we must imaginatively respond. We also face contradiction, paradox and dilemma in various contexts and this forces us into dialogical reflection on conflicting impulses, so that it is not always possible to predict in advance how people will respond. This is something I will explore at greater length in the next chapter as I turn to a theme touched upon here: the emotional dimension of power relations.

7

Emotions and Power Relations

At the end of the last chapter I concluded that emotions are not always well managed in accordance with feeling rules, as they reflect evaluative stances that are integral to the self and which have consequences within the relational networks of self and others. In these networks we are affected by the emotions of others in the fluid, indeterminate and shifting possibilities of the immediate moment, with its drama and novelty, and by the emotional consequences of our own actions. In emotional terms we can act spontaneously in these indeterminate moments but this does not mean that our actions are irrational; indeed, those spontaneous actions can be full of emotional reason, following the relational pattern of the social interconnections that we, and our emotions, are embedded in, also reflecting its contradictions. In this chapter I want to continue with this theme, shifting slightly to consider the way that social relations are always power relations in some form or to some degree. The implication of this is that emotion is always interwoven in power relations, both shaping and being shaped by them. Emotions are shaped by power relations because governments and other actors and agencies try to use emotion to direct the field of social action, controlling and manipulating people. However, these attempts often fail because emotion itself shapes power relations, as people do not always respond in ways that those who attempt to govern conduct intend, or in ways that can be predicted in advance. For me, this occurs because of the complex, contradictory nature of social relations and the emotions patterned by them. Emotional responses are unpredictable because emotions are ambivalent and are constantly shifting: we can feel both love and hate for the same person or thing; can be moved by affection and anger at the same time; or emotions like sympathy, anger and grief can quickly follow on from one another and alternate. Furthermore, individuals are also differentially placed in these relations with their own biographical trajectories – including their prior values, identifications with others and sense of belonging or alienation in relation to various groups – intersecting social relations and placing them in unique relation to others, or to situations and events.

In this chapter my focus will be on two particular emotions, anger and fear, as they emerge from within power relations and in response to attempts to govern conduct. That is because the chapter will draw on evidence from a study of the way the UK government attempted to manipulate emotions in the 'war on terror', declared by some western governments after the events of 11 September 2001 in the USA. My focus is on one particular event that ensued from this: the protests against the impending Iraq war in February 2003, especially a large anti-war demonstration in London and how this was reported in the press in terms of the emotions in the crowd, and what protesters themselves had to say about their own feelings. I hope this case study will illustrate and bring to life the points I am trying to make here. Before that, though, I want to say something about the way that various social theories understand the role of emotions as powerful forces in social life and in social movements, both knitting together and threatening the social order.

Social Theory, Emotions and Collectives

In this section I do not intend to review all the different sociological and social theoretical positions on the emotions, as others have already done this. There are comprehensive and considered studies of how classical sociological figures, and those working more broadly in social theory, encompassed an understanding of emotion in their work (Barbalet, 1998; Denzin, 1984; Turner and Stets, 2006; Williams, 2001). Instead, I will focus on the thinkers who bear a particular relevance to the subject of this chapter on power, mass movements and the affects that move people to political action. The work of the sociologist Emile Durkheim is particularly relevant here, for he suggests that emotion is not an individual phenomenon, but that '[c]ollective representations, emotions, and tendencies are caused not by certain states of the consciousness of individuals but by the conditions in which the social group in its totality is placed' (Durkheim, 1895/1938: 106). Like others of his generation (Freud, for instance), Durkheim was heavily influenced by Le Bon (1896) and thought that collective emotional forces were irrational and too powerful for individual consciousness to resist. In that sense they were 'social currents', like currents of opinion, which acted as coercive forces upon individual behaviour and consciousness, shaping conduct and thought. However, in his study of religion, Durkheim (1912/1915) developed a more fully rounded view of emotions as forces that act in the constitution and reconstitution of social groups, generated by the heightened emotional intensity of collective religious rituals and performances. The symbols of the group – such as the totem – become emblems in which the emotions of dependence and vitality created in collective rituals are invested. That is because the group is 'too complex a reality to be represented in all its complex unity' (Durkheim, 1912/1915: 220), and so ends up being represented by totems, flags, beliefs, or ideas.

However, the emotional 'effervescence' produced in collective rituals serves not only to reproduce the unity of the group through such emblems or ideas, for it can also threaten to tear it apart through the irrational emotional forces it unleashes. The morality of the everyday world, which is composed of dispersed activities acted out with moderate levels of emotional intensity, is threatened with being overturned by ceremonial and ritual gatherings that 'produce such a violent super-excitation of the whole physical and mental life that it cannot be supported very long' (Durkheim, 1912/1915: 216). Although temporary, such effervescent gatherings give the participants an inkling of a possible world beyond the everyday order. Yet Durkheim could also see the role played by powerful effervescent emotions in times of permanent social change, where 'under the influence of some great collective shock, social interactions have become much more frequent and active. Men look for each other and assemble together more than ever. That general effervescence results which is characteristic of revolutionary or creative epochs' (Durkheim, 1912/1915: 210–11). However, in everyday terms, Durkheim understands that in western modernity collective effervescence now takes place mainly around political rather than religious rituals and symbols. For him, the contemporary ideal in which a high level of emotional intensity is invested is 'moral individualism': that is, respect for the dignity, value and rights of each individual (Durkheim, 1957).

Although Durkheim's ideas are helpful in beginning to understand the role of powerful effervescent emotions in the configuration and reconfiguration of social groups and mass movements, nevertheless there are some problems with his concepts. Durkheim seems to suggest that collective forces – be they currents of emotion or opinion – are always successful in creating unity among groups because of their *sui generis* power, which is too great for individuals to resist. Perhaps Durkheim created *sui generis* concepts of society because, like the clan, a modern social group is too complex a reality to be represented clearly in all its complex unity (or should that be diversity?). Furthermore, in terms of emotion, even though his later work identifies a more rational role for the emotions in evaluating beliefs and ideas in political systems – such as moral individualism – Durkheim still holds to the idea of emotions as irrational forces too complex to analyse. As he says in an anthropological study, 'when [emotion] has a collective origin it defies critical and rational examination' (Durkheim and Mauss, 1903/1963: 88).

In this book, I have already challenged this view of emotion as an irrational force that sweeps individuals along with it and, because of its irrationality, is inaccessible to social scientific study or to intelligent reflection. Furthermore, Durkheim assumes that emotions – like collective representations – are produced by the conditions in which the social group is placed 'in its totality', ignoring the very thing that I have been stressing here: that in modern societies each person will have their own relation to the social situations they face based on their own biographical trajectories and the values that have become core to them as a self, developing and changing over time. This means that the individuals of a social group will never be in the same condition as a totality, as that totality is always fragmented by the complex diversity of the group and the very complex emotional responses within it. I will illustrate this as I go along in this chapter.

A very similar position to Durkheim's is taken by contemporary theories of affect within cultural studies, although they operate on a very different philosophical basis. We have already seen in Chapter 1 how the 'affective turn' in cultural studies tends to view emotions as forces or currents that affect the social group, working below discourse and consciousness to shape bodies and actions. In this vein, Ahmed (2004) has studied emotion in terms of power and politics, as she believes that emotions work to shape the surfaces of individual and collective bodies. For Ahmed, 'emotions circulate between bodies', sticking to some bodies and sliding over others (Ahmed, 2004: 4). However, a few pages later in the same book Ahmed claims it is not emotions that circulate as such, but it is the objects of emotion that circulate, objects that are sticky or saturated with affect, and that emotion itself moves through the circulation of these objects. Ahmed is therefore offering a model of 'affective economies' much in the way that Marx understood objects to accrue monetary value through their circulation on the market, except that she understands certain objects to accumulate affective value over time through circulation. However, it is not within the economic market that these objects circulate, but through various texts – such as political speeches and commentaries, statements by political parties and groups, and newspaper reports – that Ahmed studies to gauge the accumulation of affective value, which sticks to some bodies and slides over others. Thus she says that '[m]y analysis proceeds by reading texts that circulate in the public domain, which work by aligning subjects

with collectives by attributing "others" as the "source" of our feelings'
(Ahmed, 2004: 1).

Although I will give an example to illustrate this theory in the next
section, for now I want to make some comments on this purely at a
theoretical level. My problem with this is that there is tremendous confusion over exactly what circulates in an affective economy: is it texts,
as claimed in the quotation above, or as variously stated in other parts
of the book, emotions, objects, or signs? But even if we take this at face
value without too much critical analysis, how does the affect produced
by such an economy 'stick' to some bodies and not others? Ahmed seems
to be assuming here that the naming of emotion that goes on in texts
always sticks to its intended object, aligning subjects to collectives by
attributing others as the source of our feelings, as in the way texts about
'asylum seekers' tend to 'other' these groups as objects of hate, suspicion
and fear, while those who cannot be so named are aligned to a collective
identity of nation and home/belonging. But as with Durkheim, there is
an assumption here that emotion always works on the surface to form
collectives in this way, so everyone is formed as part of the totality or, as
Ahmed sees it, as outside of it also. The diversity that exists below this
surface is ignored. And exactly what is emotion in this theory and how
is it produced by naming or by circulation? As Wetherell (2012) has said
of Ahmed's approach, it makes emotion into a mysterious or uncanny
force that circulates, or is the product of circulation, in a highly disembodied way, in that emotion seems to stick to or slide over various bodies
only after it is formed. As I have been showing in this book, only human
bodies can feel emotion and so we must be engaged, as bodily selves,
from the very beginning of the process, in the production of various
emotions. We therefore need to locate affect, 'not in the ether, or in end-
less and mysterious circulations, but in actual bodies and social actors'
(Wetherell, 2012: 159), and in their affective practices.

But this critique also links to the issue of the production of value,
for what Marx showed was that the idea that value simply accumu-
lates by the product's circulation on the market is false: ultimately the
value of a product is determined by the labour that has gone into its
production, so that value is never produced independently of human
labour, action and practice. Similarly, I have been suggesting in this
book through developing an aesthetic understanding of emotion, following the work of thinkers like Bakhtin and pragmatists like Dewey,
that human meaning, value and emotion are a product of dialogue and
interaction, albeit shaped by the social and cultural forms of meaning that already exist. Yet nevertheless dialogical interaction produces
unique moments in which social meanings are either subtly changed

or made new for that particular moment. This is how a declaration of love, which may proceed in a time-honoured fashion, may be unique and new for two lovers in love, living and feeling the unique moment for themselves. Furthermore, as Lisa Blackman (2008) has shown, the idea that emotion and affect are like energies that circulate and have a psychic pull – such as 'falling' in love or coming under someone's 'spell' – is to do with the relational connection, pattern and dynamic between two or more people. Humans can and do get caught up in relational dynamics that are hard to control or are beyond their control, but this is not because emotion is a force or current too powerful to resist: it is because these dynamics are generated relationally through the interaction of many different people – couples, families and larger social groups or collectives – and the emotion is created from within the pattern of relationship; it does not exist prior to them as a mysterious force that independently forms, fragments, or destroys such groupings. I will return to the notion of relationality and the production of emotion throughout this chapter.

For now, though, an alternative to collective approaches for understanding emotion has been to focus on precisely what Durkheim denied in his analysis: the role of individual consciousness in the production of emotion. In some recent work on the political aspects of emotions, they are understood as intelligent responses to perceptions of value and, as such, part of the system of ethical reasoning (Nussbaum, 2001). This does not preclude the possibility that emotions can operate in unpredictable and disorderly ways, because they attach us to people, objects, or ideals that we value but which are beyond our own personal control. This leaves us vulnerable to grief, anger and fear should the people or things we love be lost or threatened. Because emotions are necessary to the very act of evaluation, they are bound to play a role in our thinking about the good and the just, and therefore in evaluations of political ideas and ideals also. This is a typical approach within cognitive theories of emotion, to which Nussbaum subscribes and by which she means that emotions are 'concerned with receiving and processing information' (Nussbaum, 2001: 23). I have dealt with this kind of cognitive theory in previous chapters, particularly Chapter 2 with reference to the work of Reddy (2001), and in Chapter 4 with reference to psychological theories of affect as being central to the processing of sensory and perceptual information. However, the downfall of all cognitive theories is precisely that they focus solely on the individual and what is happening in their own consciousness, along with the reliance on information processing models drawn from computer science in order to explain this. Once more we are drawn away from the world of social relations and a view of emotion in terms of what is going on between people as opposed to what is happening in their minds.

My own response to this has been woven throughout this book. It is not to deny that things are going on in people's bodies and minds, as this is clearly happening and is central to emotional experience. Individuals do make judgements based on feelings and emotions, and, as I showed in Chapter 5, this is inextricably tied to the reflective relation people have to the world and to their own bodily self. However, emotion is not understood as fundamentally to do with cognition but is to do with our habitual, embodied responses to others and to certain situations, which in turn is tied to our relational past and the practices we engage in with others. Our emotional-evaluative responses are ingrained in us habitually, and it is only when these are no longer appropriate, or not appropriate to the situation we find ourselves in, that we become aware of them and reflect upon them, perhaps deciding on other responses or other courses of action. This view also proposes that emotions are not necessarily irrational forces but have a reason to them that is not purely mental; instead, it is a reason that follows a relational pattern. However, those relations are also power relations, and we cannot, in my view, separate people's emotional responses and judgements of value from the power relations in which they are located.

Power and Emotion: Anger, Fear and the 'War on Terror'

For Max Weber, obedience in power relations is 'determined by highly robust motives of fear and hope' and is legitimised by three ideal types of authority – the traditional, charismatic and the legal (Weber, 1919/1948: 79). How prescient his comments now seem, because fear and hope have figured largely in political rhetoric and relations post-11 September 2001. Fear has been used by western governments, especially in Britain and the United States, when they repeatedly warn of threatened or imminent terrorist attacks; and hope is raised that action in the 'war on terror' will remove these threats to peace and security. At the same time, societies of the western world are held out as beacons of democracy and freedom of speech, resting on the legal basis of the rule of law. However, in a piece on the emotional responses to 11 September, Kemper (2002) broadens this out to make predictions about six emotions – anger, sadness, fear, joy, shame and guilt – and how they affected different groups in the USA depending on their relation to the events of that day. Furthermore, these emotions are linked to power relations because *anger* results from a loss of status; *fear* from the loss of power relative to the other; *sadness* from a loss of status which is irremediable; and *joy* from a gain in status. Likewise, *guilt* is felt when one feels one has used excess power on another; and *shame* when one has acted in a way that belittles one's status in the eyes of another. In this relational view, then, the emotions are linked to one's place in the power and status structure of society, a view linked to Kemper's wider theory of how emotion emerges in social relations (Kemper, 1990). On this basis Kemper (2002) predicts that the group he labels as 'New Yorkers/Most Americans' would feel anger at the strikes on the World Trade Center and the Pentagon on 11 September, as these were centres and symbols of US power. Thus, the strikes were perceived as a loss of status that had to be restored. Given this, anger can be predicted as an important emotion in the reaction to 11 September, certainly among many citizens of the USA, who saw this as a loss of status. This would exist alongside fear and, eventually, hope.

However, as I will show here, anger did not just emerge in response to a loss of status, or in terms of shame at that loss. Instead, in countries like the US and Britain, anger became directed at the governments of these countries by sections of their own people because of what some perceived to be the mismanagement of the response to terrorist atrocities. Indeed, as Silber (2011) points out, civic anger is a moral and political emotion that can mobilise people into action, which is directed at the state and at the realm of politics more generally. Her focus on civic anger emerged from, surprisingly, a study on elite philanthropy, in which she found that philanthropy had a personal trajectory that involved factors such as family background and values, a sense of personal satisfaction and accomplishment, empathy and compassion, and a feeling of collective solidarity with others: alongside this, though, there were also intense criticism and feelings of anger at the state for a lack of competence and efficiency. Thus, elite philanthropists were motivated in their giving by a complex of emotional responses involving not only positive emotions, but also emotions like anger and disgust which are generally perceived as negative. As Silber points out, however, anger moves people into collective action and, in this way, can be a motivating emotion. It is wrong, therefore, to see anger only in terms of a loss of status.

Equally, it is wrong to see fear simply as the result of a loss of power relative to others. As Barbalet (1998) points out, the cause of fear can be structured insufficiencies of power, but even elite groups feel this when they perceive their interests are under threat. It is this, along with the prospect of undesirable events or outcomes, that is the source of fear; yet as with anger this can have motivating effects that move people to action. Organisational innovation and development can result from feelings of fear as people act collectively to redress feelings of vulnerability and shore up their interests and sense of security. Thus, when fear is viewed as a purely individual or psychological phenomenon, as in the 'fight/flight' responses, the result is seen to be immobility, withdrawal, or denial, yet when fear is seen as a social phenomenon then the possibility emerges of collective action to remove the source of fear. In such a way, for Barbalet, all the emotions, not just fear, are directly implicated in social action and in the agent's transformation of their social world.

Much, though, rests on the definition of power that different theorists take in their studies of emotion. Kemper, for example, takes what he defines as a Weberian position on power, whereby power is defined as 'all those actions designed to obtain compliance with one's own wishes, desires, and interests over the resistance of another' (Kemper, 2002: 54). In this light, power is said to include both threatened and actual physical assault, verbal abuse, deception and manipulation, or threatened and actual deprivation of another's benefits or privileges. By such means one person seems compelled to comply, against their own will, with the will of another. We could therefore study the outcomes of social interaction in terms of power by trying to discover whose position in the power structure has increased, decreased, or stayed the same as a result of that interaction. However, this ignores Weber's emphasis on the legitimisation of power and the means by which people are persuaded to comply with powerful forces.

In opposition to Kemper's approach, I want to adopt a different definition of power and a different standpoint on the emotions in power relations. Rather than remain with a definition of power that makes the relation of one individual over and against another central, and which places status as a key element in power relations, I will develop some of Foucault's insights on power, which were briefly touched on in the last chapter. These insights are interesting because they implicitly contain some notion of the emotions that are elements in the weave of power relations and that emerge within forms of government. That is because, for Foucault, power is not about repression but about control through *stimulation* in a productive fashion. Thus, Foucault says that power is 'a total structure of actions brought to bear upon possible actions: it incites, it induces, it seduces … [it is] a way of acting upon an acting subject or acting subjects' (Foucault, 1982: 220). So power is *not* an action that imposes itself directly on another person by the very force of imposition: it works more subtly as a structure of actions that aims to *affect* a field of possible actions. Thus, 'power is less a confrontation between two adversaries or the linking of one to the other than a question of government ... it designate[s] the way in which the conduct of individuals or of groups might be directed' (Foucault, 1982: 221).

However, a difficulty in adopting a Foucaultian approach for the understanding of emotion I am developing here is that Foucault's ideas on technologies of government and techniques of the self are *impersonal*. They are designed to analyse techniques purely as technological devices that are deployed in a social domain or used by individuals as ways of mastering themselves. The latter is done, for example, through the use of ethical codes that dictate the care of the self, such as diets and other regimes which form an aesthetic of the self (Foucault, 1988), or as we saw in the last chapter, through the practice of emotional intelligence which subjects people to power within organisations. What this misses, however, is the relational processes in the making and unmaking of different power regimes and thus also the dialogical and interactional relations between people in which feelings and emotions appear. As an aesthetic, it is also highly individualised and contrasts to a dialogical approach in which 'a key human project ... is an aesthetic one – to give form to the other while being authored by the other' (Sullivan, 2012: 32). This is the style of aesthetics I have been advocating here, in which humans both experience and make meaning in social interactional settings, and where, as I showed in Chapter 5, people express *both* a sense of self-power *and* vulnerability to being subjected to others' viewpoints on them – the imagination of which makes them feel certain emotions about themselves – in dialogical interrelations with others.

Given the above critique, we can begin to think about how emotion is integral to the ordering of the emergent relational field of power and government in Foucaultian terms, if not in his analytical style, because to incite, induce and seduce involves emotion. In order to incite, people must be provoked or stirred in some way, with anger being a possible response to provocation. To induce, people must be persuaded or motivated in a way that calls out for a certain type of conduct. Finally, the act of seduction must produce a desire or longing for a person, object, goal, or ideal. Thus, while status is obviously important in relations of power and is central to the experience of shame and embarrassment, these are not the only factors – or even the key factors – to be considered in the study of power and emotion. However, what I will illustrate here is that these techniques of government, and the styles of emotional manipulation that go with them, do not always work; indeed, often they backfire and the emotions that flare up are not the ones that governments intended to induce. This is something that is not suggested in Foucault's understanding of power, except that power is always seen to meet with resistance because everyone has some degree of power within power relations. Yet the notion of resistance is highly generalised: it is understood to arise whenever power and government is practised, but there is never a sense of why people are resisting and what is the ideological or the emotional-evaluative reason for that resistance.

In a Foucaultian vein, Ahmed (2004) analyses the way fear has been used as a technology of governance and as a tool for forming collectives. Post-11 September 2001 the fear of the threat of terrorism was used to align bodies with some and against others, as fear stuck to potential terrorist bodies; presumably those that were black or Asian and thus easily identified as or mistaken for being Muslim. For those who are not so identified, the other side of fear is lived out as patriotic love for the nation-state, as the sovereign power holds up civil society as a protection from the fear of terrorist threat. Although this is an interesting analysis of the way that fear can be used in technologies of power and government, once again there is an assumption that such techniques always work successfully to align bodies in such a way. But the government rhetoric of fear and hope might have a completely different compositional logic from the way in which fear and hope are lived out in the relations and affective practices of everyday life (Wetherell, 2012). And as I will suggest here, in the affective practices of everyday life, such emotional technologies of government may not even work.

This is because personal biographical trajectories intersect relations of power and also because emotions are ambivalent and closely connected with one another. As Freud illustrated, emotion is often ambivalent in the sense of 'the direction towards the same person of contrary – affectionate and hostile – feelings' (Freud, 1963/1981: 478). Such ambivalent emotions are also interconnected and can alternate with each other, so that, 'hope alternates uneasily with fear, as a single event transforms hope into grief, as grief, looking about for a cause, expresses itself as anger, as all these can be the vehicles for an underlying love' (Nussbaum, 2001: 22). It is the ambivalence and alternation of emotion, which, I shall suggest, makes emotional responses hard to predict in all relations, including power relations. This means it is difficult for governments, or any other political group, to manipulate emotion in order to govern by directing conduct. Incitement, inducement and seduction cannot be gauged precisely for everyone enmeshed in the networks of power relations, although this does not stop those in government attempting to manipulate emotions. Attempts to do this were made by the US and British governments in the post-11 September 2001 environment, when a climate of fear and hope was fostered. As I show below, however, this did not work in Britain (or in other countries) and instead sections of the population became filled with anger at the British government, especially after the war in Afghanistan and in the wake of the war on Iraq.

Unpredictable Emotions

The case study in this section of the chapter is drawn from newspaper reports of the London demonstration on 15 February 2003 against the impending Iraq war. I selected reports to study from two broadsheet newspapers in the UK – *The Times* and *The Observer*, the latter being the Sunday edition of the *Guardian* newspaper group – and did so because, historically, the former paper has been seen to broadly represent the right wing of political opinion, while the latter broadly represent the centre-left. However, what was interesting in studying the articles was that the approaching war in Iraq did not divide opinion along those traditional lines, and both newspapers published articles that were pro- and anti-war. However, the second main reason for me to focus on these newspapers, rather than the tabloid press, was that they also published reports that included, or in one case was entirely made up of, the protesters' own words. These were quotations from protesters present on the day that recorded their feelings in their own words and which, at times, revealed something different from what journalists were saying about the protests and the emotions of the crowd. This shows that the way journalists and other commentators attempt to align people to collectives and name their emotions in their texts is not always the same as the way that body-selves align themselves or feel in their actual, everyday affective practices and relations.

In addition to the case study selected here being a good example of publicly expressed powerful emotions, I have also chosen it because it illustrates reactions *against* attempts to direct conduct through the manipulation of emotion, which involved mass protest with clear public displays of emotion. The case study therefore illustrates how attempts at limiting the field of possible actions through manipulation of emotions in power relations can be both partially successful and a dismal failure, producing the opposite effect of that intended. As I said in the section above, politicians in Britain tried to create fear and hope in the 'war on terror' and thought that these emotions would be enough to generate public support for any war being waged against terror. What the case study that follows shows is that emotional responses were much more complex, illustrating how emotions work both in attempts by government to govern *and* in the opposition to those attempts by sections of the population.

Case Study: Opposition to the War on Iraq

After the attacks on the USA on 11 September 2001, the British government, led by Prime Minister Tony Blair, had been one of the main supporters, along with other alliance partners, of George W. Bush's invasion of Afghanistan and, the following year, the British and Spanish governments were among the more active supporters of going to war with Iraq in the name of the 'war on terror'. However, the evidence the alliance partners had produced to convince the public that the regime in Iraq could be linked to Islamic terrorism and was amassing weapons of mass destruction had been open to critical scrutiny, and the build-up to war in the latter part of 2002 began to divide public opinion. On Saturday 15 February 2003 a series of huge demonstrations involving millions of people were held in cities all over the world, including London. Indeed, this was one of the largest political demonstrations ever held in London with some estimating that just over 3 million people attended. What is of interest to me, though, is the way that the demonstration was reported in the newspapers selected, in terms of the emotions attributed to the crowd by reporters and what protesters said about their own emotions, and also what reporters said about the unity and diversity of the people there. While *The Times* of Monday 17 February had a lead article which claimed that 'more than six million peace demonstrators across the world have failed to sway the United States, which last night vowed to press on this week with plans for war against Iraq' (p. 1), inside was a more detailed report of the London rally. Under a headline which read, 'Middle England packs a picnic and sets off to change the face of politics', the article – written by a reporter present at the demonstration – paints a picture of a protest unified by dominant British values and identity: a middle-class, polite affair with only a smattering of troublesome and noisy political activists (*The Times*, 17 February 2003: 12–13). On the ground the march is described as a 'restrained affair', evoking the stereotype of the British as emotionally reticent. The following extract from the report gives the general tone:

> At 11-45am, people started to move. The mood was convivial, the pace tortoise-like. Here and there you could spot the usual suspects, the anarchists who love to snarl and spit violence, but they

were completely sidelined by the overwhelming garden-centre ordinariness of the crowd. (*The Times*, 17 February 2003: 12)

In the above, the reporter attempts to articulate the feeling of the crowd – the mood – which she describes as 'convivial'. The only anger reported is attributed to a group of anarchists, who are summarily dismissed as 'the usual suspects' – a known minority group – contrasted with the safe 'garden-centre ordinariness' of the majority who, it would seem, could never get cross about anything. In this report, the unity of the crowd is constructed through middle-class identity and mildness of temperament, around which a boundary is drawn leaving 'the usual suspects' on the outside to snarl and spit violence. The piece goes on like this throughout, except when the journalist reports the actual sentiments and opinions articulated by the marchers. In contrast, these reveal strong feelings and emotions on the subject of the war, especially in that people feel the British government is not listening to their concerns. The following, the words of a woman demonstrator taken from the same report, is typical of views expressed: '"I know I am going to get emotional today," she said. "It is becoming more believable now. Tony Blair is not dealing with us. He is not listening. No one is listening"' (*The Times*, 17 February 2003: 12). The report does conclude that '[t]his was not politics as usual. This was the British people saying, politely but firmly, that they want someone to listen' (*The Times*, 17 February 2003: 13). However, once again, politeness is emphasised against firmness, tempering the strength of feeling of the protesters.

On the same page of *The Times* is a report by another journalist who was at the demonstration and spent the day talking to protesters. This report is composed of the views of 10 demonstrators in their own words, without any added journalistic comment. Again, we find the expression of strong emotions in contrast to the feeling conveyed by the main report. Here are a few snippets: 'We feel strongly against the war, but we feel we didn't have an opportunity to express that'; 'It makes you despair of any of them [politicians], but the march has been exhilarating'; 'We feel so strongly about the issue it's got us to our first march' (*The Times*, 17 February 2003: 12). In these brief quotations we can see the strength of feeling articulated by these people, even if this is not always expressed as a clear emotion such as anger. There is despair because of their perceived political impotence and disgust at politicians, yet at the same time there is the feeling of exhilaration the march has given people: the collective sense of power felt in a crowd unified in a purpose and sounding out a loud and clear voice of opposition to the government.

In contrast to the report in *The Times*, the main article in *The Observer*, written by a reporter at the demonstration, stresses the diversity in the crowd rather than its middle-England uniformity. The report notes 'the colourful warmth of feeling in the extraordinary crowds' and that carrying banners there were nuns, Muslims, toddlers, lecturers, hairdressers and Nottingham County football supporters, in addition to 'the usual suspects' (that phrase again) – 'CND , Socialist Workers' Party, the anarchists' (*The Observer*, 16 February 2003: 1–2). The report of the feelings of people talked to in the crowd is similar to *The Times*, in that there was a strong feeling of not being listened to and, thus, democracy was not working properly. One person, whose words are quoted directly, says, 'No one's being consulted, and it's starting to feel worrying – more worrying than the scaremongering we've been getting about the terrorist threat' (*The Observer*, 16 February 2003: 2–3). Another report in the same edition is more up-front about the negative emotions felt in the crowd, in that 'What unites them is anger against Bush and Blair, but mainly Blair' (*The Observer*, 16 February 2003: 1). So here, solidarity is seen as being created through the emotion of anger, which has been stirred by a government not listening to a section of its people.

This links strongly to the motivating power of civic anger, as Silber (2011) pointed out in her work on philanthropy. Although the context here is very different, some of the same emotional factors are at play, particularly compassion and a sense of solidarity with ordinary Iraqi citizens who it is felt will bear the brunt of war, hence the crowd at the demonstration wanting to express the sentiment of the war not being in their name. But there is also clear anger at the realm of politics – at the then British Prime Minister Tony Blair, in particular, but at all politicians who support the war – and a feeling of frustration that they are not being listened to by a government that many will have voted for. These people will have longed for the actualisation of the 'New Labour' values expounded by the Blair government, 'of social inclusion, community and a revived sense of socially responsible compassion' (Hey, 1999: 61). Now they think those values are being betrayed, they are angry. However, what is also interesting about the London demonstration is the way that different body-selves (and I use this term here because these are not blank bodies, awaiting the inscription of the naming of their emotions in texts, but are bodily-selves with an identity and history, including prior values, habits and dispositions that incline them to feel certain ways about particular things) are aligned together in a common cause, perhaps for different emotional reasons. *The Observer* commented on the diversity of bodies and identities in the crowd – Muslims, toddlers, lecturers, football supporters, etc. – in terms of the different age, class, gender and ethnic identities that were there. Muslims in the crowd may have been drawn because they felt that a largely Muslim nation was under threat, and their anger stemmed from that. Yet this means that a diversity of different emotional reasons can align into common cause a diversity of different body-selves. Furthermore, there is not one single emotion that unifies or fragments people on the demonstration, as emotion is ambivalent and alternates. Journalists on the day noted the conviviality in the crowd along with a feeling of exhilaration; but there was also evidence of compassion, solidarity, anger, outrage and frustration (probably many more emotions as well). This is not only a complex diversity in a gathering but a complex of emotions stemming from the relation of these people to an unfolding situation of impending war.

It must also be recognised, though, that those drawn to this demonstration were still only a small fraction of the population and they were the ones likely to have the strongest feelings about the war. What of those who did not take part in such demonstrations? A hint of the complexity and difference of opinion and emotion among a more varied section of the population can perhaps be found in a report by three journalists from *The Observer* newspaper, who spent a day in The Beano Café near Kings Cross, London, talking to customers about their views on the possibility of war against Iraq. In general, they found feelings of concern and worry about the impending war for a variety of reasons: it was felt the war would really be fought over oil; that they did not trust the US government; that George W. Bush only wanted to settle scores for his father – the US president at the time of the first Gulf war; and that the British government was too subservient to the US government. While people were generally sceptical about the official reasons being given for war there was also concern over Saddam Hussein, who was seen as an evil tyrant. But there was also a feeling of *indifference* expressed by a large number of people, many of whom did not have any opinions about the war. Both the arguments and the high level of emotion expressed by pro- and anti-war activists had not really moved them. Some of these customers might have been more interested and emotionally involved in the progress of their sports team or the latest celebrity gossip than the state of world affairs. One customer expressed the following view to a journalist:

'To be honest it doesn't really affect me', he said nonchalantly, shrugging his shoulders. 'I mean, it's so far away. I'd be worried if they started calling people up to go to war, though. Or if there was a big backlash from the Muslim community in this country.' (*The Observer*, 19 January 2003: 15)

What this demonstrates is that people had different views, feelings, opinions and emotions about the war depending on their biographical relation to the situation, which included their own prior emotional-evaluative stances and their personal interests. In terms of power relations and attempts by governments to incite, induce and seduce public feeling and opinion in the months prior to the Iraq war, this had had a mixed effect, and one could even venture to say it had failed. For the people above, there seemed to be concern and worry about the actual, as opposed to official, reasons given for the build-up to war rather than actual fear of Iraq or of imminent terrorist attack. And, perhaps, for a still larger number there was simply indifference. Of course, some people would remain strongly in support of government policy on Iraq, perhaps because of a mixture of fear plus, as Barbalet (1998) pointed out about that emotion, a hope that attempts to address what was feared would remove the threat. However, the larger point I want to make here is this: *that how people responded to attempts to incite, induce and seduce was unpredictable in advance. This is because emotions have a complex pattern, embedded as they are in the multiple networks of social relations and power relations, affording different positions and possibilities for government, opposition and resistance.* In terms of the last, this is not simply a blanket resistance that mobilises in power relations wherever and whenever attempts to govern are in operation: rather, resistance has varied emotional and intellectual reasons of its own that express the complex diversity in power relations in contemporary societies.

In conclusion, then, what I have been arguing in this chapter is that different body-selves can be drawn together into temporary collectives for a variety of different reasons, ideological or emotional, creating both unity and diversity among a social group. Even a demonstration like the one in London against the Iraq war can draw together a group that is, on the surface, united in a cause, yet beneath that surface may come together for different reasons, each person having different identifications in the group along with their own personal biography. Unity is therefore not always built on 'othering' a minority group, nor does unity automatically appear from the collective of body-selves assumed, or categorised, as being the 'same'. Furthermore, the emotions that people feel, which can drive them into political action to seek social change, are complex and shifting and do not always emerge in ways that technologies of government intend. In the 'war on terror' the fear that many governments in the west tried to provoke and induce seemed to fail to materialise in the everyday affective practices and social relations of many individuals. Indeed, some people reacted with anger at the very attempt to manipulate and manage them politically and emotionally, turning that anger on their own government which was claiming to be acting in their defence by protecting society from an external threat. I hope I have demonstrated here through the example of the reaction against the 'war on terror' that emotions are best seen as complex, ambivalent, unpredictable, and ultimately as difficult to govern as the social relations they both emerge from and feed back into.

Epilogue

What I have been arguing throughout this book is that feeling and emotion are about patterns of relationship, or, more specifically, social relationships which are intersected by personal biographies that are interwoven through them. Many of the psychobiological explanations of emotion I have considered are limited precisely because they ignore patterns of relationship, including social and personal meanings, and the emotional reason that accompanies the human experience of feeling. Feelings and emotions cannot, therefore, be understood as things in themselves, such as physiological or neurological responses that *alone* can be identified as *the emotion*, for these things are part of a complex in which feeling and emotion take on a wider reason as they follow the pattern of relationship. Social relations, though, are moving patterns because they are always in a shifting state of play, so that while we bring emotional dispositions from the past into present circumstances and situations – evaluating contexts through the lens of prior values and identifications which follow the trajectory of our own biography – these relations are constantly in flux as they move into the future, so that what we feel is constantly changing. Feelings and emotions are a dynamic part of this change as they are both produced by and yet produce effects upon the relational configuration. In this sense, emotions can both unify and threaten social relations, configuring and reconfiguring them in the same process. I hope to have illustrated something of this in the last chapter, whereby strong feelings brought people together into a temporary collective to challenge and attempt to change global configurations of power relations. Even if this attempt failed at a political level, many things changed at a more local level through the political action itself and its effects on people's identities and their feelings of power.

Furthermore, social relations at a local level, which form particular situations of interaction, are not bounded entities but are multiple and intersecting networks of practices that connect up to more generalised and, sometimes, more abstract or imagined groups such as social classes and factions. At both the general and local level, social relations rest on material and economic factors which support and make possible different types of practices, as I showed in Chapter 2 where higher standards of living created lower rates of infant mortality, allowing different types of emotional bonds to form between parents and children. Material standards in themselves do not determine the emotional cultures found within patterns of relationship, but they do allow people the possibility of forging different relations and emotional cultures.

Thus the broader patterns of social relations and the local scenes of interaction are ontologically connected, yet this can only be grasped temporally. Practices at a local level are structured by both social and personal history, because they are informed by the past in terms of dispositions towards habitual patterns of action which create what we recognise as social structure – the familiar and regular patterns of relations and practices that are immediately identifiable. At the same time, however, the current moment presents us with novelty as no two situations are ever exactly the same, and, especially where there is radical novelty in situations, habits must begin to adapt themselves to these new circumstances. This is the scene of practical and subjective consciousness in which there is no division between thought and feeling in the moment, as individuals must flexibly attune themselves to shifting circumstances and to a continually unresolved future. In these moments we engage in real relations with others, where more established meanings and values are lived and felt in the immediacy of our interpersonal connections. Here, imagination and desire also come into play as we sense the pre-formations of possible new meanings and futures, which are open to articulation when new semantic figures are created to give them more form. It is in these moments that our feelings of tendency connect old ideas and experiences to new and emergent possibilities in ways that are highly sensitive and oriented to situations as they develop. In this way, feelings and emotions are prime examples of how the body and bodily sensations are fused with social meanings in the patterned relational weavings of social encounters.

It is within these encounters with others that we are *affected* – moved or changed by a feeling or an emotion in relation to someone or something, and we are always open to some degree to being affected by the emotional-evaluative stance that others take towards us. However, because of the position put forward in this book, I am against many of the propositions of those who support the 'turn to affect'. This is because, in this stance, affect comes to be seen as a force or intensity in itself that mysteriously emerges from outside social relations and, as such, is a threatening or disruptive intensity. I am arguing here that emotion can be threatening and disruptive of existing relationships and is part of the dynamic of change constantly going on within relations; but that does not mean that affect is some intensity that is not itself a product of shifting patterns of relationships, and of the conflict and contest of diversity, opposition and divergent forms of resistance within them. Equally, I do not share the view that affect is an intensity that is pre-discursive, non-conscious and non-rational, as I have been arguing here that there are forms of emotional reason which come into focus more clearly if we see emotions as relational phenomena. While this does not mean that emotion is always experienced consciously and is continuously subject to reflection, it does lead us to think about the more subtle shadings and degrees that exist between the unconscious and the conscious, the non-reflective and the reflective, the involuntary and voluntary, and the necessary relationship between them. Indeed, this is where poise becomes an issue as people are threatened by being overwhelmed by the emotional experiences that have affected them, struggling to remain in touch with themselves and in possession of the skills and capacities that give them a habitual level of control over their everyday world, keeping them in balance. Even if we argue that much of our activity is motivated by feelings and emotions that are non-reflective, as I have been doing here, this does not mean that affect is not in a necessary relation to reflection – indeed I have been arguing this is the very basis of reflection itself. Even the style of reflective thought that proceeds through rational principles has at its core abductive inference, its attendant feelings and the metaphorical imagination that is so central to human emotion. It is also impossible to separate out feeling and emotion from discourse, as all our thoughts and feelings are modulated to the tone of metaphor (so basic to the creative use of language) and unarticulated word meanings. Although the latter are not full blown discourse, they can at any moment be turned into discursive utterance within our affective practices as we are moved by the relations we have to others or to situations. And those vague feelings that cannot yet be articulated still insist somewhere in our consciousness for the words to give them form as full verbal articulation, either for ourselves or others.

Affective practice, therefore, has to do with the kind of aesthetic embodied making and experiencing of meaning that goes on within the interactive pattern of our relationships. It carries forward the moods, feelings and values that come from our past biography, orienting us within the present and towards the future. But there is always within that present moment a myriad of small and large possibilities that can surprise us, can open us to a very different future, and can challenge the way we feel and think. These are disruptive possibilities that will no doubt spark a range of ambivalent, contradictory and alternating emotions – fear, excitement, resistance and longing for the new – working themselves out in complex ways as they attempt to both close us off from, and open us up to, the change that the future brings. Emotions are part of and never independent of these relational dynamics: in fact they follow the often contradictory pattern of relationships as they take and lead us to who knows where.

What I have also been arguing here is that emotions are complexes in that they cannot be reduced to any one element that goes into their making. Emotions are complexes in the way that bodily rhythms, energies, tensions (and release of tensions), heart-rate, neural processing networks and neurotransmitters are patterned together by social relations, meanings and interactions. Indeed, neural activation patterns are recurring structures based in habitual action and experience, yet open to setting and resetting within certain limits through practice, learning and enculturation. It is this overall social patterning of bodily practice within social relations – and their attendant and emergent meanings – that we know as emotion. This complex patterning is open to individual variation within cultural differences, both regional and local; they are also open to change within the novel and dramatic circumstances of everyday life as they tend towards new articulations. Language is the main mode of adult emotional articulation, but this is supported (and at times contradicted) by the repertoire of the bodily sounding-board which includes vocal intonation, gestures, looks and body posture. Neural systems and processing support this, as visual and other forms of perception – including those forms known as feelings – are connected to and modulated by language through 'top-down' and 'cascade' processing. These things also allow us the creativity to play on, and play with, images, metaphors, meanings and words, both to experience and to create meaning.

Human persons are, then, loosely constructed selves that are continuous, various, ambiguous, ambivalent and creative, with a polyphonic and dialogic subjectivity that reflects and refracts in imagination the various meanings it has for others, the self appearing only in the communication between self and other. At the heart of the self and its perception of the world are the emotional tones that colour all our experiences. So-called objective or rational modes of thought are not emotionless, but only the more impersonal stances that are open to a dialogically reflective consciousness; one that is reflective to varying degrees within different circumstances. Yet emotion and our own feelings about our self and world remain at the heart of everything we know and everything we are. There can be no living experience of the world, of ideas, music, art, self and others, without feeling and emotion. They are as essential to being a living bodily self as movement, thought and sensation: indeed, feeling and emotion are so intimately tied to these things as they are developed through social practice as to be ontologically, if not necessarily analytically and reflectively, inseparable from them. Feeling and emotion, then, are part of a global, meaningful, bodily being-in-the-world that defines what it is to be human.

References

Ahmed, S. (2004) *The Cultural Politics of Emotion*. Edinburgh: Edinburgh University Press.

Archer, M.S. (2000) *Being Human: The Problem of Agency*. Cambridge: Cambridge University Press.

Archer, M.S. (2003) *Structure, Agency and the Internal Conversation*. Cambridge: Cambridge University Press.

Bakhtin, M.M. (1920–1923/1990) Author and Hero in Aesthetic Activity. In M. Holquist and V. Liapunov (eds.), *Art and Answerability: Early Philosophical Essays by M. M. Bakhtin* (V. Liapunov, trans., pp. 4–256). Austin: University of Texas Press.

Bakhtin, M.M. (1963/1984) *Problems of Dostoevsky's Poetics* (C. Emerson, ed. and trans.). Minneapolis: University of Minnesota Press.

Bakhtin, M.M. (1986) *Speech Genres and Other Late Essays* (C. Emerson, M. Holquist, eds. and V. W. McGee, trans.). Austin: University of Texas Press.

Bar, M., Kassam, K.S., Ghuman, A.S., Boshyan, J., Schmidt, A.M., Dale, A.M., Hämäläinen, M.S., Marinkovic, K., Schacter, D.L., Rosen, B.R. and Halgren, E. (2006) Top-down Facilitation of Visual Recognition. *Proceedings of the National Academy of Sciences*, 103 (2): 449–54.

Barbalet, J.M. (1998) *Emotion, Social Theory, and Social Structure: A Macrosociological Approach*. Cambridge: Cambridge University Press.

Barbalet, J.M. (1999) William James' Theory of Emotions: Filling in the Picture. *Journal for the Theory of Social Behaviour*, 29 (3): 251–66.

Barrett, L.F. (2006) Are Emotions Natural Kinds? *Perspectives on Psychological Science*, 1 (1): 28–58.

Barthes, R. (1977/1990) *A Lover's Discourse: Fragments* (R. Howard, trans.). London: Penguin.

Bateson, G. (1973) *Steps to an Ecology of Mind: Collected Essays in Anthropology, Psychiatry, Evolution and Epistemology*. St. Albans: Paladin.

Bennett, M.R. and Hacker, P.M. (2003) *Philosophical Foundations of Neuroscience*. Oxford: Blackwell.

Blackman, L. (2008) Affect, Relationality and the 'Problem of Personality'. *Theory, Culture and Society*, 25 (1): 23–47.

Blackman, L. and Venn, C. (2010) Affect. *Body and Society*, 16 (1): 7–28.

Bolton, S.C. (2005) *Emotion Management in the Workplace*. London: Palgrave.

Bolton, S.C. (2009) Getting to the Heart of the Emotional Labour Process: A Reply to Brook. *Work, Employment and Society*, 23 (3): 549–60.

Bourdieu, P. (1979/1984) *Distinction: A Social Critique of the Judgement of Taste* (R. Nice, trans.). London: Routledge.

Bourdieu, P. (1980/1990) *The Logic of Practice* (R. Nice, trans.). Cambridge: Polity Press.

Bowlby, J. (1969) *Attachment and Loss: Volume 1, Attachment*. London: Hogarth Press.

Brinkmann, S. (2006) Damasio on Mind and Emotions: A Conceptual Critique. *Nordic Psychology*, 58 (4): 366–80.

Brinkmann, S. (2011) Dewey's Neglected Psychology: Rediscovering his Transactional Approach. *Theory and Psychology*, 21 (3): 298–317.

Brook, P. (2009) In Critical Defence of 'Emotional Labour': Refuting Bolton's Critique of Hochschild's Concept. *Work, Employment and Society*, 23 (3): 531–48.

Burkitt, I. (1996) Civilisation and Ambivalence. *The British Journal of Sociology*, 47 (1): 135–50.

Burkitt, I. (2010a) Dialogues with Self and Others: Communication, Miscommunication, and the Dialogical Unconscious. *Theory and Psychology*, 20 (3): 305–21.

Burkitt, I. (2010b) Fragments of Unconscious Experience: Towards a Dialogical, Relational, and Sociological Analysis. *Theory and Psychology*, 20 (3): 322–41.

Burkitt, I. (2012) Emotional Reflexivity: Feeling, Emotion and Imagination in Reflexive Dialogues. *Sociology*, 46 (2): 458–72.

Burkitt, I. (2013) Self and Others in the Field of Perception: The Role of Micro-dialogue, Feeling, and Emotion in Perception. *Journal of Theoretical and Philosophical Psychology*, 33 (4): 267–79.

Burkitt, I., Husband , C., Mackenzie, J. and Torn, A. (2001) *Nursing Education and Communities of Practice*. London: ENB Research Reports Series, Number 18.

Buytendijk, F.J. (1965/1974) *Prolegomena to an Anthropological Physiology*. Pittsburgh: Duquesne University Press.

Connell, R.W. and Messerschmidt, J.W. (2005) Hegemonic Masculinity: Rethinking the Concept. *Gender and Society*, 19 (6): 829–59.

Cooley, C.H. (1922/1983) *Human Nature and the Social Order* (revised ed.). New Brunswick, NJ: Transaction Publishers.

Cromby, J. (2007) Towards a Psychology of Feeling. *International Journal of Critical Psychology*, 21, 94–118.

Cromby, J. and Harper, D.J. (2009) Paranoia: A Social Account. *Theory and Psychology*, 19 (3): 335–61.

Crossley, N. (2011) *Towards Relational Sociology*. London: Routledge.

Damasio, A.R. (1994) *Descartes' Error: Emotion, Reason and the Human Brain*. London: Papermac.

Damasio, A.R. (2000) *The Feeling of What Happens: Body, Emotion and the Making of Consciousness*. London: Vintage.

Damasio, A.R. (2004) *Looking for Spinoza: Joy, Sorrow and the Feeling Brain*. London: Vintage.

Danziger, K. (1997) The Historical Formation of Selves. In R.D. Ashmore and L. Jussim (eds.), *Self and Identity: Fundamental Issues* (pp. 137–59). New York: Oxford University Press.

Darwin, C. (1872/1965) *The Expression of the Emotions in Man and Animals*. Chicago: Chicago University Press.

Denzin, N.K. (1984) *On Understanding Emotion*. San Francisco: Jossey-Bass.

Dewey, J. (1894/1971) The Theory of Emotion. In J. A. Boydston (ed.), *The Early Works of John Dewey, Volume 4, 1893–1894: Early Essays and the Study of Ethics: A Syllabus* (pp. 152–88). Carbondale: Southern Illinois University Press.

Dewey, J. (1910) *How We Think*. Boston: D.C. Heath & Co.

Dewey, J. (1922/1983) *Human Nature and Conduct: The Middle Works of John Dewey, Volume 14* (J.A. Boydston, ed.). Carbondale: Southern Illinois University Press.

Dewey, J. (1929/1958) *Experience and Nature* (2nd ed.). New York: Dover Publications.

Dewey, J. (1934/1980) *Art as Experience*. New York: Perigee Books.

Dewey, J. and Bentley, A.F. (1949) *Knowing and the Known*. Boston: Beacon Press.

Dreyfus, H.L. (1992) *What Computers Still Can't Do: A Critique of Artificial Reason*. Cambridge, MA: MIT Press.

Dreyfus, H.L. and Dreyfus, S.E. (1986) *Mind over Machine: The Power of Human Intuition and Expertise in the Era of the Computer*. Oxford: Blackwell.

Duncan, S. and Barrett, L.F. (2007) Affect is a Form of Cognition: A Neurobiological Analysis. *Cognition and Emotion*, 21 (6): 1184–211.

Durkheim, E. (1895/1938) *The Rules of Sociological Method* (G.E. Catlin, ed., S.A. Solovay and J.H. Mueller, trans.). New York: Free Press.

Durkheim, E. (1912/1915) *The Elementary Forms of the Religious Life: A Study in Religious Sociology* (J.W. Swain, trans.). London: George Allen & Unwin.

Durkheim, E. (1957) *Professional Ethics and Civic Morals* (C. Brookfield, trans.). London: Routledge and Kegan Paul.

Durkheim, E. and Mauss, M. (1903/1963) *Primitive Classification* (R. Needham, trans.). London: Cohen and West.

Ekman, P. (1992) An Argument for Basic Emotions. *Cognition and Emotion*, 6 (3/4): 169–200.

Ekman, P. and Friesen, W.V. (1971) Constants across Cultures in the Face and Emotion. *Journal of Personality and Social Psychology*, 17 (2): 124–9.

Elias, N. (1939/2000) *The Civilizing Process: Sociogenetic and Psychogenetic Investigations* (revised ed.) (E. Dunning, J. Goudsblom, S. Mennell, eds. and E. Jephcott, trans.). Oxford: Blackwell.

Elias, N. (1969/1983) *The Court Society* (E. Jephcott, trans.). Oxford: Blackwell.

Elias, N. (1978) On Transformations of Aggressiveness. *Theory and Society*, 5 (2): 229–42.

Elias, N. (1987) On Human Beings and their Emotions: A Process-sociological Essay. *Theory, Culture and Society*, 4 (2–3): 339–61.

Elias, N. (1988) Violence and Civilization: The State Monopoly of Physical Violence and its Infringement. In J. Keane (ed.), *Civil Society and the State: New European Perspectives*. London: Verso, pp. 177–198.

Emerson, C. (1991) Freud and Bakhtin's Dostoevsky: Is there a Bakhtinian Freud without Vološinov? *Wiener Slawistischer Almanach*, 27: 33–44.

Emerson, C. (1993) American Philosophers, Bakhtinian Perspectives: William James, George Herbert Mead, John Dewey, and Mikhail Bakhtin on a Philosophy of the Act. Transnational Institute, Moscow, March.

Emirbayer, M. (1997) Manifesto for a Relational Sociology. *American Journal of Sociology*, 103 (2): 281–317.

Emirbayer, M. and Mische, A. (1998) What is Agency? *American Journal of Sociology*, 103 (4): 962–1023.

Flaubert, G. (1857/2007) *Madame Bovary: Provincial Lives* (G. Wall, trans.). London: Penguin.

Foucault, M. (1969/1989) *The Archaeology of Knowledge* (A.M. Sheridan-Smith, trans.). London: Routledge.

Foucault, M. (1975/1979) *Discipline and Punish: The Birth of the Prison* (A. Sheridan, trans.). Harmondsworth: Peregrine Books.

Foucault, M. (1982) The Subject and Power. In H.L. Dreyfus and P. Rabinow, *Michel Foucault: Beyond Structuralism and Hermeneutics* (pp. 208–26). Brighton: Harvester.

Foucault, M. (1988) Technologies of the Self. In L.H. Martin, H. Gutman and P.H. Hutton (eds.), *Technologies of the Self: A Seminar with Michel Foucault* (pp. 16–49). Cambridge, MA: MIT Press.

Freud, S. (1930/1961) *Civilisation and its Discontents* (J. Strachey, ed. and J. Riviere, trans.). London: Hogarth Press.

Freud, S. (1963/1981) *Introductory Lectures on Psychoanalysis.* Harmondsworth: Pelican.

Freund, P. (1998) Social Performances and their Discontents: The Biopsychosocial Aspects of Dramaturgical Stress. In G. Bendelow and S.J. Williams (eds.), *Emotions in Social Life: Critical Themes and Contemporary Issues* (pp. 268–94). London: Routledge.

Gergen, K.J. (1994) Emotions as Relationship. *Realities and Relationships: Soundings in Social Construction* (pp. 210–35). Cambridge, MA: Harvard University Press.

Gibson, J.J. (1979/1986) *The Ecological Approach to Visual Perception.* Mahwah, NJ: Lawrence Erlbaum Associates.

Giddens, A. (1984) *The Constitution of Society: Outline of the Theory of Structuration.* Cambridge: Polity Press.

Giddens, A. (1991) *Modernity and Self-identity: Self and Society in the Late Modern Age.* Cambridge: Polity Press.

Ginsburg, G.P. and Harrington, M.E. (1996) Bodily States and Context in Situated Lines of Action. In R. Harré and W.G. Parrott (eds.), *The Emotions: Social, Cultural and Biological Dimensions* (pp. 229–58). London: Sage.

Goffman, E. (1959/1990) *The Presentation of Self in Everyday Life.* London: Penguin.

Goleman, D. (1996) *Emotional Intelligence: Why it Can Matter More than IQ.* London: Bloomsbury.

Goleman, D. (1998) *Working with Emotional Intelligence.* London: Bloomsbury.

Gregg, M. (2010) On Friday Night Drinks: Workplace Affects in the Age of the Cubicle. In M. Gregg and G.J. Seigworth (eds.), *The Affect Theory Reader* (pp. 250–68). Durham, NC: Duke University Press.

Harré, R. (1986) An Outline of the Social Constructionist Viewpoint. In R. Harré (ed.), *The Social Construction of Emotions* (pp. 2–14). Oxford: Basil Blackwell.

Harvey, R. (1999) Court Culture in Medieval Occitania. In S. Gaunt and S. Kay (eds.), *The Troubadours: An Introduction* (pp. 8–27). Cambridge: Cambridge University Press.

Heidegger, M. (1927/1962) *Being and Time* (J. Macquarrie and E. Robinson, trans.) Oxford: Blackwell.

Heidegger, M. (1977) The Age of the World Picture. *The Question Concerning Technology and Other Essays* (W. Lovitt, trans., pp. 115–54). New York: Harper Colophon Books.

Henriques, J. (2010) The Vibrations of Affect and their Propagation on a Night Out on Kingston's Dancehall Scene. *Body and Society*, 16 (1): 57–89.

Hey, V. (1999) Be(long)ing: New Labour, New Britain and the 'Dianaisation' of Politics. In A. Kear and D.L. Steinberg (eds.), *Mourning Diana: Nation, Culture and the Performance of Grief* (pp. 60–76). London: Routledge.

Hochschild, A.R. (1983) *The Managed Heart: Commercialization of Human Feeling*. Berkeley: University of California Press.

Hochschild, A.R. (1998) The Sociology of Emotion as a Way of Seeing. In G. Bendelow and S.J. Williams (eds.), *Emotions in Social Life: Critical Themes and Contemporary Issues* (pp. 3–15). London: Routledge.

Hughes, J. (2005) Bringing Emotion to Work: Emotional Intelligence, Employee Resistance and the Reinvention of Character. *Work, Employment and Society*, 19 (3): 603–25.

Hughes, J. (2010) Emotional Intelligence: Elias, Foucault, and the Reflexive Emotional Self. *Foucault Studies*, 8: 28–52.

Iacoboni, M. and Dapretto, M. (2006) The Mirror Neuron System and the Consequences of its Dysfunction. *Nature Reviews: Neuroscience*, 7 (12): 942–51.

Illouz, E. (2007) *Cold Intimacies: The Making of Emotional Capitalism*. Cambridge: Polity Press.

Jablonka, E. and Lamb, M.J. (2005) *Evolution in Four Dimensions: Genetic, Epigenetic, Behavioural, and Symbolic Variation in the History of Life*. Cambridge, MA: MIT Press.

James, W. (1884/1971) What is an Emotion? In G.W. Allen (ed.), *A William James Reader* (pp. 41–57). Boston: Houghton Mifflin.

James, W. (1890/1950a) *The Principles of Psychology, Volume One*. New York: Dover.

James, W. (1890/1950b) *The Principles of Psychology, Volume Two*. New York: Dover.

James, W. (1892/1985) *Psychology: The Briefer Course* (G. Allport, ed.). Notre Dame, IN: University of Notre Dame Press.

James, W. (1894/1994) The Physical Basis of Emotion. *Psychological Review*, 101: 205–10.

Joas, H. (1980/1985) *G.H. Mead: A Contemporary Re-examination of his Thought* (R. Meyer, trans.). Cambridge: Polity Press.

Johnson, M. (1987) *The Body in the Mind: The Bodily Basis of Meaning, Imagination, and Reason*. Chicago: Chicago University Press.

Johnson, M. (2007) *The Meaning of the Body: Aesthetics of Human Understanding*. Chicago: University of Chicago Press.

Johnson-Laird, P.N. and Oatley, K. (1992) Basic Emotions, Rationality and Folk Theory. *Cognition and Emotion*, 6 (3/4): 201–23.

Kehew, R. (ed.). (2005) *Lark in the Morning: The Verses of the Troubadours* (E. Pound, W.D. Snodgrass and R. Kehew, trans.). Chicago: Chicago University Press.

Kemper, T.D. (1990) Social Relations and Emotions: A Structural Approach. In T.D. Kemper (ed.), *Research Agendas in the Sociology of Emotions* (pp. 207–37). Albany: SUNY Press.

Kemper, T.D. (2002) Predicting Emotions in Groups: Some Lessons from 11 September. In J.M. Barbalet (ed.), *Emotions and Sociology* (pp. 53–68). Oxford: Blackwell.

Le Bon, G. (1896) *The Crowd: A Study of the Popular Mind* . New York: Macmillan.

Léglu, C. (1999) Moral and Satirical Poetry. In S. Gaunt and S. Kay (eds.), *The Troubadours: An Introduction* (pp. 47–65). Cambridge: Cambridge University Press.

Levy, R.I. (1984) Emotion, Knowing and Culture. In R. Shweder and R. LeVine (eds.), *Culture Theory: Essays on Mind, Self and Emotion* (pp. 214–37). New York: Cambridge University Press.

Lorenz, K. (1963) *On Aggression* (M.K. Wilson, trans.). New York: Harcourt, Brace & World.

Luria, A.R. (1966) *Human Brain and Psychological Processes* (B. Haigh, trans.). New York: Harper & Row.

Lutz, C. (1986) The Domain of Emotion Words on Ifaluk. In R. Harré (ed.), *The Social Construction of Emotions* (pp. 267–88). Oxford: Basil Blackwell.

Lutz, C. (1988) *Unnatural Emotion: Everyday Sentiments on a Micronesian Atoll and their Challenge to Western Theory*. Chicago: University of Chicago Press.

Lutz, C. and Abu-Lughod, L. (1990) Introduction. In C. Lutz and L. Abu-Lughod (eds.), *Language and the Politics of Emotion* (pp. 1–23). Cambridge: Cambridge University Press.

Marsh, P., Rosser, E. and Harré, R. (1978) *The Rules of Disorder*. London: Routledge and Kegan Paul.

Massumi, B. (2002) *Parables for the Virtual: Movements, Affect, Sensation*. Durham, NC: Duke University Press.

Mead, G.H. (1913/1964) The Social Self. In A.J. Reck (ed.), *Selected Writings: George Herbert Mead* (pp. 142–9). Chicago: Chicago University Press.

Mead, G.H. (1924/1964) The Genesis of the Self and Social Control. In A.J. Reck (ed.), *Selected Writings: George Herbert Mead* (pp. 267–93). Chicago: Chicago University Press.

Mead, G.H. (1934) *Mind, Self, and Society: From the Standpoint of a Social Behaviourist* (C.W. Morris, ed.). Chicago: Chicago University Press.

Merleau-Ponty, M. (1945/2012) *Phenomenology of Perception* (D.A. Landes, trans.). London: Routledge.

Merleau-Ponty, M. (1960/1964) The Child's Relation with Others. *The Primacy of Perception: And Other Essays on Phenomenological Psychology, the Philosophy of Art, History and Politics* (W. Cobb, trans., pp. 96–155). Evanston, IL: Northwestern University Press.

Merleau-Ponty, M. (1964/1968) *The Visible and the Invisible* (C. Lefort, ed. and A. Lingis, trans.). Evanston, IL: Northwestern University Press.

Nussbaum, M.C. (2001) *Upheavals of Thought: The Intelligence of Emotions*. Cambridge: Cambridge University Press.

Observer, The (2003) 16 February, http://observer.guardian.co.uk/iraq/story/0,12239,896511,00.htm and http://observer.guardian.co.uk/iraq/story/0,12239,896714,00.html (accessed 8 October 2013).

Ooi, C.-S. and Ek, R. (2010) Culture, Work and Emotion. *Culture Unbound: Journal of Current Cultural Research*, 2: 303–10.

Paden, W.D., Sankovitch, T. and Stäblein, P.H. (eds.) (1986) *The Poems of the Troubadour Bertran de Born*. Berkeley: University of California Press.

Parkes, C.M. (1972/1975) *Bereavement: Studies of Grief in Adult Life*. Harmondsworth: Pelican.

Paterson, L. (1999) Fin'amor and the Development of the Courtly Canso. In S. Gaunt and S. Kay (eds.), *The Troubadours: An Introduction* (pp. 28–46). Cambridge: Cambridge University Press.

Pearce, W.B. and Cronen, V.E. (1980) *Communication, Action and Meaning*. New York: Praeger.

Peirce, C.S. (1902/1966) Philosophy of Mind. In C. Hartshorne and P. Weiss (eds.), *Collected Papers of Charles Sanders Peirce: Volume VII, Science and Philosophy* (pp. 223–397). Cambridge, MA: The Belknap Press of Harvard University Press.

Peirce, C.S. (1903/1934) Lectures on Pragmatism. In C. Hartshorne and P. Weiss (eds.), *Collected Papers of Charles Sanders Peirce, Volume V: Pragmatism and Pragmaticism* (pp. 11–131). Cambridge, MA: The Belknap Press of Harvard University Press.

Plutchik, R. (1962) *The Emotions: Facts, Theories, and a New Model*. New York: Random House.

Plutchik, R. (1980) *Emotion: A Psychoevolutionary Synthesis*. New York: Harper & Row.

Putnam, H. (1999) *The Threefold Cord: Mind, Body, and World.* New York: Columbia University Press.

Reck, A.J. (ed.) (1964) *Selected Writings: George Herbert Mead.* Chicago: Chicago University Press.

Reddy, W.M. (2001) *The Navigation of Feeling: A Framework for the History of Emotions.* Cambridge: Cambridge University Press.

Reddy, W.M. (2009) Saying Something New: Practice Theory and Cognitive Neuroscience. *Arcadia: International Journal for Literary Studies,* 44 (1): 8–23.

Robinson, D.N. (2004) The Reunification of Rational and Emotional Life. *Theory and Psychology,* 14 (3): 283–93.

Rosenwein, B.H. (2010) Problems and Methods in the History of Emotions. *Passions in Context,* 1: 1–32.

Sabini, J. and Silver, M. (1982) *Moralities of Everyday Life.* Oxford: Oxford University Press.

Sankovitch, T. (1999) The Trobairitz. In S. Gaunt and S. Kay (eds.), *The Troubadours: An Introduction* (pp. 113–26). Cambridge: Cambridge University Press.

Sartre, J.-P. (1939/1994) *Sketch for a Theory of the Emotions* (P. Mairet, trans.). London: Routledge.

Scheff, T.J. (1990) *Microsociology: Discourse, Emotion, and Social Structure.* Chicago: Chicago University Press.

Scheff, T.J. (2011) *What's Love Got to Do With It? Emotions and Relationships in Popular Songs.* Boulder, CO: Paradigm Publishers.

Scheper-Hughes, N. (1992) *Death Without Weeping: The Violence of Everyday Life in Brazil.* Berkeley: University of California Press.

Seigworth, G.J. and Gregg, M. (2010) An Inventory of Shimmers. In M. Gregg and G.J. Seigworth (eds.), *The Affect Theory Reader* (pp. 1–25). Durham, NC: Duke University Press.

Sheets-Johnstone, M. (2009) *The Corporeal Turn: An Interdisciplinary Reader.* Exeter: Imprint Academic.

Shusterman, R. (2008) *Body Consciousness: A Philosophy of Mindfulness and Somaesthetics.* Cambridge: Cambridge University Press.

Silber, I.F. (2011) Emotions as Regime of Justification? The Case of Civic Anger. *European Journal of Social Theory,* 14 (3): 301–20.

Sorenson, E.R. (1976) *The Edge of the Forest: Land, Childhood and Change in a New Guinea Protoagricultural Society.* Washington, DC: Smithsonian Institution Press.

Stacey, R.D. (2011) *Strategic Management and Organisational Dynamics: The Challenge of Complexity* (6th ed.). London: FT Prentice-Hall.

Stanislavsky, C. (1937) *An Actor Prepares* (E. R. Hapgood, trans.). London: Geoffrey Bles.

Styron, W. (1990/2004) *Darkness Visible: A Memoir of Madness*. London: Vintage.

Sullivan, P. (2012) *Qualitative Data Analysis Using a Dialogical Approach*. London: Sage.

Swabey, F. (2004) *Eleanor of Aquitaine, Courtly Love, and the Troubadours*. Westport, CT: Greenwood Press.

Theodosius, C. (2008) *Emotional Labour in Health Care: The Unmanaged Heart of Nursing*. London: Routledge.

Todes, S. (2001) *Body and World*. Cambridge, MA: MIT Press.

Turner, J.H. (2007) *Human Emotions: A Sociological Theory*. London: Routledge.

Turner, J.H. and Stets, J.E. (2006) Sociological Theories of Human Emotions. *Annual Review of Sociology*, 32: 25–52.

Vološinov, V.N. (1927/1976) *Freudianism: A Marxist Critique* (I.R. Titunik, N.H. Bruss, eds. and I.R. Titunik, trans.). New York: Academic Press.

Vygotsky, L.S. (1934/1987) Thinking and Speech. In R.W. Rieber and A.S. Carton (eds.), *The Collected Works of L.S. Vygotsky: Volume 1, Problems of General Psychology* (N. Minick, trans., pp. 39–285). New York: Plenum Press.

Weber, M. (1919/1948) Politics as a Vocation. In H.H. Gerth and C.W. Mills (eds.), *From Max Weber: Essays in Sociology* (H.H. Gerth and C.W. Mills, trans., 1991 ed., pp. 77–128). London: Routledge.

Werblin, F. and Roska, B. (2007) The Movies in Our Eyes. *Scientific American*, 296: 72–9.

Wertheimer, M. (1959) *Productive Thinking* (enlarged ed.). New York: Harper and Brothers.

Wetherell, M. (2012) *Affect and Emotion: A New Social Science Understanding*. London: Sage.

Whitman, W. (1892/1975) Sea Drift. In F. Murphy (ed.), *Walt Whitman: The Complete Poems* (pp. 275–91). London: Penguin.

Williams, R. (1977) *Marxism and Literature*. Oxford: Oxford University Press.

Williams, S.J. (2001) *Emotion and Social Theory: Corporeal Reflections on the (Ir)Rational*. London: Sage.

Wilshire, B. (1982) The Dramaturgical Model of Behaviour: Its Strengths and Weaknesses. *Symbolic Interaction*, 5 (2): 287–297.

Wittgenstein, L. (1958) *Philosophical Investigations* (2nd ed.) (G. Anscombe, trans.). Oxford: Blackwell.

Wouters, C. (1989a) Emotions and Flight Attendants. *Theory, Culture and Society*, 6 (1): 95–123.

Wouters, C. (1989b) Response to Hochschild's Reply. *Theory, Culture and Society*, 6 (3): 447–50.

Wouters, C. (2007) *Informalization: Manners and Emotions since 1890.* London: Sage.

Yee, E. and Sedivy, J.C. (2006) Eye Movements to Pictures Reveal Transient Semantic Activation During Spoken Word Recognition. *Journal of Experimental Psychology: Learning, Memory, and Cognition*, 32 (1): 1–14.

Yun, H.A. (2010) Service Workers: Governmentality and Emotion Management. *Culture Unbound: Journal of Current Cultural Research*, 2: 311–27.

Index

Dostoevsky, Fyodor 112, 114–15
dramaturgical approach 128–31, 133, 134,
    135, 139, 140, 141, 142–3, 145, 147
    see also scripts
dreams 106
Dreyfus, H.L. 96
Dreyfus, S.E. 96
dualism 23, 44, 79, 97
Duncan, S. 10–11, 95–6, 103
Durkheim, E. 37, 151–3, 154, 155

Ek, R. 124
Ekman, P. 26–8, 29, 84
Eleanor of Aquitaine 29, 30–1
electrical impulses 89–90
Elias, N. 20, 38–9, 40–2, 43, 44, 45,
    127–8, 147
embarrassment 121–2, 159
emergency situations 105, 125, 140, 142,
    143–4, 149
Emerson, C. 107, 118
Emirbayer, M. 19–20, 21
'emotion memory' 120, 130, 131
'emotional animus' 110, 114, 123, 146
emotional attitudes 28–9
'emotional attunement' 140
'emotional blackmail' 74
emotional conflict 5, 16, 21–2, 85–6
emotional culture 143–4, 145–6, 169
emotional 'effervescence' 152
emotional-evaluative dialogue 113–15,
    118–19
emotional honesty 143, 147
emotional intelligence 100, 101, 146–7,
    148, 159
emotional intensity 151–2
emotional labour 125, 138–9
emotional labour and feeling rules
    nursing 138–46
    in paid work 124–35, 137, 147
    resistance 126–7, 130–1, 148–9
emotional management
    contradictory feelings 135–7
    emotional intelligence 100, 101,
        146–7, 148
    emotional labour 125–6, 127, 128,
        130–1, 138, 147
    emotional work 126
    failure and resistance 126–7, 130–1,
        148–9
    feeling rules 132
    impression management 129
    nursing 139–46
emotional reason 47, 95, 101, 123, 137,
    150, 164–5, 168, 170

'emotional reflexivity' 146–7, 148
emotional situations/scenarios 18, 20–1,
    22, 57–8, 59–60, 139–44, 148–9
emotional style 25, 42–3, 148
emotional vocabulary 1, 49, 62, 71, 74, 87
    see also naming emotions through
        language
emotional work 125, 126, 131, 135–7
emotions
    and cognition relationship 45,
        95, 97
    definition 7, 8–9, 56, 132, 133
    and feelings relationship 7–8, 83,
        87–8, 168
    quality of feelings and emotions 11,
        12–13, 60–1, 63, 68, 72
    quantification in commonsense
        language 1–2
    and rationality/reason relationship 23,
        44, 79, 95–6, 100–1, 102, 123,
        170, 171
'emotive meaning' 74, 76–7
'emotives' 44–5, 95
empathy/empathy deficits
    and body-brain 86
    brain damage 101
    dialogic self 108
    emotional intelligence 147
    and emotional reason 101
    emotional work in private and public
        life 127–8
    and mirror neurons 98
    nursing 140, 143–4
    in philanthropy 157
    and self power in children 134
    and stream of experience 108
employment
    emotional labour and feeling rules 124–35,
        137, 138, 147
    flexible capitalism and emotional
        reflexivity 146–9
enjoyment 26
erotic and romantic love *see* romantic and
    erotic love in Western society
ethical codes 159
Europe
    civility, civilisation and transformations
        in emotions in14th–18th century
        Europe 38–45
    romantic and erotic love in the 12th
        century 29–36, 37–8
    war songs in 12th century 39
evolution 25–6, 52, 80, 83, 133
exhilaration 163, 165
expectations 55, 132, 135–7, 138